Drugs, Thugs, and Diplomats

D1554197

Anthropology of Policy

Drugs, Thugs, and Diplomats

U.S. Policymaking in Colombia

Winifred Tate

Stanford University Press
Stanford, California

Stanford University Press

Stanford, California

Material reprinted from Winifred Tate, "Accounting for Absence: The Colombian Paramilitaries in U.S. Policy Debates," in *Sex, Drugs and Body Counts: The Politics of Numbers in Global Crime and Conflict*, edited by Peter Andreas and Kelly M. Greenhill. Copyright © 2010 by Cornell University. Used by permission of the publisher, Cornell University Press.

Material by Winifred Tate reprinted with permission from "Human Rights Law and Military Aid Delivery: A Case Study of the Leahy Law." *Political and Legal Anthropology Review* 34 (2): 337–54, 2011; "Proxy Citizenship and Transnational Advocacy: Colombian Activists from Putumayo to Washington, DC." *American Ethnologist* 40 (1): 55–70, 2013; and "Congressional 'Drug Warriors' and U.S. Policy Towards Colombia." *Critique of Anthropology* 33 (2): 214–33, 2013.

Printed in the United States of America on acid-free, archival-quality paper

Library of Congress Cataloging-in-Publication Data

Tate, Winifred, 1970- author.

Drugs, thugs, and diplomats : U.S. policymaking in Colombia / Winifred Tate.

pages cm — (Anthropology of policy)

Includes bibliographical references and index.

ISBN 978-0-8047-9201-1 (cloth : alk. paper) — ISBN 978-0-8047-9566-1 (pbk. : alk. paper)

1. United States—Foreign relations—Colombia.   2. Colombia—Foreign relations—United States.   3. Drug control—United States.   4. Drug control—Colombia.   5. Military assistance, American—Colombia.   6. Counterinsurgency—Colombia.   7. Paramilitary forces—Colombia.   8. Colombia—Politics and government—1974–   I. Title.   II. Series: Anthropology of policy (Stanford, Calif.)

E183.8.C7T29 2015

327.730861—dc23

2015004650

ISBN 978-0-8047-9567-8 (electronic)

Designed by Bruce Lundquist

Typeset by Westchester Publishing Services in 10.5/15 Brill

This book is dedicated to
the women of the Women's Alliance of Putumayo, Weavers of Life,
and, in particular, to Nancy Sánchez

And to my family:
Scott, Beatrice, and Owen

Contents

Acknowledgments

I HAVE INCURRED MANY DEBTS during the years spent gestating this book, only some of which I can acknowledge here. First, I must thank those who schooled me in foreign policy advocacy while at the Washington Office on Latin America. I was extremely fortunate to have the opportunity to work with some of the most thoughtful, perceptive, and smart people around, including Adriana Beltran, Peter Clark, Rachel Farley, Laurie Freeman, Dave Mattingly, Rachel Neild, Eric Olson, Bill Spencer, George Vickers, and Coletta Youngers. I also thank my colleagues on the Colombia Steering Committee, especially Lisa Haaguard, Alison Giffen, and Adam Isacson, for their political insights.

I first conceptualized the project while a postdoctoral fellow in the Culture, Identity, and Politics Program at the Watson Institute for International Studies at Brown University. Among the many Brown colleagues who deserve my thanks are Peter Andreas, Keith Brown, James Der Derian, Cathy Lutz, Simone Pulver, and Kay Warren. Under the auspices of the Watson Institute, I organized a workshop on the Anthropology of Foreign Policy, and I am grateful for the thoughtful contributions of the participants, especially Catherine Besteman, Keith Brown, Jason Cross, Gregory Feldman, Hugh Gusteron, Catherine Lutz, María Clemencia Ramírez, Nina Siulc, Stacey Van Der Veer, David Vine, Kay Warren, and Janine Wedel. My research benefited greatly from time spent with the document collection at the National Security Archive in Washington, D.C., where I was fortunate to work with Michael Evans.

In Colombia, Nancy Sánchez was my first guide in Putumayo. María Clemencia Ramírez was extremely generous with her time, contacts, and insights. I am grateful beyond words for the patience, guidance, and wisdom of the Women of the Alliance, especially Fatima, Elena, Carmen, Amanda, Ana, Yesenia, and the many others who spent hours with me.

Financial support for research in Colombia was provided by a grant from the U.S. Institute for Peace; faculty development funds from Colby College; and a postdoctoral fellowship in the Drugs, Security, and Democracy Program of the Open Society Foundation and the Social Science Research Council. During a sabbatical in Colombia, the Political Science Department of La Universidad de los Andes provided me with an institutional home.

I was fortunate to benefit from conversations and comments shared with me while presenting parts of this project at Lawrence University; Franklin and Marshall College; the International Affairs Program at the New School for Social Research; Vassar College; the Off-Centered States conference in Quito, Ecuador (sponsored by Emory University, the Carnegie Corporation, and FLASCO-Ecuador); the Cold War and Afterwards seminar of the History Department at New York University; the Human Rights in the United States conference at the University of Connecticut; the Issues in the Critical Study of Armed Forces workshop at the Watson Institute for International Studies at Brown University; the Empire and the Americas Conference: Rethinking Solidarity workshop at the University of New Orleans; the Conference on International NGOs at the Universidad de los Andes in Bogotá; the Politics of Numbers workshop at the Watson Institute for International Studies at Brown University; and at meetings of the American Anthropological Association and the Latin American Studies Association.

At Stanford University Press I greatly benefited from the graceful guidance of Michelle Lipinski; Anthropology of Policy series editors Cris Shore and Susan Wright provided thoughtful comments and much needed feedback. While this book was still in process, I benefited from the insightful comments on all or partial drafts from Jeffrey Anderson, Teo Ballvé, Chandra Bhimul, Catherine Besteman, Heath Cabot, Michael Evens, Paul Gootenberg, Britt Halverson, Jenna Hunter-Bowman, Ben Fallaw, Adam Isacson, Erica James, Ramiza Koya, Mary Beth Mills, David Nugent, María Clemencia Ramírez, Maple Razsa, David Strohl, Bill Tate, and Kimberly Theidon. I greatly appreciate all their wise counsel over the years. I also benefited from conversations with Sibylla Brodzinsky, Jessica Cattelino, Elena Florez, Daniel Garcia-Peña, Olga Gutierrez, Bridget Guarasci, Sherine Hamdy, Arlene Tickner, Alex Wilde, and Jessica Winegar. I thank Alex Fattal, Julie Chu, and Caroline Yezer for their particularly wise thoughts in the final round. All remaining errors are, of course, my own.

Drugs, Thugs, and Diplomats

Figure 1   Community residents wave from the bank of the Putumayo River, 1999.
Photograph by Winifred Tate.

Introduction
Anthropology of Policy

WORKING WITH COLOMBIAN HUMAN RIGHTS groups in the 1990s was first exhilarating, then depressing, but most of all frustrating. As a volunteer and then freelance researcher, I was immersed with my colleagues in a frantic world of daily emergencies. Paramilitary gunmen occupied villages for days, killing and dismembering their victims. Activists were pulled off of buses and shot by the side of the road. Families fled their homes in the cover of darkness with only what they could carry. Our job was to document atrocities, producing lists of the dead and, when possible, obtaining eyewitness testimony of events. We found that paramilitary forces working with local military commanders were responsible for the majority of cases. Faced with grieving families and fleeing survivors improvising shelter in urban shantytowns, merely producing the mounting piles of documentation seemed heartbreakingly inadequate. In late-night conversations with my Colombian colleagues and friends, we voiced our collective frustration, despair, and outrage over our inability to halt the violence, achieve justice, or even attract international attention and aid. Such conversations frequently ended with references to the United States as a powerful foreign power that seemed to be secretly dictating Colombian policy, as well as to my own provenance as a *gringa*. We were all well versed in the long history of U.S. support for abusive military forces in Latin America. My friends challenged me to find the real power: to go to Washington, D.C. Instead of criticizing the effects, they told me to go to the source: the policies producing this violence and misery.

And so, when offered a chance to "do policy work," I went to Washington. In 1998, I began work as the Colombia analyst at the Washington Office on Latin America (WOLA), a small advocacy organization dedicated to promoting human rights in Latin America. WOLA's mission was, and is, changing U.S. policy toward Latin America. Founded in 1974 by U.S. activists horrified by official U.S. support for military dictatorships in the Southern Cone, WOLA has shifted its focus over the years to address the major U.S. policy initiatives in the region. No longer simply listing deaths and describing violence, I would now be trying to change U.S. policy in order to address the issues in the Southern Hemisphere at their roots. Its staff, myself included, viewed WOLA's mission as critiquing existing programs, offering alternatives, and connecting grassroots activists to policy-making. Often, we had to settle for changing the debate, rather than the policy itself, by providing analysis and information for the media, volunteer organizations, and activists far from Washington who lacked the insider knowledge critical to participation in the process. As the Colombia policy analyst, I developed advocacy campaigns with the Colombia Steering Committee, a coalition of nongovernmental organizations (NGOs) working on Colombia. In this role I wrote policy memos, conducted research trips, led delegations to Colombia, briefed members of Congress and their staff, and gave media interviews. Along with other NGO staff in Washington, I served as a gatekeeper for Colombians, deciding whom to invite to Washington, setting up their meetings, and serving as a translator—literally from Spanish to English, during their presentations, but also in a larger political sense, as I attempted to instruct them in the ways of Washington and to fit their stories into existing policy narratives.

Early in my initial six-month contract, the U.S. government prepared to launch a major aid package, which came to be known as "Plan Colombia." At the time, Colombia was widely described as a country in crisis; it was facing an economic downturn, escalating guerrilla war, and a growing illegal drug trade. When Colombia's then newly elected president, Andrés Pastrana, visited Washington in October 1998, President Bill Clinton promised to expand the bilateral agenda beyond drugs to include human rights, trade, and peace. During that and subsequent visits, Pastrana requested support for the nascent peace process with the guerrillas and assistance for his "Marshall Plan" for rural Colombia. His proposal involved economic and development aid for the small farmers growing coca, in hopes that the international community would respond to the devastation caused by drug production and trafficking just as it had to ravaged Europe after World War II. Instead, in 1999 Congress tripled assistance for militarized counternarcotics programs, making Colombia the third largest recipient of U.S. military aid after Israel and Egypt. At the same time, the Clinton administration convened the Plan Colombia Interagency Task Force to design an aid package.

Passed in 2000, the "Emergency Supplemental in Support of Plan Colombia" was going to help Colombia do it all: reduce drug trafficking, defeat leftist guerrillas, support peace, and build democracy. More than 80 percent of the assistance, however, was military aid, at a time when the Colombian security forces were linked to abusive, drug-trafficking paramilitary groups. The bulk of this assistance—$600 million—was destined for the "Push into Southern Colombia" and was used to train and equip elite battalions of the Colombian army. Although U.S. officials classified the entire Colombia proposal as counternarcotics aid, many of the military campaigns in southern Colombia, a stronghold of the country's largest leftist guerrilla group, were identical to counterinsurgency operations. Over the next five years, more than US$5 billion was spent under the umbrella of Plan Colombia.

Although a relatively minor project compared to the massive ongoing U.S. interventions in the Middle East, Plan Colombia is a critical site for interrogating U.S. policy formation. Pundits and policymakers have heralded Plan Colombia as a success: U.S. aid brought the country "Back from the Brink," according to one Washington think tank 2007 report.[1] Plan Colombia is now a model for U.S. efforts in Iraq, Afghanistan, and elsewhere. It also demonstrates the continuities among the major paradigms of U.S. foreign policy at the turn of the twenty-first century: the lingering Cold War preoccupation with defeating communist insurgents and the "drug war" against the illicit narcotics trade, both of which set the stage for the "war on terror's" focus on nonstate actors employing particular tactics. Cold War histories weighed heavily in these debates through the eruption of contentious memories of the U.S. role in Central America, particularly El Salvador.[2] In the most literal sense, these debates involved many of the same people and organizations. The State Department and Pentagon officials now focused on Colombia had been instrumental in designing and implementing U.S. Cold War programs in Central America. U.S. activists and their allies opposing the plan employed institutional channels and political practices developed during the Central America peace movement. Plan Colombia also demonstrates the endurance of Cold War ideological apparatus, discursive practices, and mobilization strategies involved in formulating U.S. policy. The dominant role of military institutions and expertise in establishing the parameters of policy is one such central thread that can be traced throughout these paradigms. Another is the mobilization by policy officials of affective dimensions of solidarity and fear to justify specific programs.

I worked at WOLA for three years as Plan Colombia was designed and its implementation began. My job—lobbying policymaking officials and explaining U.S. policy to activists around the country—seemed straightforward enough. But as I worked, I saw the contradictions between the bland platitudes issued by U.S. officials in staged press conferences and the material resources—helicopters, miniguns, chemical herbicides—sent in their name. I did not see the proposals, hopes, or experiences of Putumayan residents reflected in these policy formulations. I began to question both what I observed and what I participated in. What exactly is "policy"? How does policy get "made"? What constitutes successful policy, and how are such assessments generated?

My quest to answer these questions took me back to Washington, but now as an anthropologist instead of an advocate.[3] In late 2001, I had returned to Colombia to research human rights activism, completing my doctorate in anthropology in 2005. Beginning in 2008, I focused on policy as an object of anthropological analysis. I sat in on congressional hearings, read declassified embassy cables, interviewed congressional aides and my former colleagues, and traveled to the U.S. Southern Command military headquarters in Miami to question officers and civilian contractors.[4] In Putumayo, I listened to coca farmers in remote villages, attended public meetings with small town mayors, and joked with priests over hot bowls of *sancocho*, the chicken and plantain soup typical of the region. As I considered policy not as an advocate circulating recommendations but as an ethnographer intent on the study of policy production, my object of investigation seemed to disappear before my eyes. Distinguishing and isolating foreign policy seemed more and more like grasping at smoke. What I found was not policy as a specific guideline or articulated vision. Instead, there were stories, multiple narratives of justification and positioning that knit together existing programs of governance.

In this book, I argue that foreign policy is not a discrete, fixed plan for future political action. Rather, policymaking consists of producing narratives that justify political action in the present and unite disparate bureaucratic projects. This is not an investigative exposé of the financial interests that shape how the U.S. government operates. Rather, I am concerned with how policy narratives play a central role in making politics legible; that is, coherent and comprehensible. In his discussion of how we can study the state, anthropologist Michel Trouillot argues for a focus on "the ways in which state processes and practices are recognizable through their effects." He goes on to define the "legibility effect" as "the production of both a language and knowledge for governance and of theoretical and empirical tools that classify and regulate collectivities."[5] Contemporary policymaking is a central site for this process, beginning with the process of what Susan Greenhalgh calls policy problematization, through which particular social relationships, identities, and practices are defined as requiring institutional intervention from the state.[6] Policymaking as a political project must first establish the problems to be resolved in order to manage, regulate, and shape both individual behavior and collective social life.[7]

At the same time, a central task of policy production is to generate alliances and support among competing bureaucracies.[8] Efforts to marshal the fullest range of institutional allies and to create coherence among disparate programs that are already underway produce strategic ambiguity as a necessary feature of contemporary policymaking. This ambiguous discursive scaffolding provides an appearance of institutional coherence and consensus among disparate programs, allowing distinct and even apparently contradictory programs to appear as a seamless unified initiative. Such ambiguity also limits dissent and opposition. Understood this way, policy is a state effect: not produced in anticipation of state programs but through the recategorization of existing efforts at governance and state relations.[9]

This book presents a biography of an aid package as a way to analyze foreign policy production, the conditions under which it was produced, and the ways in which multiple actors attempted to shape it. The "natives" in this anthropological tale of contemporary American political life are self-proclaimed policymakers, among them congressional staff, embassy officials, military officers, and Foreign Service personnel. Their social worlds were connected through the chain of bureaucratic command, the circulation of diplomatic correspondence, and the institutional framework of the Plan Colombia Interagency Task Force—convened by the State Department to coordinate the efforts of the various agencies involved in its creation, including the Pentagon, the CIA, the U.S. Agency for International Development, and the Justice Department. Numerous congressional delegations visited Colombian military installations and toured coca fields by helicopter, and high-ranking administration officials met repeatedly with government representatives in Bogotá. In Washington, the Colombian diplomatic corps was instrumental in shaping the package according to their own agenda, even while working within the constraints of the American political system.[10]

Broadening the analytical field in the study of policy to include the targets of policy, their political allies, and others excluded from these efforts is one of the central contributions of an anthropological approach to policymaking. Although they were frequently absent from official policy narratives, U.S. activists and advocates and Colombian local officials, activists, and target populations all attempted to participate in policy production. They employed a range of political tactics, including protests, lobbying, and the production of alternative policy visions. Marginalized Colombians, including Putumayan state officials, activists, and coca farmers—the targets of Plan Colombia—built transnational political coalitions and presented their proposals and claims in a variety of knowledge genres in their ongoing efforts to shape policy production. Understanding these attempts requires a focus on what could be considered hidden sites of policymaking, far from Washington office buildings.[11] In this case, they were hidden in plain sight in southern Colombia, in mayors' offices and peasant forums held in damp concrete school buildings. Coca farmers, priests, and politicians in the region operated publicly and held strong opinions about how policy operated, but these policy actors were excluded from Washington as criminal and dangerous.

Foreign policy production necessarily obscures and misrepresents events in the regions that are its policy targets. This is particularly true of U.S. foreign policy, which emanates from a hegemonic power with a long history of viewing Latin America as its backyard. Thus, an additional central objective of this project, alongside illuminating the cultural dimensions of policy production as a sphere of social life, is to explore the ways in which ethnographic research among the target populations of policy interventions reveals not only competing policy agendas but also the inaccuracies of official policy formulations.

Lila Abu-Lughod's project applying her ethnographic expertise to the creation of policy around Muslim women is an important model for this dimension of the critique of policy. Although Abu-Lughod does not explicitly address the issue of policymaking, her 2013 book *Do Muslim Women Need Saving?* centers on the ways in which mobilizing discourses of particular policies—in this case, concern for Muslim women as justifying military interventions—employed frameworks that fundamentally misconstrue local cultural logics, social practices, and material conditions in the targeted countries. Drawing on more than thirty years of fieldwork with Muslim women in the Middle East and writing in conversation with contemporary political theorists including Edward Said and Wendy Brown, Abu-Lughod interrogates the multiple ways in which Muslim women are positioned as needing saving, through concern about veiling, honor crimes, and particular sexual and marriage practices attributed to "Islamic tradition." She argues that such campaigns fulfill Orientalist fantasies and justify imperialist interventions, but do not contribute to understanding the complexities and multiplicities of Muslim women's experiences, which include but are not limited to suffering and oppression. The practices frequently condemned as representing traditional culture are often the result of transnational economic inequalities, are viewed as aberrations by Islamic authorities, and are negotiated by women within the context of family and community entanglements far beyond the binary of "free" or "oppressed." Her work brings a deep ethnographic engagement to the critique of particular policy framings, using anthropology to illuminate the ways in which these discourses fundamentally misrecognize and distort the experience of policy by its targets and their political claims.

Politics, Proxies, and Sentiment

Policy is produced in a wide range of settings, from relatively small single institutions to complex transnational networked organizations, and has come to shape and dominate human encounters with bureaucracies in ever-proliferating spheres of social life. Anyone who has been treated at a hospital, enrolled in school, or gotten a driver's license has encountered the social world of policy. Here, my focus is on policy production by state officials and agencies. My project examines one particular realm of such policy production known as "foreign policy": how governmental agencies and officials set their agenda for relationships with other governments. I am interested in understanding the cultural assumptions that shape how the U.S. government sets the official agenda for interaction and exchange with Colombia. As such, this is a story about contemporary U.S. views of illegal drugs, military aid, state-sponsored development initiatives, and nation-building, as well as the histories of these views. At the same time, policymaking is a dynamic process occurring through transnational circuits and involving U.S. and Colombian officials as well as activists and targeted populations.

Policy analysts frequently present policy as a concrete, linear process, in which the responsible authorities identify an existing problem and design a proposal to address the issue. They imagine policy as responsive, diagnostic (usually of situations "in the world," on the ground, and outside of the policymaking institutions), and a blueprint for governance. Such an imagined policy process is temporally organized, moving from the beginning (recognition of the problem) to policy formulation and implementation, and culminating in assessment of whether the policy was successful in addressing the problem. These assumptions often underlie writing about policy, including many of the accounts of official policymakers, media reporting, and much of the political science and policy studies literature.

However, policy action does not have discrete beginnings and endings; such temporal markers must be produced through the stories told about policy. The issues addressed through policy are also never separate from state action. The situations defined as problems targeted by "drug policy," for example, are produced in part through the actions of the state to rein in, regulate, and control illegal economies and the reconfiguration of political power. They are produced, in other words, by previous policies.

Policymaking involves profound emotional work.[12] Ethnographic research reveals how both oppositional activists and policymaking officials (primarily U.S. congressional staff) locate the origins of their policy practice in emotional transformations and commitments. Policymaking is frequently imagined as the dispassionate, rational assessment of specific forms of expert knowledge. Here, I explore the ways in which policy mobilization involves the opposite: emotional commitment, couched and explained in terms of affective relationships and passionate obligations. Anthropologists have long argued that, in the words of Michelle Rosaldo, "feelings are not substances to be discovered in our blood but social practices organized by stories that we both enact and tell."[13] For example, in her work in Melanesia, Catherine Lutz argues against a universal theory of affect, instead exploring the distinct emotional ranges and registers in different cultural contexts.[14] The work of critical and feminist international relations theorists examines how emotions constitute a fundamental realm of contemporary political practice.[15] These emotions, "inner states described as feelings," as defined by Crawford, include anger, disgust, pride, despair, and joy.[16]

Policy narratives are also ghost stories, haunted by the dead who call out to us. As Judith Butler reminds us, grievable deaths are those that are made visible in the public sphere, and this process of public mourning reveals and generates political values.[17] It was through this process of politicized and partial public mourning that I first became aware of the role of sentiment and affect in policymaking. In the course of my advocacy work, U.S. and Colombian officials frequently instructed me that the true victims were not the human rights defenders and peasant communities under attack by right-wing paramilitary groups allied with the Colombia security forces. The true victims were others, and I should be devoting my political resources to them, the victims of kidnapping and the police killed in the line of duty. As I explored the ways in which state officials described their policy visions, I became increasing attuned to how policy reflects and produces "structures of feeling," the "characteristic elements of impulse, restraint, and tone; specifically affective elements of consciousness and relationships: not feeling against thought, but thought as felt and feeling as thought."[18]

My discussion of policymaker solidarity expands Butler's discussion of the "politics of moral responsiveness" in the case of the Middle East to debates over Latin America. She argues that politics is expressed through support of those "who are recognizable to us;" here I chart how that recognition is constituted and performed.[19] This process is central to how solidarity is imagined and enacted, drawing on a moral landscape engendered through travel and embodied in commemorative acts focusing on memorialization of particular wounded and dead. This political identification plays a central role in the way that policymakers mobilize and justify support for particular policies. Anthropological analysis thus reveals the multiple ways in which policymaking works through the mobilization of sentiment and solidarity. The politics of recognition is a fundamental structuring logic of U.S. political culture and is a central way in which Americans imagine themselves as acting in concert with transnational political projects in other countries: it is a justifying logic of intervention, particularly in the case of neocolonial U.S.-Latin America relations.[20]

Policy stories are also a central site in which the future is deployed in the present, haunted not only by the past but also by the fears of possible things to come. Policies are future oriented, but contain the possibilities of multiple futures.[21] Through scenarios, modeling, and other forms of threat assessment and prediction, dystopian visions are constructed as possible futures that present policy must militate against. These imagined futures constrain and shape the possibilities for action in the present. Some of the possible futures that weigh most heavily on the present are threats, imagined future dystopias, and the making real of worst-case scenarios. These threats of futures not yet realized, and the work done to conjure them, are a critical site for the analysis of how policy problems are constituted and how they can be solved through state action.

This study of policymaking requires examining bureaucracies in relation to each other, an ethnographic approach that is oriented both toward the horizontal, across a particular political field, and to the vertical—from the most powerful state agents to the subjects of governance. At the same time, an anthropology of policy is attuned to the ways in which policy-mobilizing discourses work in myriad spheres, what Susan Greenhalgh calls "policy assemblages."[22] In this case, I analyze a broad political field that includes distinct governmental agencies, NGOs, and other institutional realms; a range of knowledge genres and forms of expertise; and the dynamics of Colombian armed conflict. Dissecting the role of these assemblages in policymaking requires an examination of bureaucratic practice, encounters between officials and citizens, and the material products and processes of governance.[23]

Scholars of state formation frequently examine the ways in which states classify and make legible a range of populations and social practices. Here I reverse the gaze: what is the work done by the state to make the state's own action legible both outwardly—by subjects and publics—and inwardly, by the range of bureaucratic agencies that constitute the state? Policy, as a form of state speech, not only wields particular power as a transformative speech act but also works through concealment and denial. Policy narratives make political action legible, locating specific programs within broader spheres of political value. Yet they also erase, elide, and obscure. Here, I ask how these stories perform the work of "enframing"—naturalizing domination, as Timothy Mitchell describes how "modes of power are presented as outside local life, time and community."[24]

Policy in many ways embodies the ideal of the modern state, laying out its action plan in ways that are transparent, accountable, and equally accessible to all. Yet each of these attributes has emerged as a political artifact of late capitalism and "free-market" democracy. These demands for transparency are entangled with historically situated notions of accountability, auditing, and systems of measurement.[25] In Latin America, transparency became a locus of political concern during the decades-long process of democratization following military authoritarianism and civil wars; a similar process occurred in Eastern Europe during the post–Cold War era. These processes of accounting necessarily obscure as well as reveal, however.[26] Ethnographic inquiry in the policymaking process reveals both the ways in which the existing power structures subvert the public stance and performance of transparency and accountability and the ways in which transparency and accountability engender new forms of occult power and alternative politics. In this case, I am particularly concerned with how transparency projects organized around audits and particular forms of knowledge production can hide the workings of state power through proxies and other concealment strategies.[27]

Democratization during the 1980s, 1990s, and on to today has been equated with the return to procedural electoral democracy and the emergence of the neoliberal state, with its emphasis on reduced state services, unregulated (though frequently subsidized) corporate activity, and the privatization of previously state-managed enterprises, including health care and education.[28] The resulting outsourcing of multiple spheres of governance has been well documented throughout Latin America. State proxies providing these services include NGOs (some of which are vast multinational networks) and for-profit consulting firms. Flexibility, intended to yield dynamic and efficient services, is the salient dimension of the relationship between state agencies and these proxies.[29] However, this flexibility also provides political cover for state officials, who are distanced from the state effects of action by these proxies. State officials' ability to deny any knowledge or role thus also emerges as a critical impetus for outsourcing and the use of proxies.[30]

Security is one of the central state functions that is currently part of this global process of privatization.[31] Military entrepreneurs, defined as violence professionals who move in and out of state employment as part of governance consolidation projects and in order to secure territorial control for their private business interests, have been instrumental to historical processes of state formation in many areas.[32] At the end of the twentieth century, Western democracies, particularly the United States, have increasingly turned to the use of contractors and private military forces to achieve their geopolitical ends. Throughout Latin American, fear of crime and rising homicide rates have made private security one of the fastest growing industries; in the United States, fear of terrorism and crime produced a massive expansion of government oversight and intervention, much of which has been conducted and managed by private contractors.[33]

I focus on the privatization and outsourcing of a particular form of national security: counterinsurgency violence. Although the Colombian paramilitaries have since become infamous, this form of privatized violence marked an important international shift. The use of paramilitary forces as state proxies and as the primary agents of counterinsurgency violence was a direct result of emerging demands for transparency generated by U.S. human rights legislation in the

1990s. Precisely because of the demands for accountability that accompanied the U.S. government's growing investment in the drug/counterinsurgency war, the Colombian security forces could not unleash the brutal counterinsurgency tactics used by other Latin America militaries to defeat their domestic rivals. Rather, they outsourced this violence to private armies funded in part by drug-trafficking money; these private armies then coordinated their actions with the local military commanders who were outside of their chain of command. Colombian official state policy was denial: in some cases that this violence was occurring at all, in all cases that local commanders facilitated these paramilitary operations. Although much of the anthropological work on governance has focused on what Akhil Gupta calls the "biopolitical project of counting and classifying the population minutely,"[34] here I argue that we must attend to what the state refuses to see and account for. In many regions, including rural Colombia, the state is actively engaged in the work of erasing any register of the forms and practices of political violence; this process is fundamental for understanding both projects of governance and policy production.

Understanding how some knowledge is produced and authorized as acceptable expertise is another central task for an anthropology of policy.[35] Policymaking involves categorizing policy issues out of existing social actors and practices. This process is oriented toward the needs and strategies of existing bureaucracies. Categorizing these needs and strategies as "foreign policy," however, requires substantial cultural and material work. Expert knowledge and authorization to participate in policy debates are circumscribed and bounded by these institutional needs. The domains of authorized expert knowledge shift over time, in terms of what knowledge is labeled "expert" and how it is situated, celebrated, and incorporated (or excluded) into policy discourses and practices.[36] In the case of drug policy, these domains have shifted from medical doctors during President Nixon's initial programs, to cultural critics under Reagan, and to military contractors, former and current military officers, and weapons experts during the Clinton administration—as part of the long process of the militarization of drug policy that I trace here.

Charting the cultural and material work of excluding particular forms of knowledge, which are categorized as "not policy expertise," discredited, illegitimate, or otherwise unacceptable, alerts us to alternative possibilities. I examine how specific populations, including the coca farmers who were the targets of intervention, produced political claims and policy mandates despite their marginalization and exclusion as criminals. Similarly, different ways of understanding drug consumption—as an illness, social identity, or as a form of care—were also eliminated from these debates.

Methodological Dilemmas in the Anthropology of Policy

This book presents an analysis of the mobilizing logics of policymaking—"studying through" the policy—rather than a community-bound study of institutions. In this study I apply the anthropological method to policymaking to understand the cultural assumptions and frameworks central to this U.S. foreign policy program, as well as resistance to it. By tracing relationships and practices through interviews and observation with participants in the policymaking process, as well as examining the efforts by target populations to participate in policy formation, I study through the internal cultures of a variety of institutions.

This project began with my work as a paid policy analyst.[37] My work experience led me to conceive of the initial phase of my fieldwork, in the broadest sense, as anthropological "deep hanging out." In a wide-ranging, amorphous, highly contested, and policed political field, being positioned within any one institution will necessarily limit one's perspective, and working with an NGO is no exception. It did, however, give me the opportunity to participate in spaces where some of the "hanging out" occurred—such as strategy meetings with sympathetic congressional staffers, a delegation of two members of Congress and congressional aides to Colombia, and a Bogotá dinner with the assistant secretary of state for human rights, democracy and labor. From 1998 to 2001, I was immersed in the ebb and flow of the daily debates, the media, and the world of policymaking. This experience served as a foundation for my later research, providing a set of questions and a map of the political terrain and policy actors that would have been difficult to distinguish or construct from the outside. In this study I draw on the reflections, insider knowledge, and networks developed during that time.

My ongoing research in Putumayo has also been shaped by my work history in terms of both institutional location and political affinities. My first trip to the region, in 1999, was as a representative of WOLA on a trip accompanied by representatives of Colombian NGOs. Colombian anthropologist María Clemencia Ramírez provided invaluable contacts and support as she accompanied me on some of my subsequent research trips. Since 2004, much of my research in the region has been supported by the *Alianza Departamental de Mujeres del*

Putumayo–Tejedoras de Vida (the Women's Alliance of the Department of Putumayo–Weavers of Life; hereafter the Alliance), a loose network of women, many of them public school teachers and community activists, created in an effort to collectively address political and domestic violence. Although I continue to interview a range of people in the region, the Alliance assists me with contacts and my travel arrangements, and guarantees my security—to the degree that it can be.[38] My perspective is deeply informed by the Alliance's analysis and projects, rather than reflecting the larger and more complete universe of local perspectives that might have been gained during a traditional extended fieldwork stay.[39]

To theorize this positioning I employ the concept of "embedded ethnography," which I first heard discussed in a paper presented by Stephen Jackson at a seminar on studies of humanitarian aid. It is a valuable concept because it highlights the issue of institutional positioning as a central factor in the production of knowledge about modern transnational processes. Ethnographers who assume positions within organizations not simply as researchers but also in institutional roles gain valuable insight that enriches their anthropological analysis.[40] The term "embedded ethnography" keeps in the frame the degree to which research is embedded within particular institutional processes. This reflection is not new, drawing on a long tradition of reflexive anthropology, but is important given the methodological difficulties inherent in doing research in complex transnational bureaucracies.

Scholarly work on bureaucratic processes produced in part from embedded experiences includes books by Susan Greenhalgh, David Mosse, and Karen Ho. Ho draws on what she calls "institutional kinship," based on her connections in elite schools, specifically Stanford and Princeton, but also drawing on a year of employment within the financial sector, which she took on with the intention of laying the groundwork for future ethnographic fieldwork. In her introduction to *Liquidated*, she writes, "The job on Wall Street led me directly into the belly of the financial markets; taking that path made this book possible."[41] She argues that her employment was "not covert research" and distinguishes, as I do, between her journal and reflective writing and her fieldnotes. Ho's employment and institutional locations positioned her within networks, allowing her a range of access; her work enabled her to experience the social world of banking, including being "liquidated" herself and preparing an analysis in anticipation of firing others. Greenhalgh turned from more than a decade of work as a think tank policy expert to the study of the policy—the one-child rule in China—she had been critiquing. Like Ho, she writes about how her experience was most valuable in terms of the insights she gained into the process and becoming a trusted part of knowledge networks that then became the foundation of her interview-based fieldwork. David Mosse produced an ethnographic account of development policy in a project sponsored in India by DFID (the British equivalent of USAID) that he participated in for more than a decade as a consultant. Through his close long-term and intertwined relationship with the project, he was able to explore the ways in which policy and implementation are not separate but rather mutually constitutive. In my case, my work experience in Washington opened doors for me, offering insights into the policymaking landscape, including "hidden" sites and the importance of imagined affective relationships in transnational policymaking.

Embedded ethnography can resemble activist anthropology, but with crucial differences. Embedded anthropology, like activist anthropology, assumes a political affinity with the organization within which the researcher is positioned. However, the relationship between the anthropology and the embedded work is fundamentally different. Activist anthropology assumes and embodies a political commitment to the organization or community within which the anthropologist locates her work. An activist anthropologist explicitly promotes an anthropology that will advance the goals of this community in some way. Activist anthropology remains a debated concept, with multiple visions and contested conceptions of how such partnerships between anthropologist and community/organization function (here I am representing the field broadly in the interest of drawing general comparisons).[42] In embedded anthropology, the researcher is institutionally positioned within the organization in a specific institutional role—not as an anthropologist, but as an employee (or in some cases, a volunteer) fulfilling a specific job. The anthropology comes later. The job and the research shape each other: although taking on the position may or may not have been motivated by the research, the scope of the research is influenced by the job. But the job and the research are not organically connected: unlike activist research, embedded ethnography does not maintain the institution as an ongoing referent and is not driven by a desire to serve an activist agenda.

Yet embedded anthropology is produced through and is generative of political and emotional commitments. Analytically, my identification with specific institutional projects, as well as my own emotional responses to our policymaking failures, made me attentive to emotion, resonance, and the ways in which politics is felt by activists and officials alike. Such commitments can become entanglements, producing not just access and empathy but also alienation and estrangement. Conducting fieldwork among former colleagues and navigating the slippery boundaries produced by multiple positions within a single political field can produce differing and sometimes conflicting expectations. This has been an ongoing issue in my own work. In one case, I attended a meeting along with the U.S. ambassador to Colombia and U.S. NGOs while I was both conducting fieldwork and was closely identified with WOLA. As we left the embassy, a former colleague remarked to me that it seemed I was now more interested in asking questions and was no longer the articulate advocate I had once been. Similarly, I faced confusion and resentment from the women of the Alliance as I explained that my current position as an academic in Maine put me far from the contacts with international funding sources and human rights groups that they hoped to access through me. In Mosse's case, a number of his former colleagues on the development project he went on to analyze ethnographically challenged his account as violating their moral community and epistemological project, leading him to insightfully reflect on the "exit" difficulties inherent in what he calls "insider ethnography."[43] Although he, like I, may have a sense of a broader shared political project, these anthropological efforts are not collaborative projects, nor do our former colleagues necessarily share the assumptions, conventions, or conclusions of the ethnographic genre.

In addition to the issues presented by embeddedness, access has been a challenge on multiple levels. Simply locating people can be difficult, especially among transient institutions such as the State and Defense Departments. I used Facebook and Google searches to find people, including retired generals and former congressional staff. Not everyone agreed to meet with me. In some specific policy initiatives, only a small number of individuals knew particular salient facts or witnessed meetings and processes—and sometimes these individuals would not talk to me. Arturo Valenzuela, a foreign policy advisor at the National Security Counsel and now a professor at Georgetown, never returned my calls. When I tried to interview General Barry McCaffrey, his assistant told me he had no available slots for an hour-long phone interview during the next two-year period. In some cases, this unavailability reflected the fact that time and information are money. Many former officials became high-priced lobbyists; one reminded me during an interview that an hour-long conversation with him usually cost more than $500 and that I was getting his insights for free. Access also depended on the timing of policymaking cycles, which could vary by day and week according to the legislative agenda. If Congress was in session, staffers were going to be rushed and pulling all-nighters; if in recess, staffers had more free time and were more likely to respond to requests for interviews. The electoral cycle also played a role. Individuals running for office or considering doing so were generally less available and sometimes less forthcoming.

Career cycles were also important; people were much more free to talk while not institutionally constrained, either because of retirement or because they were cycling out of appointments during changes in administrations. In my project, the Democratic Clinton administration developed the aid package. Many of the senior officials who were instrumental in developing the package left the government during the subsequent Republican administration and went to work as consultants and lobbyists. I was able to interview some officials during this window of being outside official government employment, which gave them more freedom to speak with me. Many then returned to government to work in the Obama administration, restricting my access once again.

Differential access plays a central role in the kinds of ethnographic texts that anthropologists produce. In response to an article draft describing an advocacy trip to Washington by Putumayo activists, one anonymous reviewer asked me, "What are the sights, the sounds, the smells?" In that case, I was able to fill in some of the sensory details requested because I had accompanied the activists during their five-day stay in Washington; the late-night hotel conversations, confessions over meals, and angry outbursts in shared cab rides were some of the most illuminating moments of their stay. Although restricted by security concerns and other considerations, my fieldwork in Putumayo included many hours spent in the homes of women activists. We engaged in multiple conversations over the course of years, with interviews taking place across extended social and kin networks while we were informally socializing. My interviews with policy officials in Washington, in contrast, were bounded by time constraints imposed by the subjects and frequently occurred over the phone or in public spaces such as coffee shops. I had no access to the social world of these policymakers, no opportunity to attend church or eat meals with them, to have what Hugh Gusterson describes as polymorphous engagement across social and institutional spaces.[44] This limitation complicated my ethnographic description and in some places replicated the policy divide separating those who were acted upon from those who made decisions in the service of institutions that did the acting. Difficulties in writing ethnographically rich and compelling descriptions did not reflect the qualities of the sites, but rather the quality of the access.

My archival research included government reports and the declassified document collection at the National Security Archive (referred to as the Archive) where I was fortunate to be a research fellow with the Colombia program from 2007–8. The Archive is a private NGO document collection housed at the Gelman Library of George Washington University, which contains declassified government documents obtained through the Freedom of Information Act. Work with these documents has limitations, such as long waits for documents to be released and their significant redaction, including blacked-out sentences, paragraphs, and even entire blank pages.[45] Yet the Archive collection includes thousands of documents, including previously restricted institutional reporting assessing foreign agencies and providing policy analysis as well as embassy cables. These cables form the bulk of the collection and consist of meeting notes and reporting sent from the field to the State Department. Although these documents offer fruitful material for ethnographic analysis, it was beyond the scope of this project to examine their production, their role in the practice in governance, and their forms and functions.[46] However, I used these texts in several ways. One was to fill in missing sections of the historical record by providing details of events, agendas, and meetings. They were also useful as prompts during interviews. These documents also served as fieldnotes, albeit written by others with a separate agenda, but revealing in both what they said and did not say, as well as for the institutional conflicts they illuminated.

Demystifying Drugs and Drug Policy

Drug policy is a transnational field that creates opportunities and motivates multiple actors, including politicians, peasant farmers, and entrepreneurial traders; tracing its evolution required excavating the history of U.S. drug policy and Colombian responses to it. At their most basic, drugs are simply substances that alter brain chemistry. Throughout human history, drugs have been employed—as found in nature or synthetically manufactured—for religious, medicinal, and recreational purposes. Yet their regulation has become a central preoccupation of contemporary American political life, as these substances have shifted in cultural, legal, and economic value and status; from medical treatment to leisure use; and from domestic to commercial production. Although antidrug policies may claim to work to protect U.S. citizens, efforts to regulate the consumption of chemical stimulants have been based on racially biased social engineering goals. These policies emerge from deeply rooted concerns about urbanization, immigration, and racial and social mobility.[47] Antidrug laws are closely connected with attempts to improve, police, assimilate, or exclude particular kinds of threatening populations. These bodies out of place and out of control include newly urban immigrants, unhappy women, white youth rejecting social norms, and black youth feared as a criminal underclass.[48] These efforts have been reinforced by institutional alliances including government agencies, reformist civic organizations, and scandal-mongering media. Their results include new forms of drug commodification and use.

South Americans have grown coca for more than five thousand years, especially along the subtropical foothills of Peru and Bolivia, the ecological niche where the plants flourish. The crop was widely cultivated before the arrival of the Europeans throughout the Incan Empires, which stretched along the Andes mountain range from southern Chile to southern Colombia. Traditionally, coca leaves are used in rituals of reciprocity and religion, steeped as tea or chewed. The leaf is mixed with ash, lime, or other substances and sucked while held between the cheek and gum. The effect is similar to the stimulant of caffeine; the practice also reduces hunger and provides valuable nutrition, including minerals and vitamins. Coca leaves historically were offered as tribute to rulers and gods and were probably also consumed by the general population, particularly indigenous people doing hard labor at high altitudes in the silver mines after the Spanish invasion and conquest. Coca chewing remains an important symbolic and religious practice in indigenous communities in Bolivia and Peru among Quechua and Aymara people; in Colombia it is only used by the comparatively miniscule groups of Páez/Nasa in the Cauca region, the Witoto in the Amazon, and the Kogi on the Atlantic Coast.[49] Colombia, the country most associated with coca cultivation, is not now and has never been a country with a large-scale coca-chewing culture.

Cocaine, the name given to chemically processed coca, has, like many now illegal drugs, morphed from miracle cure, to festive diversion, to deadly threat.[50] The powerful stimulant properties of coca's alkaloids were first isolated in 1860. Beginning in 1884, cocaine enjoyed its first commercial success as a topical anesthetic that proved critical for the development of early surgical practices. By the late 1890s, cocaine and fluid coca extracts were widely used in the United

States as tonics sold to treat drug addiction, alcoholism, depression, fatigue, and general ailments and in beverages, most famously in Coca-Cola.[51] The early efforts to regulate cocaine and coca use are indicative of the kinds of political movements that would come to inform drug policy in the twentieth century. Groups supporting cocaine prohibition in the early twentieth century included coalitions of private and governmental organizations ranging from physicians and their emerging professional societies; government agencies attempting to expand their regulatory reach (including municipal, state and federal agencies, boards of health and boards of pharmacies); journalists (whose published exposés of abuse drew outrage while employing sensationalist fear-mongering narratives); and private social welfare organizations, including temperance groups and community welfare associations particularly concerned with children. The growing hegemony of the United States following World War II and the postwar decolonization movement cleared the way for increasingly internationalized legal regimes and enforcement agencies championed by the United States. The United Nations became a channel for U.S. antidrug lobbying, culminating in the 1961 UN Single Convention on Narcotic Drugs, a binding counternarcotics platform that equated coca with cocaine and had a profound impact on producer countries.[52] During the Cold War, the United States expected loyalty from Latin American governments, requiring they enact parallel drug policies, and intelligence sharing and joint enforcement efforts increased. At the same time, Cold War political transformations pushed cocaine trafficking into new routes. A Chilean network of suppliers, connecting Bolivian producers to U.S. consumers, was crushed following the 1973 coup, when a DEA agent convinced the new president General Augusto Pinochet to jail or extradite the country's top traffickers.[53]

Colombia was happy to fill the resulting gap, as the U.S. market for cocaine ballooned during the late 1970s. In 1974, only 5.4 million Americans reported having tried the drug; by 1982, that figure reached nearly 22 million.[54] Cocaine became the era's signature glamorous party drug; in the period's most fabulous nightclub, New York's Studio 54, the dance floor décor featured a neon man in the moon sniffing glittery dust from a spoon. To move the drug north, some Colombian traffickers repurposed old shipping routes after a government crackdown on a wave of marijuana trafficking in the early 1970s contributed to a shift to the more profitable—and easier to handle—cocaine trade. The serendipitous meeting in a Connecticut jail cell of George Jung, a small-time pot dealer from New England, and Carlos Ledher, a Colombian car thief who would rise to be a founding member of the Medellín Cartel, led to the dramatic expansion of cocaine sales along the West Coast of the United States. In the 1970s and 1980s, little of this cocaine was produced in Colombia. Initially, coca leaf and paste grown and processed in Bolivia and Peru were refined in and shipped through Colombia to the United States.

Over the next two decades, however, Colombia became a major producer of coca leaf as well as a transshipping route for cocaine. Transnational drug policy contributed to the move to Colombia in what some critics of drug policy call the "balloon effect," in which pressure on production and trafficking in one region simply pushes those activities into another, much as a balloon squeezed on one side will expand on the other. Within Colombia, landless peasants without recourse to state services along the agricultural frontier welcomed the profitable crop, and the country soon produced more than 50 percent of the world's total. The southern state of Putumayo reigned as the epicenter of coca production for the global cocaine trade between the late 1980s and mid-2000s.

For local farmers, coca meant economic opportunity and empowerment, as well as exclusion and violence. The country's oldest and largest guerrilla group, the Revolutionary Armed Forces of Colombia (FARC), in the 1980s began by taxing coca production by traffickers, but in the 1990s expanded to charging *gramaje*—a per gram surcharge—on the coca paste produced by small farmers, using this money to more than quadruple its forces by the end of the 1990s, including substantial urban militias. At the same time, paramilitary groups under the umbrella of the United Self-Defense Forces of Colombia (AUC) began a brutal campaign to gain territorial control while transforming themselves from regional renegades into a powerful military and political force. Money from the drug trade allowed them to evolve from small groups linked to local military commanders into private armies. The fusion of counterinsurgency ideology and illegal narcotics revenue produced one of the most lethal fighting forces in Latin America, which attacked suspected guerrilla sympathizers, leftist political activists, and Colombian authorities attempting to investigate drug trafficking. Beginning in 1994, the United States sprayed thousands of acres of Colombia with glyphosate, a commercial herbicide that kills a wide range of plant life.[55] Farmers in Putumayo complained that this fumigation destroyed food crops, caused respiratory illness and skin problems, and eliminated their only means of support, while coca cultivation simply moved into new areas.[56]

U.S. counternarcotics and counterinsurgency operations converged in Putumayo. Counterinsurgency involves, as the name suggests, a conflict against insurgent forces, characterized by the use of guerrilla tactics (including psychological warfare, sabotage, and terrorism) because of the asymmetrical power relations between the forces. Although conventional warfare—between states and conducted by uniformed troops on well-defined battlefields using conventional (as opposed to nuclear or biological weapons) weapons—is frequently imagined as the dominant form of war, counterinsurgency war has been a primary means of American war fighting since the country's foundation. Beginning with the guerrilla tactics employed by General George Washington's forces against British troops during the war for independence, U.S. troops then waged irregular warfare for more than a century against the Native American populations at home, and abroad in wars in the Philippines, Cuba, Vietnam, Central America, and elsewhere. Viewed in historical context, the forms of fighting in the European theater during World Wars I and II are the exception, rather than the rule, despite receiving the vast majority of military attention and funding.

Throughout the twentieth century, the United States supported Latin American militaries in their counterinsurgency efforts.[57] This support included the provision of material aid (weapons, helicopters, surveillance equipment) and training, both in-country and for U.S. based programs such as those at the Western Hemisphere Security Institute for Security Cooperation (formerly the School of the Americas).[58] The U.S. government supported military regimes that overthrew elected reformist governments (in Guatemala in 1954, and Chile in 1973) and that established dictatorships throughout the Southern Cone in the 1970s and 1980s, justifying their brutality by referring to nonexistent or weak insurgencies. During the Cold War, counterinsurgency practices were frequently folded into death squad operations targeting opposition leadership and suspected guerrilla sympathizers as part of the National Security Doctrine promoted by the United States. Unlike conventional warfare, which focused on combat between standing armies of opposing nations, the National Security Doctrine focused on internal threats and unconventional warfare, in which asymmetrical forces fighting as proxies for the superpowers waged war primarily off the battlefield, through sabotage, psychological operations, and guerrilla attacks.

The relationship between human rights, counterinsurgency operations, and counternarcotics efforts has come to the fore in the post–Cold War period. Even as human rights and international humanitarian law standards have entered into public debate over the conduct of warfare and have been widely and publicly accepted as the foundations of professional military conduct, the central tenets of counterinsurgency warfare—with its emphasis on military-controlled joint civil-military operations and focus on involving the civilian population in war—remain in fundamental conflict with the human rights norms and standards that have gained increasing public currency. Some argue that the primacy of the counternarcotics and counterinsurgency mission overrides human rights concerns. Putumayo, and the debates over Plan Colombia, is an unfortunately ideal terrain for exploring these issues.

An Anthropology of Policy

The first chapter, *Domestic Drug Policy Goes to War*, begins with the history of how illegal narcotics emerged as a national security threat, requiring the warfighting machinery of the United States to be applied in concert with foreign militaries throughout the Western Hemisphere and the reorientation of the military-industrial bureaucracy. Increased military roles bolstered a range of institutional interests, including the U.S. Southern Command's efforts to increase its mission profile, Democrats' concerns about appearing "soft on drugs" and the expansion of the military industrial complex into narco-enforcement operations. The ideological articulation of these efforts in Colombia culminated around the labeling of Revolutionary Armed Forces of Colombia as a narcoguerrilla meta-threat. Chapter 2, *Human Rights Policymaking and Military Aid,* tells the story of how an increasingly professionalized human rights lobby attempted to transform its documentation of abuses into specific policy reforms. I focus on the Leahy Law, which prohibits U.S. military counternarcotics assistance to foreign military units facing credible allegations of abuses, and its unintended consequences.

The next two chapters turn to Colombia. Chapter 3, *Paramilitary Proxies*, examines evolving forms of counterinsurgency violence, arguing that the paramilitaries emerged as state proxies in part because of the human rights legislation that demanded accountability from official actors. These forces were considered evidence of an absent state; the dominant policy in the Washington narrative minimized their military brutality while naturalizing them as the authentic expression of a frustrated middle class. Colombian state denials of their sanction of paramilitary groups were a form of state terror for residents experiencing their daily brutality. Chapter 4, *Living Under Many Laws*, describes the strategies employed by Putumayans to shape its political future while living in a region contested by multiple actors claiming the right to govern. This chapter explores local state officials' and civilian residents' experience during the dramatic transformation of Putumayo in the coca boom of the 1990s. Although Putumayo has been widely characterized as an "outlaw" region by U.S. and Colombian politicians, in fact local residents have been deeply enmeshed in long histories of political organizing with diverse connections to national and transnational networks.

Chapter 5, *Origin Stories*, employs origin stories produced through oral history interviews with policymakers to reveal agency and institutional actions that are frequently hidden in public policy debates. The officials I interviewed described Plan Colombia as emerging from a range of policy priorities: a domestic counternarcotics policy intended to address the Clinton administration's perceived morality crisis, a peace plan to bolster Colombian president Andrés Pastrana's negotiations with the FARC, and a counterinsurgency program to defeat the Colombian guerrillas. This strategic ambiguity enabled the range of institutional alliances to coalesce in support of military aid.

Support for military aid and the redefinition of the Colombian security forces as a central ally were generated through official delegations to Colombia and the construction of distinct sensory, affective, and moral geographies. In Chapter 6, *Competing Solidarities*, I analyze how solidarity is produced through travel to Colombia and channeled through existing identities and institutions. I argue that solidarity is a central ideological and affective apparatus in foreign policymaking for both supporters and opponents.

Chapter 7, *Putumayan Policy Claims*, features *Putumayense* elected officials and local residents who resisted such criminalization and exclusion and attempted to present policy alternatives through association with NGOs, protests, and formal lobbying. During this period, local residents had to contend with multiple actors claiming state powers of governance and sovereignty, including evolving networks of regional, national, and transnational NGOs; elements of regional, national, and foreign governments (including the United States); and illegal armed actors (both guerrillas and paramilitaries). Despite this complex political panorama, peasant farmers attempted to participate in policy formation through both electoral politics and adversarial mobilizations.

U.S. intervention in Colombia has been widely praised as a success to be replicated in other sites. "Colombia is what Iraq should eventually look like, in our best dreams," Robert Kaplan wrote in *The Atlantic* online in 2007. Similar arguments have been presented in official statements, think tank reports, and editorials. In the conclusion, *Plan Colombia, Putumayo, and the Policymaking Imagination*, I analyze these claims to success and what constitutes "the Colombian miracle," as the title of a 2010 article in the *National Standard* put it. The life stories of three residents of Putumayo challenge this triumphal narrative, offering in its place sober assessments of damage in the region.

Part I

Militarization, Human Rights, and the U.S. War on Drugs

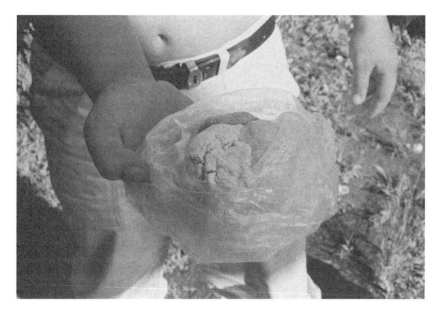

Figure 2 Coca paste in Putumayo manufactured by a peasant farmer, 1999.
Photograph by Winifred Tate.

Chapter 1
Domestic Drug Policy Goes to War

IN THE 1990S, the war on drugs in the United States went from being a metaphor to a real war involving combat helicopters, military advisors, and dedicated army battalions. The zero tolerance paradigm that the United States embraced domestically in the 1980s provided the ideological architecture for the subsequent militarization of domestic drug policy abroad. Although rooted in the long history of the regulation of drug consumption that has targeted particular marginal populations, zero tolerance emerged as a dominant policy apparatus during the Reagan administration. This paradigm viewed all illegal drugs as irreparably damaging to white middle-class youth. The overwhelming force of the military was required to prevent these commodities from passing through U.S. borders or to ensure their physical destruction during production and transit. Militarization and zero tolerance of drug use emerged from and employed the same set of cultural logics based on a totalizing ideal of overwhelming force and control. Both relied on conjuring dystopian futures through imagined threats. Both created new social relationships based on exclusionary visions that draw boundaries around enemies and allies, demand allegiance, and signal traitorous betrayal at any sign of opposition.

Dwight Eisenhower warned of the growing "military-industrial complex" in a 1961 speech at the close of his presidency. "This conjunction of an immense military establishment and a large arms industry is new in the American experience. The total influence—economic, political, even spiritual—is felt in every city, every State house, every office of the Federal government," he told the nation.[1] In the past three decades, a small but growing anthropological literature has focused on the evolving institutions, social practices, and cultural values facilitating the increasing domination of military institutions, technologies, and logics in multiple spheres of social life.[2] As the pioneering scholar of militarization Cynthia Enloe reminds us, this process is not inevitable, nor is it transparent.

A gun may be militarized or not, as may a toy or can of soup.[3] Scholars have focused their inquiry around specific geographies, such as Catherine Lutz's study of Fayetteville, North Carolina; masculinities, in the case of Aaron Belkin's study of the entwined histories of U.S. gender ideologies and imperial projects; or the production of subjectivities as violence workers, as in Ken MacLeish's analysis of soldiers' communities in Fort Hood.[4] Here I focus on the militarization of a policy. I am interested in the way in which an issue—defined as "drug policy"—comes to be dominated by military institutional practices, logics, and expertise.

This history is part of a larger genealogy of contemporary national security threats.[5] To study such a genealogy involves tracing how threats and fear are produced and circulate, the role they play as structures of feeling within U.S. policymaking, and their state effects. Joseph Masco argues that the imaginaries of fear are central to the securitization of contemporary political life and the militarization of national security threats in the case of nuclear war and the so-called war on terror, tracing their deployment in discourses, technologies, and infrastructures.[6] As Jutta Weldes reminds us in her masterful analysis of the events that became known as the Cuban missile crisis, threats do not simply arise, but are produced in relation to particular state identities and assumptions about national roles and character, and within distinct time scales. These threats are deployed to produce particular affective dispositions, political subjectivities, and scientific practices, as anthropologists have argued in the case of possible nuclear annihilation, biological hazards, and geological disasters.[7] In this complex political terrain, the threat posed by the consumption of illegal drugs has come to encompass not only social values and the bodily integrity of particular youth populations but also national security. This threat now emanates from distant producers and traffickers. Fighting these new enemies requires the United States to secure new allies, in this case, the Colombian military forces.

Militarization of the drug war is only one small piece of the broader militarization of U.S. foreign policy. Spending on civilian diplomatic missions has decreased while that on the military has grown. This shift is reflected in the distribution of financial resource within state agencies. The State Department's operating budget was cut 20 percent during the 1970s and 1980s, resulting in 22 percent fewer Foreign Service personnel and smaller embassy staffs around the world; more than thirty embassies and consulates shuttered their offices by the late 2000s. The difference in size between the civilian and military bureaucracies is enormous; compare the institutional weight of 6,000 Foreign Service officers and 2,000 USAID staff versus 1.68 million active-duty military personnel. The number of musicians employed in military bands is larger than the total staff of the State Department.[8]

The military presence abroad has expanded through a growing network of U.S. bases and participation in advising missions and training operations.[9] Many tasks that had been assigned to civilian agencies have been transferred to the military so that U.S. regional military commanders play a growing role in establishing mission mandates and developing in-country relationships. These shifts have had profound political consequences, as military leaders use "military-to-military relations to seduce countries into the U.S. sphere of ideas and geopolitical interests."[10] Although overwhelmingly endorsed by U.S. civilian politicians, such arrangements also generate conflict between civilian leadership and military programs in the countries where they are carried out and in the case of U.S. civilian critics of these efforts.[11]

In this chapter, I trace the emergence of the zero tolerance framework and how the U.S. Military Southern Command (SouthCom) successfully lobbied for an expanded military role in counternarcotics operations in the post–Cold War period. For much of the 1990s the Colombian National Police were the major U.S. partner in counternarcotics operations. Despite critiques of the military as an abusive, inefficient, and corrupt garrison force, in the late 1990s, the Colombian military was poised to replace the Colombian police as the primary recipients of U.S. assistance. Military aid became a solution to the Clinton administration's political vulnerability generated by Republican concern about domestic drug consumption and the ongoing culture wars. Increasing assistance to the Colombian military rather than the police allowed the Democratic administration to differentiate itself from the Republicans who were championing the Colombian National Police.

The expansion of militarized counternarcotics programs to primarily support the Colombian army required ideological and institutional work including the creation of new enemies justifying a military response. Yet these new enemies were not entirely new: U.S. policymakers merged the lingering Cold War fears of communism with the escalating concern of hyperviolent traffickers. To these policymakers the Revolutionary Armed Forces of Colombia (FARC) embodied both of these historical enemies. The *narcoguerrilla* label, used by U.S. Foreign Service officials to categorize insurgents throughout the continent during the Cold War, signaled the convergence of the FARC and the drug trade.

The designation proved to be very sticky and was frequently recirculated by pundits and media outlets.[12] This chapter also traces the erroneous assumptions at the heart of this policy narrative. The narcoguerrilla moniker falsely implied that the guerrillas were the drug traffickers at the center of the drug trade, in the process erasing the larger presence of paramilitary traffickers allied with the Colombian military.

Officials' fear of bureaucratic vulnerability played a central role in the mobilization of institutional support for these projects. Focused on the possible loss of political power, prestige, and control, this sense of vulnerability orients officials toward viewing themselves as charged with protecting their own vulnerable and besieged institutions. Efforts to promote the militarization of international drug programs were fundamentally bureaucratic processes, focused on gaining resources for the ongoing support and expansion of existing institutional programs. "Bureaucracy has been studied as a rationalizing apparatus, instigating discipline and organizing audit procedures, with no room for affect," Yael Navaro-Yashin writes. Yet as her research with the Turkish-Cypriot civil service reveals, bureaucracy "produces and incites specific modes of affectivity in its own right." As an "emotive domain," these institutional practices involve desire, reverence, resentment, irony, restraint, apathy and dissatisfaction.[13] Fear, which is central to the affective experience of bureaucratic vulnerability, favors particular policy options—in this case, militarization. The U.S. military feared funding declines in the post–Cold War era; SouthCom wanted leverage for its expanded presence in Latin America and to bolster its role relative to other military divisions. The Clinton administration worried that attacks from Republican congressional leadership would further delegitimize the administration.

As an ethnographer the meetings that were the foundational practice of these bureaucratic efforts were off-limits to me; in some cases they were held in classified spaces (defined as secret allegedly to safeguard national security), and in every case they were subject to the institutional policing of attendance, the literal concern over who had a seat at the table. Those who did agree to speak with me insisted on anonymity—that they were speaking "on background" or could be identified only by general position or military rank. Much of this fieldwork was conducted over the phone or in meetings in chain restaurants and cafes. The tone and style of this chapter reproduce this disembodied institutional logic as recounted by participating officials.

Those office spaces I was able to access for interviews reflected both the imperial and bellicose aspirations of these institutions and their bureaucratic banality. Entering the U.S. Embassy in Bogotá requires traveling to a large compound, passing the outside perimeter wall and then through bronze doors two stories high, which open to a gray granite lobby with a four-story atrium and Marine guards behind bulletproof glass. But once inside, I discussed the history of counternarcotics operations and military training in beige cubicles, personalized only by coffee mugs. Approaching the neatly mowed campus of the Joint Interagency Task Force South, which coordinates counterdrug missions off the Florida Keys, I encountered a homemade submarine sitting in a circle of crushed gravel lined with white stones. I was instructed that no picture taking was allowed (national security again?), but was proudly told the story of the capture of this vessel, its lone sailor, and hundreds of pounds of cocaine. Inside, the walls of the offices where I received my briefings were featureless particleboard decorated with smudgy white boards. A few days earlier I had spent the day at the Miami headquarters of SouthCom, an anonymous glass and concrete office building along a highway surrounded by parking lots. In my fieldnotes, I reflected at the end of that visit on "the shabby similarity of all the Army offices I have been in," with the same generic institutional accouterments, while "[all the people I see while waiting] are dressed the same, in desert camouflage uniforms with boots—although clearly office style, with the Major's uniform including two pens in pen holders sewn into the forearms." However, the offices of higher ranked officers and civilian advisors did feature accessories that signaled a connection to Latin America: an oversized coffee-table book of photographs of Colombia, handmade *artisanía* clocks, or baseball caps emblazoned with logos in Spanish of military units. Because of my limited access to these spaces and the daily practices of the officials who worked within them, I do not focus on these realms in this book, but rather trace the institutional narratives and histories that made possible the militarization of drug policy and made it legible as a rational public project.

Emergence of the Zero Tolerance Paradigm

President Richard Nixon (1969–74) declared the first U.S. "war on drugs" in 1971. His administration focused on the rising rates of heroin addiction among veterans of the wars in Southeast Asia. In contrast to drug consumers who were associated with crime and social deviance, as soldiers these addicts were viewed as worthy subjects for rehabilitation. For the first and only time in American history, treatment on demand was made available, and medical professionals drove drug policy.[14] However, Nixon's antidrug rhetoric still linked drug consumption and crime as part of his larger law-and-order agenda, defining drug treatment as an anticrime program and exacerbating social fears of criminal drug users. At the same time, Nixon and other conservatives were increasingly critical of the escalating recreational drug use among youth during the 1960s that was linked to political opposition and social unrest. Richard Nixon told an anxious public, "To erase the grim legacy of Woodstock, we need a total war on drugs."[15]

Concern about white middle-class drug use came to a head in the 1980s with the creation of what became the "most powerful lobbying group in the country."[16] In the late 1970s, a small group of concerned parents had organized Families in Action, which expanded to become the National Federation of Parents for Drug Free Youth and was soon a major player in drug policy debates. After the election of Ronald Reagan, these lobbyists worked with the First Lady to redefine drug policy around the adage *"just say no."* Reacting to the widely perceived decline in parental authority and so-called traditional values, this first wave of what became the culture wars of the 1980s was not concerned with teenage drinking or cigarette smoking, but rather saw white middle-class youth as profoundly vulnerable to illegal drug use. "We had a sense of something invading our families, of being taken over by a culture that was very dangerous, very menacing," said Marsha "Keith" Schuchard, who became a founder of the parent's movement because of her outrage against marijuana use.[17] Describing "serious behavioral changes" in their children and decrying the "deterioration of values," this group produced a widely circulated booklet, *Parents, Peers, and Pot*, which contained a scalding critique of "youth culture" and its tendency to undermine "the traditional authorities who could nurture a young person's ability to reject drug use."[18]

In the view of these parent groups, any exposure to drugs inevitably led to extreme addiction. Their publications wildly exaggerated the negative health effects of marijuana and its dangers. By rejecting the scientific consensus that marijuana use was relatively benign (the view held at the time by several senior drug policy officials in the Carter administration, who supported the decriminalization of marijuana consumption), these parent groups proclaimed themselves "the real counterculture." "The parents' movement turned [the previous] policy upside down. Their concern was not with inner-city addicts, but with suburban teenagers, not with heroin but with pot, and not with treatment but with 'zero tolerance.' "[19] According to Michael Massing's account of the evolution of U.S. drug policy, these parents and policymakers felt that "the notion of recovery meant that addicts could get well—a message that, they felt, undermined their warning to young people not to use drugs." This view was echoed by prominent drug policy officials, including the first "drug czar" appointed by the first President Bush, literature professor William Bennett. According to his aides, the Office of National Drug Control policy "was not directed at hard-core addicts. They consumed the vast bulk of the drugs, and contributed a significant part of the crime, but they weren't the main threat to your kids becoming drug users."[20] The white parents' movement and Reagan-appointed policymakers rejected science-based studies of addiction in their focus on preventing white middle-class children from gaining access to drugs, attempting to terrorize them into rejecting consumption.

Cocaine addiction and the crack economy did have real and devastating effects on many communities during this period, particularly among inner city African Americans. However, press coverage and public narratives of drug use during this period relied on racist stereotypes and inaccurate understandings of the nature of addiction and failed to examine the larger systems of social and economic exclusion that generated much of the social damage attributed to individual drug use.[21] Media coverage of drug consumption during this period exacerbated fears of its dangers. The widely publicized death of University of Maryland basketball star Len Bias in June 1986 of a heart attack connected to cocaine use greatly raised concern about the negative impact of such consumption. Drug-trafficking violence became a staple of American popular culture through TV police procedurals such as *Miami Vice* (1984–89), and movies such as the 1984 blockbuster *Romancing the Stone*, which showed Colombia as an undeveloped third world danger zone. While a 1981 *Time* magazine cover featured a martini glass full of white powder, by the mid to late 1980s the covers focused on the dark side of drugs: the "bloody business" of the "cocaine wars" (1985), drugs as the "enemy within" (1986), the "kids who sell crack" (1988), and "crack kids" (1991). National hysteria over the negative effects of cocaine consumption reached its zenith in the panic over "crack babies," described as an "emerging biological underclass" resulting from drug use by pregnant women. Despite numerous later studies demonstrating that "crack baby" syndrome did not exist, the prosecution of pregnant women for their drug use continues.[22]

During the 1980s, Congress created legislation to address the moral panic over drug use, particularly crack cocaine. The 1986 Anti-Drug Abuse Law mandated grossly unequal sentencing structures for powder cocaine (associated with white use) and crack cocaine (associated with African American use and sale). According to the law, a five-year mandatory minimum prison sentence was triggered by possession of 5 grams of crack (10–50 doses) versus 500 grams of powder cocaine (2,500–5,000 doses). This legal structure, combined with discriminatory enforcement practices, resulted in the jailing of a profoundly disproportionate number of African Americans (primarily men) for drug offenses. Law enforcement powers expanded, as counternarcotics legislation eroded civil rights and multiplied the punishments faced by drug offenders, including subsequent ineligibility for student loans and many forms of public assistance, including public housing, and draconian parole regimes. Counterdrug efforts also contributed to the reconfiguration of American legal practices through the use of informants and plea bargains, culminating in the largest per capita incarcerated population in the world.[23]

Bringing the Military In

At the same time that mandatory minimum sentences were written into law, drug consumption was defined as a national security issue requiring a militarized response. In 1986, President Ronald Reagan issued National Security Directive 221, formally declaring drugs a national security threat. According to a CBS News/*New York Times* poll conducted in March 1988, 48 percent of U.S. residents viewed drugs as the principal foreign policy challenge facing the United States; 63 percent thought the fight against drugs should take precedence over the anticommunist struggle.[24] The Fiscal Year 1989 National Defense Authorization Act gave the Pentagon a legislative mandate for counternarcotics operations for the first time— an important precedent for Plan Colombia that would take shape ten years later. The 1989 Omnibus Anti-Crime Bill dramatically expanded the domestic drug enforcement bureaucracy, creating the Office of National Drug Control Policy. The bill also made the Department of Defense the lead federal agency for interdiction efforts in support of law enforcement agencies. In August 1989, President George H. W. Bush issued National Security Directive 18, which specifically directed the military to assist law enforcement agencies to halt the flow of drugs as part of the national counterdrug effort. That same year, Bush declared that the "gravest domestic threat facing our nation today is drugs." The United States expanded funding for "source country" operations, prioritizing interdiction (the capture of illegal drugs en route) and the destruction of drug production facilities and cultivation. In a September press conference, Bush promised U.S. funds, equipment, logistical support, and personnel from the DEA, the CIA, and other agencies as part of the "Andean Strategy." The zero tolerance paradigm had set the stage for the deployment of helicopters and miniguns for Colombian soldiers as the solution to escalating American parental fears of their children's drug use.

The U.S. military has been prohibited from domestic deployment since the period of Reconstruction when Southern officials' fears of a permanent Northern occupation resulted in the Posse Comitatus Act of 1878. Posse Comitatus has played a critical role in maintaining foreign defense as the primary mission of the U.S. military forces and preventing their domestic deployment. As a result, many U.S. military officers initially resisted the idea of military participation in counternarcotics operations. However, the war on drugs eroded the distinction between domestic and foreign deployment. Legislation passed in 1981 allowed the Department of Defense to support counternarcotics efforts through the provision of equipment, information, training, and advice, but it retained the prohibition on military participation in search, seizure, and arrests.

Despite the 1981 legislation, many officers felt that military involvement in counternarcotics operations skirted the intentions of the Posse Comitatus Act. They objected to adding a law enforcement mandate to institutions designed to conduct combat operations and noted the political difficulties of assuming responsibility for tackling what many viewed as a deeply politicized domestic policy issue. Former Department of Defense (DOD) drug coordinator Lt. Gen. Stephen Olmstead reflected this view in his 1992 comments published in *The Defense Monitor*: "What I find is: Let's make the Army the scapegoat. We don't know what the answer is to the drug problem, so let's assign it to the Army and let them try to solve it." Military officers testified before Congress that focusing on reducing demand would be a more appropriate strategy than employing military and police operations to limit supply. One senior Defense Department official told me that the counternarcotics mission "was completely driven by Congress." In his recounting of the history, "there had always been pressure on DOD," but it had been resisted, until "the mission was entirely forced down their throats."

Military resistance to the counternarcotics mission was driven partly by the career aspirations of young officers. In the military, career success and promotions in rank typically stemmed from expertise in conventional warfare, not what were viewed as law enforcement operations. Many officers were motivated by what one called the "the big stuff, the really cool stuff." In the case of the Navy, this was not pursuing small boats and handing them over to the Coast Guard for search, but the possibility of "contact time" with a Soviet submarine. "To catch druggies was not as sexy as the Cold War," one naval officer involved in counternarcotics operations in the Florida Gulf told me.

Even after the military's acceptance of the counternarcotics mission, the deep divide in institutional missions and mandates between military forces and law enforcement agencies remained. Their very different forms of training and capabilities have resulted in distinct institutional cultures and forms of expertise. The military mission is focused on applying overwhelming force for a total victory. Law enforcement, in contrast, is directed toward community protection based on criminal investigation and evidence gathering. As one senior SouthCom military officer involved in counternarcotics operations put it,

> We describe it as mowing the lawn: the mission is always there, every week you have to go out and mow the lawn. That is the Coast Guard, you are always going to have to do coastline patrol, patrol fisheries, do drug missions. You are mowing the lawn every week. The military abhors mowing the lawn. The military wants to pave it over. To finish, to pave it, to do it and to never have to mow the lawn again. The same with the mission: the military wants to go in and kill guys, and now you tell me that I can't kill the enemy. With drug trafficking organizations, I have the target, we know where he is, he is a declared enemy, and . . . we have to turn over the tactical control of assets to the Coast Guard, who then intercept and arrest him.

Over the next decade, however, the U.S. military, in particular SouthCom, did an about-face and enthusiastically embraced counternarcotics operations. Framed as a national security threat, the counternarcotics mission represented an ideological raison d'être for the military just as its primary adversary and principal imagined threat had disintegrated without the opportunity for direct military engagement. "Drugs represented the 'Communism' of the 1990s," wrote retired colonel Richard Downie in his assessment of counternarcotics doctrine.[25] Drug consumption, like Marxism, was amorphous and insidious, corrupting American values from within, and drug traffickers enjoyed boundless resources and military weaponry, a view promoted by U.S. counternarcotics agencies and military officials. The Center for Strategic and International Studies concluded in its 1995 report "Global Organized Crime: The New Evil Empire" that such criminality posed a "greater international security challenge than anything western democracies had to cope with during the Cold War."[26] In the absence of the Soviet threat and the lower possibility of nuclear annihilation, U.S. national security experts focused on "non-specific threats," which required reconceptualizing the logics of military deployment and technologies.[27] Military doctrine at the time developed what became known as MOOTW, clumsy shorthand for "military operations other than war," which included peace-keeping and humanitarian missions and fighting terrorism, immigration, and drug trafficking.[28] As one senior Defense Department official told me, "On drugs, the military was no, no, no and then yes, yes, yes."

The Role of the U.S. Southern Command

Of the five geographic commands, SouthCom embraced the counternarcotics mission most enthusiastically. In part, this enthusiasm was a reflection of the high levels of narcotics production in the Andean region, which was under its jurisdiction. However, it also reflected the relative position of SouthCom within the military, as the smallest and least funded of the five U.S. geographic commands. During the Cold War, the most prestigious assignments were in Europe and Asia, which also saw the largest troop buildup and big-budget bases. South-Com had been limited to a supervisory role in the proxy wars in Central America, which military officials regarded as an unrecognized success despite activists' human rights critique. One SouthCom officer referred to the command as the "red-headed stepchild" within the military's institutional hierarchy. SouthCom's relative power can be measured by its small Washington, D.C., field office, which is housed not in the Pentagon (the thirty-acre Defense Department headquarters), but instead in an overflow office building several miles away.

The secretary of defense and the chairman of the Joint Chiefs of Staff are responsible for issuing implementation instructions for the military's involvement, and Secretary of Defense Dick Cheney assigned SouthCom the mission of planning combat operations and working with host countries in Latin America in 1989.[29] General George Joulwan (SouthCom commander, 1990–93) attempted to fully exploit the bureaucratic possibilities of the counternarcotics mission. His predecessor, General Maxwell Thurman (SouthCom commander, 1989–90), was widely quoted as calling the drug war "the only war we've got." However, Thurman did little to implement the counternarcotics focus during his tenure as commander, focusing instead on the U.S. invasion of Panama in

December 1989; he was then sidelined by illness. Joulwan was a politically astute bureaucrat interested in expanding SouthCom's institutional power. Colleagues nicknamed him "King George" because of his authoritarian and flashy style, including using a bulletproof green Mercedes as his vehicle in motorcades. Joulwan made SouthCom the operational-level headquarters for the drug war, coordinating U.S. military intelligence assets for counternarcotics operations with a focus on the Andean ridge countries. For SouthCom, long accustomed to a backseat view of the primary conflict theaters of the Cold War, this new constellation of security threats seemed designed to keep them a relevant fighting force. When asked why SouthCom embraced the counternarcotics mission, one Southcom officer told me, "Because it was *our* mission. We had no Fulda Gap, the valley in Germany where the Russians would attack . . . all the others had real world missions. SouthCom saw theirs as a lead in DOD drug fight."

The drug war was a means to stave off lowered military budgets. During the defense budget cuts and military downsizing in the immediate post–Cold War era, new missions were a bureaucratic imperative. Counterdrug missions "might give us something to do," one general told reporters from the *Los Angeles Times* in 1989. In the same article, the chairman of the Joint Chiefs of Staff, Admiral William Crowe, told the reporter, "Certainly I think we'll put more emphasis on the drug war. And if there are resources tied to it, why, you'll see the Services compete for those and probably vigorously. We take some pride in being accomplished bureaucrats, as well as military men. And I think it is legitimate for military men to try and perpetuate their institution." Programs that were slated to be cut were reclassified as critical infrastructure for counternarcotics operations. As one Defense Department official described to me:

Because the Cold War was over, budgets were coming down, and the Cold War programs were vulnerable. There was a vast landscape of programs and weapons systems that were on the endangered list. Take any one of them, [for example] the ARL, the Airborne Low Reconnaissance Program. It was an intelligence platform, it was set up in the 1980s for counterinsurgency monitoring in Central America, but now the funding was going down, Central America was cooling off, so they said, this is not counterinsurgency, this is counterdrug, they can do it by law.

This official was referring to one of the multimillion dollar programs funded for SouthCom through the counternarcotics budget; such programs included the Caribbean Basin Radar Network, the Command Management System, and the

Airborne Low Reconnaissance Program. Military equipment and programs initially designed for the Cold War were now deployed in—and their budgets justified by—militarized transnational law enforcement efforts. Defense contractors began to play an expanding role in developing counternarcotics and law enforcement hardware in the post–Cold War era in what a *Wall Street Journal* article called the "Cold War of the '90s."[30] Major U.S. military research centers, including the Los Alamos laboratories, began including counternarcotics technologies as part of their agenda; weapons makers and other corporations sponsored national conferences on the issue.[31] During my interviews, a senior Defense Department official called the drug war a "public check book." SouthCom officers actively pursued these resources, lobbying congressional offices and the media that their counterdrug mission was a critical national security issue.

Resurgent Moral Panics and the Clinton Administration's Drug Crisis

Even as military officers lobbied for greater involvement in counternarcotics operations, Plan Colombia was not inevitable. For several years early in the first Clinton administration, a shift in international drug policy appeared possible. Other foreign policy issues, such as the Gulf War (1990–91) and U.S. entanglements in Kosovo, were considered higher priorities. Some policy analysts posited then that foreign counternarcotics operations could wither from neglect. The Clinton administration conducted an extensive classified review of drug eradication and interdiction programs, concluding that efforts to date had been ineffective.[32] Andean antidrug aid declined from $387 million to $174 million for FY 1993. Some drug policy analysts went so far as to predict that the war on drugs would be reconceived.

However, support for a zero tolerance, militarized drug policy returned with a vengeance with the 1994 midterm elections as the Republicans regained a majority in the House of Representatives, part of a drug war backlash. Their position on illegal drugs was part of their stance on a broad spectrum of so-called social issues, including abortion, homosexuality, and pornography, in which conservatives advocated greater personal responsibility through government regulation and intervention. Along with support for Christianity, gun ownership, and patriarchal social relationships, these political positions emerged as central political concerns in the "culture wars" of the 1980s and 1990s. Future drug czar John P. Walters (appointed during the George W. Bush administration and serving from 2001–09) wrote a 1994 backgrounder, "How the Clinton Administration Is Abandoning the War Against Drugs," published by conservative think tank the Heritage Foundation. He concluded that Clinton "offered no moral or political leadership or encouragement to those in America and abroad fighting the drug war." The report went on to claim that Clinton made the Office of National Drug Control Policy (ONDCP) a "backwater," cutting its funding and reducing personnel by 80 percent; it critiqued both the administration's decision to include legalization in its discussion of policy options and the Attorney General's stated goal of reducing sentences subject to mandatory minimums.

The 1994 midterm election wielded a dramatic blow to the Clinton administration's political agenda, in both pragmatic and ideological terms. The Republicans regained the majority in the House of Representatives, and with their majority in the Senate they effectively controlled the legislative agenda and the hearing schedules within congressional committees. In the U.S. Congress, assistance for the Colombian National Police was championed by a cohort of Republican representatives known informally as the "drug warriors" and institutionally linked through the Congressional Drug Caucus. Although a voluntary group without legislative powers, the caucus convened hearings and served as an important network. After the 1994 midterm election, the drug warriors came to occupy institutionally powerful positions in the House. Among them were Speaker of the House (1995–98) Newt Gingrich (R-GA), Speaker of the House (1999–2006) Dennis Hastert (R-IN), head of the House Government Reform Committee (1997–2003) Dan Burton (R- IN), chair of the House International Relations Committee (1995–2001) Benjamin Gilman (R-NY), and Asa Hutchinson (R-AR 1997–2001), who served as one of the prosecutors of the Clinton impeachment trial; he was subsequently named director of the DEA. These positions allowed them to control the legislative agenda, and they used this power to convene hearings debating drug policy and assistance programs for Colombia and to sponsor congressional delegations to Colombia.

Creating Allies: From the CNP to COLMIL

The Colombian National Police were the clear beneficiaries of a "bifurcated" policy that emerged during the mid-1990s crisis in U.S.-Colombia diplomatic relations. Revelations released by a DEA agent in 1994 that president-elect Ernesto Samper had received campaign contributions from the Cali Cartel led to his ostracism by U.S. officials. Although he took office and completed his term, the crisis severely weakened the Samper administration. The United States "decertified" Colombia in the yearly report from the State Department that assesses transnational cooperation with U.S. counternarcotics operations, and it revoked Samper's visa.[33] At the same time that U.S. officials expressed hostility toward Samper, they provided ongoing enthusiastic support to the Colombian National Police (CNP) and especially Police Chief Rosso José Serrano. U.S. pressure had been instrumental in Serrano's promotion to chief, replacing a general rumored to be implicated in corruption.[34] Once in office, Serrano carried out a highly publicized purge of the police forces and created elite counternarcotics units that were rigorously vetted, making him the celebrated favorite of U.S. policymakers. CNP supporters working in Congress described the force in messianic terms and as coming "out of the dark ages." Congressional aides recalled that many viewed Serrano as a superhero, one remarking that he lacked only a cape as he strode confidently through the halls of Congress.

Congressional Republican's rhetorical and material support of the CNP emerged from their celebration of these policemen as a heroic force protecting the U.S. public through their counternarcotics efforts and as the purest expression of commitment to a shared counternarcotics goal. Members of Congress frequently described their support of the CNP as motivated by the threat of drugs to American children, locating their care in their own patriarchal position as fathers and the protectors of children in their districts. The chair of one congressional hearing described its subject as being "the heroic efforts of certain Colombians in the drug war . . . but it is also about the youth of America, our children, and, frankly, our future." This larger frame drew direct connections between American young people and the Colombian National Police.

Republicans accused Clinton administration officials of not caring about the impact of drugs on American youth and implicated them in the deaths of Colombian policemen because of their failures to deliver congressionally mandated assistance. Republican members of Congress objected to the failure of the U.S. Embassy to expand its counternarcotics staff even when provided with earmarked funding from Congress. They drew attention to delays in aid delivery caused by bureaucratic procedures and legal standards. They blamed the Clinton administration for the suspension of aid required by the U.S. decertification of Colombia and the delay in aid delivery following the passage of what became known as the Leahy Law, requiring human rights screening before military aid delivery (analyzed further in Chapter 2).[35]

In congressional hearings, the expertise of the congressional drug warriors—gained through their travel to Colombia, close connections to the CNP and other officials, and intimate knowledge of military weapons technology—was positioned against State Department officials' concern with legal protocol, human rights safeguards, and bureaucratic procedure.[36] Human rights were discussed as a threat to U.S. policy, an issue explored further in the next chapter. In one of the most dramatic examples, during a 1997 House hearing of the Subcommittee on National Security, International Affairs, and Criminal Justice, Congressman Hastert accused the U.S. ambassador to Colombia of "protecting the human rights of people who want to transgress against the children of this country" by attempting to implement the Leahy Law.[37] Ambassador Myles Frechette replied that he was following official policy and adhering to administrative rules established within the State Department bureaucracy. In response, Representative Bob Barr (R-GA) demanded that State Department officials consider

whether or not those brave men [Colombian police officers] would be alive today had it not been for the bloviation, the obfuscation and the delays which we have been witnessing with the last many months in providing the helicopters, the guns, the ammunition, the armor plating, the vests and all the other equipment that is designed to save lives.

At the same time that the CNP was being celebrated, internal U.S. reporting rebuked the Colombian military as inept, corrupt, and abusive. A 1994 CIA report on counterinsurgency operations reported that the Colombians suffered from limited mobility and insufficient troop levels, calling the 125,000-member army "primarily a static garrison force." It also described the military's "harsh treatment of *campesinos*" and "spotted record" in terms of human rights: "The military has a history of assassinating leftwing civilians in guerrilla areas, cooperating with narcotics-related paramilitary groups in attacks against suspected guerrilla sympathizers, and killing captured combatants."[38] Other reports reached similar conclusions. U.S. policymakers also viewed the Colombian military as extremely corrupt—not only engaging as a matter of course in institutional embezzlement and kickbacks but also becoming involved in drug trafficking.[39] In 1997, then U.S. Ambassador Myles Frechette categorically stated that the United States would provide no counterinsurgency aid, because of "too many human rights concerns" and lack of "any evidence of a coherent anti-guerrilla strategy."[40]

One senior congressional staffer's assessment of the military was even more blunt. "We regarded the Colombian military as a criminal organization," he told me. "They were unprofessional, unaccountable, inefficient." A 1998 State Department memo echoed these concerns and included a list of suggestions for the Colombian military:

It needs to do less protecting of incompetent officers and more promoting of good ones faster . . . Less on simply lashing out at perceived "enemies of Colombia" and more on developing and using credible and defensible intelligence gathering and interrogation techniques instead of 12-volt batteries and rubber hoses . . . the Colombian Army doesn't pass the test with human rights groups, the U.S. Congress, or the media.

As the 1990s drew to a close, however, U.S. military leaders began to focus on Colombia as a critical place to begin expanding military-military relationships. Support for the Colombian military provided a clear political advantage for the Clinton administration, enabling it to outflank Republican support for the CNP. Military forces were seen as inherently superior to police: they had a larger force with national jurisdiction, more advanced weaponry and intelligence capabilities, and fewer legal limitations on their operations. Yet the political work positioning the Colombian military as worthy U.S. allies did not focus on rehabilitating their image and U.S. official assessments of their competence. Rather, U.S. officials focused on reimagining the enemy. Their struggle was no longer centered on drug-trafficking cartels (itself a problematic label that did not reflect the flexibility and complexity of such organizations), but instead positioned the Colombian military as fighting on the frontline between ruthless narcoguerrillas and U.S. citizens. In the logic of militarization, the question was not whether providing military equipment and training was the appropriate policy response, but to which agency it should be delivered. Further, the destination of this aid was determined not by a discussion of the agencies in question, but was the result of partisan wrangling as Republicans and Democrats jockeyed for the position of being *most* supportive of military aid to the Colombians.

Categorizing military aid as support for the Colombian army's counternarcotics missions calmed the fears of policymakers, particularly Democrats, who were skeptical of entanglements in counterinsurgency operations abroad. Since the 1970s, public debates over U.S. involvement in military operations abroad had been dominated by what is widely known in U.S. foreign policy circles as "Vietnam syndrome," a concern about replicating the ongoing political and military costs of the U.S. defeat in the Vietnam War. Counterinsurgency partnerships were seen as profoundly politically risky, involving reliance on foreign military forces whose conduct could not be controlled and on ambiguous strategic objectives that could not be clearly achieved. During the Clinton administration, this debate was revived by the 1993 deployment of Marines to Somalia in what was defined as a humanitarian mission to capture warlords in Mogadishu. What was intended to be a dramatic surgical strike ended up a tragic humiliation, as dead U.S. soldiers were dragged through the streets. The incident dominated foreign policy discussion of possible U.S. military intervention in foreign conflicts from Rwanda to Colombia. "People said, 'we don't do counterinsurgency any more.' So people who did counterinsurgency recognized that they had to do something else, so counterdrug became the new buzzword," one Pentagon advisor told me. "People said, we want to do something in Latin America, and we can't do counterinsurgency, so let's do counterdrug operations."

Yet there were no clear lines delineating humanitarian, counternarcotics, and state-building missions from counterinsurgency on the ground, particularly in cases such as Colombia. The first effort to maintain a division between counternarcotics and counterinsurgency operations was done along geographic lines: the aid could not be used outside "the box," the "core" coca-growing region as defined by the U.S. Embassy. The "box" formulation was abandoned by the late 1990s, but officials continued to try to distinguish between counterinsurgency and counternarcotics operations. "We thought at the time that there was no difference between counterterror and counternarcotics [operations]," one State Department official told me in a phone interview. "But Congress took the division very seriously, so we had to take the distinction very seriously." Michael Skol, who served as deputy assistant secretary of state for Latin America before he resigned in 1996 to run a lobbying firm, described the debates as necessary "in order to get the military counternarcotics aid through the US Congress," calling the promises made by State Department "silly" and the resulting arguments "tortured . . . The Democrats vs. the Republicans in Congress, that was where the big fight was." He went on to dismiss the discussions as an "almost theological dilemma" about providing assistance that could be used against the guerrillas, saying "it was counting the number of guerrillas who could dance on the end of a counternarcotics bullet." That is why the narcoguerrilla label was so valued: it allowed policymakers to circumvent these debates: by definition, all counterinsurgency operations were counternarcotics operations if the enemy was both a trafficking and insurgency organization.

Creating Villains: The Narcoguerrillas

As Clinton officials and U.S. military officers began advocating for increased military aid, they began to argue that counterinsurgency and counternarcotics operations were one and the same. The Revolutionary Armed Forces of Colombia (FARC) was discussed in Washington not simply as benefiting from drug trafficking but as *the* central player in the industry following the death of Medellín trafficker Pablo Escobar and the dissolution of the Cali organization in the mid-1990s. Assessing how this conflation emerged, as well as the ways it obscured what was happening in Colombia, requires an understanding of the emergence of the FARC, its role in the drug trade, and the role of the media in the creation of a moral panic focused on the guerrillas. Even though the vast majority of the drug trade was being conducted by right-wing paramilitary forces, U.S. officials focused almost exclusively on the guerrillas. In the remaining sections of the chapter I explore how this policy logic emerged and was perpetuated through the construction of a custom-made villain: narcoguerrillas.

Used by U.S. and Colombian officials to refer to the FARC in public interviews and testimony, the "narcoguerrilla" label had deep roots in Washington political discourse about Marxist opposition movements in Latin America. Lewis Tambs, then U.S. ambassador to Colombia, is credited with coining the term in the mid-1980s. Government officials warned that insurgencies throughout the region were using drug trafficking to finance their operations. Widely used during the final years of the Cold War, such labeling discursively linked communist groups with criminal drug-trafficking elements. It delegitimized such movements' political claims by categorizing them as criminal organizations, and it justified the escalation of military aid to their opponents by alleging the narcoguerrillas' access to the nearly limitless resources of the drug trade. Such concerns were aired during discussions during the 1980s about increasing military aid to Central American forces fighting Marxist insurgencies or Marxist-identified governments. "Drugs have become the natural ally of those that would choose to destroy democratic societies in our hemisphere through violent means," cautioned then-U.S. customs commissioner William Von Raab in a 1984 Senate hearing.[41] He claimed then that Cuba and Nicaragua were using the regional drug trade to finance insurgencies throughout Latin America. The next year, the Joint Chiefs of Staff cited the narcoguerrilla threat when it unanimously recommended that the U.S. military take action to combat drug trafficking in Central America, including the imposition of naval and air blockades. By the end of the decade, the rise of the brutal Shining Path in the coca-producing regions of Peru brought the focus on narcoguerrillas to the Andes.

The 1980s' posturing about narcoguerrillas as a central threat to U.S. interests in Latin America was revived in reference to Colombia in the 1990s, specifically focusing on the FARC. During his tenure as director of the Office of National Drug Control Policy, General (ret.) Barry McCaffrey testified numerous times before Congress, always emphasizing the growing role of the FARC in the drug trade. As early as 1996, McCaffrey told Congress that U.S. counternarcotics operations in Colombia had "generated violent responses from narco-guerrillas." Statements to the press by the U.S. ambassador to Colombia, as well as officials from the Defense and State Departments, continually stressed the narcoguerrillas as the primary threat to U.S. interests in the region.

Within Colombia, senior members of the armed forces used the phrase as well. The efforts to brand the FARC as narcoguerrillas was part of a larger propaganda war whose central purpose was to delegitimize the insurgency's claims to an ideological commitment to uplifting Colombia's marginalized classes and achieving eventual political recognition. In 1996, then head of the Colombian Armed Forces Harold Bedoya wrote the forward to *The FARC Cartel*, a book written by a Colombian army major and published with the army's endorsement. The text was simultaneously released in English and Spanish and circulated to U.S. policymakers. When I worked at WOLA I received a copy as a gift from the Colombian military attaché. The text is a poorly edited compilation of media articles, documents allegedly captured by military commanders, quotations from demobilized guerrillas and experts, and accusations of FARC profiting from the narcotics trade. General Fernando Tapias, commander of the Colombian Armed Forces, told the Associated Press in 2000, "I do not believe that anyone in Colombia or the world can doubt the links between drug trafficking and the rebel group." Large and growing estimates of FARC income from the drug trade also began to circulate, as high as between $600 million and a billion dollars a year—unverifiable statistics that were implicit arguments for large budgets to match the menace.

For SouthCom commanders, the FARC was the new cartel. One SouthCom senior official described to me the shifting dynamics of the illegal cocaine trade and the FARC's evolution as a transformation from "an ideological group with true intentions of overthrowing the government" to "strictly a narcotrafficking group that is interested in profits and self-preservation . . . When the big cartels were dismantled the FARC were the ones who vertically integrated the drug trade, they were responsible for consolidating the entire drug industry." In a 2008 fieldwork interview, former assistant secretary of state for narcotics and law enforcement Rand Beers reported that the "FARC surfaced as a drug trafficking organization before the AUC [paramilitaries], at least in Washington."

Narcoguerrilla Fallacies

Fieldwork in southern Colombia and the growing Colombian scholarship on the FARC reveal the specific ways in which the category "narcoguerilla" mischaracterized conditions in southern Colombia. Understanding these dynamics is critical for tracing the political work implicit in the use of the narcoguerrilla label and demonstrating what was obscured in this process. First, the label denied the political logic of the FARC as a guerrilla insurgency. Second, the moniker erased the actual existing structure and actors within the evolving drug trade. Finally, the narcoguerrilla narrative overestimated the FARC's military strength, exaggerating the threat the group posed to the state. In the policy debates over Plan Colombia these elements were critical in building a justifying apparatus for militarization.

Throughout its history, the FARC has maintained that it is a political and military organization oriented toward the overthrow of the state in defense of the rural poor. The FARC originated in peasant self-defense forces. Rural communities organized in part by the Communist Party developed into armed enclaves as early as the 1930s; peasant families often fled landowner persecution en masse into previously unsettled lands, a process later described as "armed colonization."[42] Their leaders combined robbery with peasant resistance in an amorphously defined political banditry. Over the next decade, these poorly trained self-defense forces developed into Colombia's first guerrilla organizations. In the process, they were disavowed by the national Liberal Party, targeted by ferocious counterinsurgency campaigns, and isolated from Colombia's industrializing economy. Although weakened by amnesty offers from the government that enticed many leaders into civilian life and battered by overwhelming counterinsurgency campaigns, these armed enclaves survived into the 1960s as "independent republics" operating outside the control of the central government. Guerrilla leaders, radicalized by the military campaigns against them, formalized their vision in a meeting on July 20, 1962, declaring themselves the southern bloc and issuing a national agrarian platform. Two years later, at the second national conference of guerrilla groups, the leadership adopted a Marxist platform and announced the birth of the Revolutionary Armed Forces of Colombia (FARC).

The FARC remained a loose federation of poorly organized peasant fronts for its first two decades of existence, but increased resources from its "taxation" of the illegal narcotics trade financed its growth, enabling it to become the country's largest guerrilla force by the late 1990s. In 1982, at its VII Conference, the FARC decided to focus on expansion, which entailed new military, political, and financial strategies. It shifted its tactics from traditional guerrilla warfare of ambush and retreat to more conventional military attacks and to holding territory, particularly around major cities. This transformation was signaled by its new name, FARC-EP, *Ejercito del Pueblo*, or the People's Army. Inspired by the Sandinista triumph in Nicaragua in 1979 and emboldened by the growth of social movements and labor strikes in Colombia during the 1970s, the group declared ambitious plans to take power in eight years. A truce and bilateral ceasefire signed with the government during ultimately unproductive peace talks from 1984–87 allowed the FARC-EP to build political support, visibility, and critical social networks through its participation in the legal political party, the Patriotic Union.[43] The FARC-EP also increased its recruitment of urban cadres, including workers, intellectuals, students, lawyers, and priests.[44] It used its military power to assert social control, mediating disputes and enforcing local contracts, as well as organizing community improvement projects. "The FARC is not a drug cartel; it is not a Mafia," conservative Colombian political analyst Alfredo Rangel insisted in a 1999 interview. "It is an armed political group that has opted to go to war to bring about radical change in the country's social, economic and political system."

The FARC's economic relationship to the coca trade transformed over time. At first the group focused only on building its political base. As the extravagant resources of the coca trade became more widely known, however, the FARC expanded its "taxation" system to include coca, first collecting taxes from the middlemen and traffickers, and then from the peasant farmers themselves. This tax was known as the *gramaje*—a price per gram of coca paste, and nowhere did the gramaje come to dominate local economic relations as it did in Putumayo. The dramatic profits available to the FARC were the product in part of U.S. counternarcotics policy, because interdiction efforts targeting the small planes bringing coca paste from Bolivia and Peru into Colombia contributed to the dramatic increase in coca growing in Colombia—much of it in areas that were historic FARC strongholds. University of Miami professor Bruce Bagley described the FARC as taxing peasants and "contracting" protection services to trafficker organizations. Although some fronts "may even have begun to operate their own processing facilities," he found "there was, however, no indication that FARC personnel engaged in international drug smuggling activities outside of Colombia."[45] Some internal U.S. government documents reported similar findings, despite the dominant public discourse of narcoguerrillas. A January 1998 background memo prepared for Undersecretary Pickering concluded that "while the guerrillas, the FARC especially, are heavily involved in protecting drug crop cultivation and some processing, they have not formed a new 'cartel.'" Outspoken Ambassador Frechette gave the same message to the Colombian minister of defense, according to a 1997 State Department cable:

Not all [guerrilla] fronts are involved in narcotrafficking and those that are cannot be said to constitute a cartel. In the U.S. view, the notion of the "FARC cartel" was put together by the Colombian military, who considered it a way to obtain US assistance in the counterinsurgency.

Although drug profits clearly financed the FARC's military expansion and its escalating attacks, the vast majority of those exorbitant profits were going not to the FARC, but to the Northern Valle Cartel and other trafficking organizations. The initial cocaine boom was dominated by two sprawling networks based in Medellin and Cali, which were labeled "cartels" despite the fact that these organizations were more like loose networks and were unable to control drug prices through monopoly control of a market. After these groups' leadership was killed or jailed in the mid-1990s, a new generation of mid-level capos organized new trafficking structures, most notably the Northern Valle Cartel. Their vertically integrated illegal operations employed new and constantly changing shipping routes for moving cocaine through Central America, Mexico, and the Caribbean. Their political affiliations were not with left-wing guerrillas, but rather with right-wing paramilitary forces. These ties between illicit drug operations and right-wing paramilitary organizations solidified as high-level traffickers became paramilitary chiefs (see Chapter 3).

During this period, the FARC undeniably increased its criminal operations and abuses of civilians—partly in response to the growing strength of the paramilitaries during the late 1990s and their incursions into FARC-controlled areas.

FARC militias attacked suspected collaborators and imposed draconian punishments on local residents. At the same time, the financial demands of increased military operations contributed to the FARC's further criminalization. Colombia became the world leader in kidnappings, with more than 3,700 people reported kidnapped in 2002 alone; approximately 70 percent of these kidnappings were attributed to the guerrillas, and two-thirds of those were financially motivated.[46] According to Colombian governmental statistics, the FARC and the National Liberation Army (a much smaller group) received approximately US$1.2 billion in ransom between 1991 and 1998.[47] Fear of kidnapping dominated discussions of security in Colombia. During so-called miraculous fishing (*pesca milagrosa*) expeditions, guerrillas set up improvised roadblocks and conducted mass kidnappings based on their victims' presumed wealth.

In 2000, the FARC issued communiqués announcing new "laws." The first, Law 001, addressed plans for agricultural reform including land expropriation by the guerrillas, whereas Law 002 set a "tax" on any assets over US$1 million, with those failing to pay the tax threatened with kidnapping. The FARC also began holding numerous so-called prisoners of war, including hundreds of captured soldiers, police officers, and high-profile politicians, in an effort to pressure the government to make concessions; many were captive for more than a decade.[48]

Many U.S. officials were deeply concerned about the growing guerrilla strength and remained focused on counterinsurgency. According to a senior Defense Department and SouthCom official, "What drove Colombia policy was that the situation kept getting worse—not the drug side but the guerrilla side." He described Defense Intelligence Agency personnel as "focused on counterinsurgency," closely monitoring FARC activity, and noted with alarm the FARC's increasing activity and new weapons capability by the end of the decade. "In the mid 1990s, the counterinsurgency guys start jumping up and down about the FARC. They had brand new uniforms; they were better equipped than the Colombian military." The Defense Intelligence Agency and the International Institute for Strategic Studies told Colombian officials that, in their opinion, the Colombia army was losing the war and would be defeated within five years.[49]

However, despite the FARC's real gains in military and operational capabilities, media accounts, as well as some Colombian and U.S. policymakers, consistently exaggerated the strength of the FARC and its ability to pose a serious threat to the Colombian state. In one of the clearest examples, the guerrillas were repeatedly described in the press and by officials in public statements as

controlling 40 percent—often rounded up to "half"—of the country. Few reporters clarified, however, that this "control" was over the southern jungle low-
lands, which make up approximately 40 percent of Colombia's territory, but
houses less than 10 percent of the population, none of its industry, and remarkably little infrastructure. Plan Colombia supporter Tom Marks suggested that
the frequent discussion of the FARC's control of half of the country was a distortion of a 1997 army report, which stated that 13 percent of the country's mayors had direct links to the guerrillas, with another 44 percent engaging in some
degree of collaboration. A background memo prepared for Undersecretary
Pickering in 1998 presented a more accurate assessment, reporting that the ELN
and the FARC combined "control about 13% of the Colombia's 1070 municipalities, where they act as de facto government, and are active in two thirds of the
country."

Similarly, the series of dramatic assaults against military barracks, during
which hundreds of soldiers and police were killed or taken as prisoners, were
often cited as proof of the FARC's increasing military strength. These attacks
were symbolically important and were the initial phase of the FARC's strategy
to strengthen its control over the southeast region of the country. However, few
accounts of these attacks specified that the towns in question were in fact remote outposts, located in jungle lowland regions far from urban economic and
political power centers. These dramatic incidents did not result in administrative control of significant territory, nor did they demonstrate the military
strength to take—or even launch an offensive against—any one of the country's major cities. Although the widespread practice of kidnapping, particularly
the "miraculous fishing" expeditions carried out on major roads, did generate
widespread panic, daily life in cities was largely unaffected, and many rumored
attacks never took place. For example, while living in Bogotá in 2002, I heard
radio reports of possible imminent attacks against the water system, including
rumors of poisoning, but never heard of a confirmed attack. The FARC never succeeded in staging anything other than standard guerrilla bombings and acts of
sabotage in major cities.

Despite its multiple inaccuracies, the cultural and policy work performed by
the narcoguerrilla thesis had profound effects. By reconfiguring the complex and
multi-actor illegal drug trade into a simple linear process dominated by Marxist
guerrillas, U.S. counternarcotics policy was reduced to a goal of eliminating the
insurgency. Counterinsurgency and counternarcotics campaigns became one

and the same, while the role of drug-trafficking paramilitary groups allied with the Colombian military was strategically elided. This policy logic was championed by a Democratic administration facing its own panic over sexual impropriety and policy critiques focused on fears of escalating drug consumption. The moral landscape mapped in congressional hearings pitted Republican drug warriors as passionate defenders of America's youth against an inept and immoral administration, unable or unwilling to implement policies designed to protect the Colombian National Police. Drug policy became a way of differentiating the political parties, a part of a larger political struggle framed as a culture war.

Conclusion

This chapter has traced how drug trafficking became one of many "nonspecific threats," not localized in a nation-state enemy, but used to categorize particular political practices, relationships, and claims as dangerous.[50] The production of enemies by state agents seeking to legitimate ongoing repressive interventions into specific communities is a fundamental practice of militarization and has been analyzed in numerous contexts, including the construction of black and Latino youth as criminal threats to the social order[51] and foreign nationals as enemy combatants in the war on terror.[52] This fear works as an apparatus of governance, in part through the ways in which specific populations are positioned as threats in embodied encounters, imagined relations, and media representations.

No longer simply a matter of getting schoolchildren to "just say no" or imprisoning retail sellers, institutional commitments to ending drug consumption involved operations against a rebel force in a distant jungle. For U.S. policymakers, Colombian narcoguerrillas constituted not a physically present threat but rather an existential one through their multidimensional opposition to an amorphous U.S. value system. The incorporation of the guerrillas as narco metavillains into U.S. popular culture was laid out in a 2001 Arnold Schwarzenegger movie, *Collateral Damage*, which featured a Colombian narcoguerrilla family as the central villains. Schwarzenegger plays a fireman whose family is blown up in a Los Angeles bombing carried out by a Colombian guerrilla leader known as "the Wolf." Infuriated that the U.S. government will not avenge the death of his family, Schwarzenegger travels to Colombia, where he meets drug dealers, debates politics with rebels, and attempts to rescue the Wolf's wife and child, only to discover that the wife is a committed terrorist herself, willing (spoiler alert!) to use her child's toy as a bomb.[53]

The narcoguerrilla label reflected the U.S. military's institutional interest in justifying its budgets and programs in the post–Cold War context. This label also performs significant ideological work, assembling multiple political resources under the umbrella of an amorphous analytic frame. In this process, residual fear is mobilized and redeployed in new arenas. The immediate precedent for the classification of Colombian rebel groups as narcoguerrillas was the panic over drug trafficking Communists in 1980s Central America, but the label also resonates with a much longer history of fear mongering over the nexus between criminal networks and political opposition. It delegitimizes efforts to oppose and critique militarization and positions the targets as outside the realm of appropriate policy debate, instead naturalizing a total military response.

Drug policy is only one of many arenas of social and political life that has became dominated by military logics and resources. The expansive reach of the "military definition of the situation," in the words of C. Wright Mills, has deep roots in U.S. political culture, even as its acceleration during the past half of the last century brought military logics into an ever-increasing range of social worlds. The militarization of drug policy involved cultural and ideological shifts that justified new institutional practices and policies, as well as the concentration of resources within particular bureaucracies and private industries. In the post–Cold War search for new mandates and missions, the drug war served as an impetus for military expansion in Latin America. At the same time, militarization was fundamental in drug policy problematization, establishing the parameters of the issue to be resolved and defining the appropriate institutions for policy action. Defining particular commodities and people as national security threats set out the scope of both the problem and its solution through military hardware and combat operations, explored further in the later chapters. In the case of drug policy, prohibitionary policy was in some ways a self-fulfilling prophesy; the violence generated by the enormous profits of the black market was then categorized as the threat justifying militarization. Finally, militarization of the policy process involved foreclosing alternative political futures, in this case those engendered through the categorization of drug consumption as religious ritual, creative endeavor, act of care, or disease.

Chapter 2

Human Rights Policymaking and Military Aid

THE PLAN COLOMBIA AID PACKAGE was profoundly shaped by a new dynamic in U.S. political life: the human rights lobby and its efforts to create human rights policy through legislation. During what became known as the "human rights era," in the immediate post-Cold War period coalitions of activists, advocates, congressional staff, and government officials worked together on human rights policymaking.[1] No longer only the battle cry of opposition activists and exiles, human rights were championed by presidents, advanced by a growing network of government bureaucracies, and financed by wealthy foundations. Activists wanted to use their human rights reporting not simply to shame governments but also to influence the policymaking process. Such efforts required new relationships, bureaucratic practices, and forms of expertise. This chapter is concerned with the unintended consequences of such efforts, as well as the fissures and contradictions revealed within the state and among nongovernmental actors as human rights becomes folded in—or in some cases, shoved in—to the articulation of policy and the institutional practice of state bureaucracies.

How is human rights policy made, and what does it do?[2] I explore these processes through a case study of the Leahy amendment to the Foreign Operations Appropriations Act of 1997. The "Leahy Law" or "Leahy," as it came to be known, was later expanded in scope. As worded, Leahy appears straightforward: the law prohibits U.S. counternarcotics assistance to foreign military units facing credible allegations of human rights abuses unless the government takes effective measures to address the allegations. The law was created through a coalition process involving NGO advocates, grassroots activists, and their allies in the U.S. Congress. Leahy exemplified the ways in which the focus on policymaking emerged from and in turn transformed human rights practice itself. Participation in policymaking generated ongoing debates among activists, even as it became a central marker of professional status and a primary criterion for institutional support and assessment. Many activists were also critical of human rights policymaking as failing to represent their political views, as well as resulting from antidemocratic and exclusionary processes. Supporters, however, argued that such legislation was a critical advance in the reorientation of policymaking toward human rights. Conversely, for some promoting military aid, human rights concerns constituted a threat to their political agenda. Shaped by the transnational diplomatic context of a growing U.S. military presence in Colombia, the law shifted U.S. policy, but not in the ways that the activists and policymakers who designed the law intended.

The movement of human rights from the realm of activist demands to policy formation involved the reconfiguration of activist practices and identities, as well as emergent forms of political action organized around participation in the policymaking process. Lobbying and advocacy required the development of new genres of political claims in the form of specific policy formulations. No longer strictly oppositional and reactive, human rights activists had to create proactive strategies that articulated specific proposals for support. Rather than speak in the utopian language of human rights recommendations, these activists now had to function within the Washington universe of the politically possible, defined in terms of past actions and achievable outcomes. Their work was reoriented toward a lobbying culture organized around "the ask," which articulates a specific action so that politicians can claim the results as an example of their political power, responsiveness and leverage.

Human rights legislation established legal requirements for the government officials and agencies charged with its implementation. Yet even as human rights concerns were brought into the realm of national legislation, ambivalence over how such laws bound bureaucratic practice was written into the law. The unwillingness to let human rights standards trump national security concerns was codified in the form of presidential waivers. The president could, and President Clinton and subsequent presidents did, ignore the human rights requirements by arguing it was in the interest of national security to continue sending military aid. These competing agendas—ongoing military aid in the name of national security versus human rights standards limiting such aid in the case of abuses— were also exposed in the debates over implementation, assessment, and compliance. In the process, concern about bureaucratic vulnerability was revealed as a central dynamic in policymaking. Policy formulations positioned specific agencies as institutionally subordinate and strengthened others, exposed some to contradictory mandates, and in some cases obligated officials to administer programs that they found objectionable. Policymaking and implementation exposed the institutional and power hierarchies between civilian and military state institutions, between U.S. and Colombia officials, and between residents of Putumayo and the Colombian central government.

As U.S. governmental agencies took up and framed their political interventions in terms of human rights, these projects became subsumed to the bureaucratic imperatives of surveillance, routinization, and measurement, as well as to the dominant political processes of militarization. The Leahy vetting program worked and continues to work through systems of assessment and classification, as officials distinguish between credible and non-credible allegations, forms of violence, and authorized and unauthorized military units. The indicators employed in this process are never neutral, but emerge from and generate profoundly politicized systems of valorization.[3] As Leahy was interpreted and implemented, these indicators were designed to ensure the ongoing flow of military aid.

Origins of U.S. Congressional Human Rights Policymaking

Congressional willingness to intercede in foreign affairs, traditionally the purview of the executive branch (the president and representatives in the State Department), was transformed after the Vietnam War.[4] After hearing revelations that the administration had presented inaccurate information during the war and in the Watergate briefings, members of Congress began taking a more activist orientation toward foreign policy and international affairs. "The notion that the government [the State Department] was constantly lying to you was appalling," one congressional staffer recalled. "It was a shock to the political system. Before, there was the idea that these were serious people and they would tell the truth." Members of Congress expanded their oversight role through conducting hearings and imposing reporting requirements. Also in the 1970s, Congress first became involved in discussions of explicitly labeled "human rights" as a foreign policy issue. Members of Congress developed a number of mechanisms to pursue human rights concerns, including applying country-specific conditions (standards that had to be met for aid to flow) to assistance for a number of nation-states, including Argentina, Chile, Uruguay, Nepal, Sri Lanka, Turkey, the Philippines, Indonesia, and Guatemala. The Congressional Human Rights Caucus was founded in 1983 to organize briefings and congressional testimony on human rights issues. Rather than simply rely on government officials' statements, Congress began to turn to outside experts for testimony and reports, a fundamental factor in the growth of Washington "think tank" culture.[5] Congress also set up a system of thematic "caucuses" to provide research and analysis on specific issues, staffed and funded through resources donated by interested members from funds allocated to their congressional offices. The Arms Control and Foreign Policy Caucus was the themed caucus that was most directly involved in international human rights issues; it worked closely with other groups including the Black Caucus.[6] Former Arms Control and Foreign Policy Caucus staff Caleb Rossiter described their role as "inside agitators."

The U.S. role in Central America was a key locus of congressional foreign policy disputes in the 1980s.[7] The Reagan administration funded the Salvadoran army in its counterinsurgency war and the Contras in their fight against the leftist Sandinista government of Nicaragua. Both forces perpetrated atrocities and failed to meet the legal standards for aid recipients set by the U.S. government. However, the State Department's Bureau of Human Rights and Humanitarian Affairs, created in 1977 to be the U.S. government's official human rights agency, supported the administration's agenda of sending military aid to abusive forces. President Ronald Reagan ensured this support by weakening the bureau, limiting the number of employees to twenty and appointing leadership hostile to human rights concerns.[8] The Bureau's director, Elliot Abrams, repeatedly denied the role of U.S.-funded Salvadoran military in massacres; he later pled guilty to two misdemeanor counts of lying to Congress about the Reagan administration's illegal support of the Nicaraguan Contras.[9] Given the Reagan administration's unified front, human rights activists turned for support to the Democratic opposition. The Democratic majority in the House of Representatives allowed them to convene hearings, conduct investigations, and call votes on amendments to the aid.[10] The congressional caucuses played an important role in the debates and produced independent reports on military aid issues based on weeks of in-country research by caucus staff.

Activists within the movement to change U.S. policy in Central America developed a repertoire of political tactics focusing on congressional lobbying that continue to shape how advocacy groups approach human rights policymaking today. This movement was a massive and heterogeneous amalgamation of distinct ideological and organizational groupings that included religious, labor, solidarity, and humanitarian groups. Although these organizations had a variety of political visions and activist profiles, many shared a pragmatic orientation toward reducing U.S. military aid to the region.[11] The movement focused on Congress because of the partisan policy dynamics in play at the time. The Republican Reagan administration designed and championed the policy of military aid, which was largely supported by Republican members of Congress. However, Democrats were opposed to the policy, and its majority in the House of Representatives for much of this period facilitated alliances between activists and opposition members of Congress. Activists therefore chose to focus on the most important congressional tool for shaping international relations: the budget appropriations process. One staffer called this approach the "blunt, big stick," because such efforts could not alter the policy design, but rather limited program implementation by reducing or conditioning the money allocated. Activists working with sympathetic members of Congress mobilized in support of a series of amendments to reduce military aid to the Nicaraguan Contras and Salvadoran security forces.

Activists pursued a two-pronged strategy: targeting congressional offices directly and working with grassroots activists in their districts to apply constituency pressure on particular representatives. The Central America Working Group (CAWG) coordinated these lobbying efforts; by the late 1980s, the coalition had more than fifty members representing peace organizations around the country whose members received political training from CAWG staff.[12] In their efforts to reach congressional offices directly, activists developed new genres of reporting, such as the "hill drop," fact sheets distributed to all members of Congress addressing specific legislative concerns and providing talking points. At the same time, they recruited more activists by providing the analytical tools to understand U.S. policy as a grievance that must be remedied through action. Educational efforts tied to legislative action included arranging "witnessing" tours— political tourism orchestrated by NGOs to spark personal transformation—and bringing activists and survivors of human rights abuses on speaking tours within the United States. The CAWG also held conferences and teach-ins, which often featured instruction on how to lobby members of Congress, media outreach (such as how to build media contacts, provide interviews to reporters, and write op-eds), and connecting with and expanding existing activist networks. Many of these educational efforts also taught activists the particulars of policy advocacy, including how to develop specific policy goals, analysis of the range of foreign policy mechanisms, and information about specific pieces of legislation, amendments, and congressional debates. Protests were timed to coincide with votes or specific legislative initiatives. Before the Internet or social media, legislative alerts and editorial board mailings were distributed by fax to activists and local media alerting them to upcoming political events. This repertoire of political practices provided the foundation for subsequent generation of activists. At the same time, however, the focus on legislative action was deeply divisive and controversial for many activists, particularly among those who viewed participation in policymaking as complicity with what they viewed as a criminal policy and favored more confrontational tactics.[13]

The Central American wars ended in negotiated settlements in Guatemala and El Salvador; the Sandinistas were voted out of office in Nicaragua. By the mid-1990s, the Central America peace movement had largely dissolved. The region was rarely in the news and no longer the focus of human rights debates, which prioritized the complex conflicts in Africa and the Balkans. Latin America was frequently described as on the path to democratization. The end of the Cold War signified the lack of a central and coherent meta-narrative of U.S. foreign policy missing the urgency of the apocalyptic visions of a Soviet triumph that justified proxy wars and the motivating possibilities of socialist social change. Activists turned to other concerns, their personal lives, and careers; in some cases, they began to champion other political causes.[14] For a small number, however, fighting for human rights was now a career and profession in itself. This cohort of advocates took the lobbying practices developed by CAWG staff—the hill drop, editorial board mailings, the legislative alert—as central strategies in their efforts to orchestrate human rights policy.

Practicing Professionalization

In the post–Cold War era, many human rights groups faced major institutional changes as human rights moved—to some degree—into the political mainstream. Major foundations offered human rights funding, universities offered human rights courses, and human rights groups expanded their salaried staff. The Central America Working Group, for example, relaunched as the Latin America Working Group (LAWG). Working with five paid staff, LAWG expanded its mission to providing support for implementation of peace accords in Central America, humanitarian and development assistance, disaster relief, and opposition to the Cuba embargo. Human Rights Watch and Amnesty International, the largest and best known transnational human rights organizations, established Washington offices staffed with full-time professional advocacy directors in the early 1990s and began to orient their research toward legislative campaigns intended to shape policy. This professionalization process brought about profound changes in knowledge production practices, centered on objective reporting that depoliticized human rights knowledge, adhered to legal standards, and used a dispassionate tone rather than explicitly expressing alliance with social justice movements. Activists and advocates debated these changes as they struggled to define what constituted authentic and effective human rights practice at the close of the twentieth century.

Human rights groups operating in Washington became one part of a growing legion of lobbyists attempting to influence congressional debates. Operating on shoestring budgets, they were faced with the question of how to become "power players" where access to government influence was the only game in town. For grassroots and membership groups, a central part of their political influence derived from their ability to motivate constituents in particular congressional districts to pressure their representatives in Congress. This model of participation in policymaking relied on claims of citizenship to justify grassroots participation. This calculus assumed that, as residents in a democracy whose taxes funded governmental programs and whose officials claimed to act in their name, citizens had a right and obligation to shape policy. Amnesty International (AI) was the largest membership human rights group, with local chapters throughout the country. In addition to writing letters to repressive governments on behalf of political prisoners, AI campaigns now began to target U.S. policymakers to pressure them to support specific policy initiatives. Similarly, the Latin America Working Group was a coalition of groups such as churches and solidarity committees that were able to mobilize their membership to lobby their representatives. These human rights groups provided political action blueprints for citizen-activists.

Even for membership organizations, however, much of their policymaking participation rested on the logic of expertise, not citizenship. Credibility is widely described as the central political resource available to human rights groups that are unable to provide campaign contributions or other material rewards to officials. Profound and specialized knowledge about a situation and its impact served as currency. To be a credible expert required accurate information about violence in remote regions. Groups that trafficked in exaggerated, untrue, or incomplete tales were quickly excluded from official policy circles. Simply reporting valid information, however, was insufficient for acceptance as a credible human rights organization.

In the broader political field of policymaking, credibility functioned as a form of social capital involving not only accuracy but also institutional origins, qualities, and larger political agendas.[15] Hierarchies of credibility reflected broader assumptions about status and worth. The U.S. government considered Colombian government agencies to be inherently more credible than NGOs. Among the NGOs, the hierarchy of credibility was as follows: international over national groups, national groups over regional ones, and professionally run over volunteer led.[16] These hierarchies of credibility also applied among and within governmental agencies. The U.S. government considered U.S. governmental agencies to more credible than Colombian agencies; officials from both governments found human-rights–focused agencies (such as the Bureau of Democracy, Human Rights, and Labor [DRL] in the State Department, and the Colombian Human Rights Ombudsman) to be less credible than other agencies.

Institutional agendas—"the ask"—were also part of the credibility calculus. As one human rights researcher told me, "We were listening to people, [finding out] what works, the arguments they are using that we could use to advance a human rights agenda that responds to their political necessities." In the Colombia policy debates, credibility rested in part on not talking about some realms of policy (drug prohibition) and ensuring that the critique included specific perpetrators (the guerrillas). Although the Washington Office on Latin America (WOLA) was one of the only groups during the 1990s that discussed the negative and counterproductive impact of drug policy in Latin America, advocating the legalization or even decriminalization of drugs was verboten. Despite the personal convictions and analysis of many staff members of human rights groups, the institutional decision not to even mention such issues was based on the need to remain credible. Accusations that human rights NGOs failed to address guerrilla violence or were harboring secret political sympathies and alliances were a mantra of those attempting to discredit them. Thus, for Human Rights Watch and other organizations, reporting on guerrilla abuses was both "a real issue we should be concerned about" and a strategy to gain credibility, "a bona fide play for the Washington work, to be taken seriously in Washington," in the words of one former staffer.

In other words, the "ask" itself became a critical site for establishing credibility. Demands that were seen as outside the realm of appropriate political practice eroded credibility and the ability of such groups to gain funding, access, and leverage. What constituted the boundaries of appropriate political practice was a subject of constant debate, however. Many human rights advocates saw pushing the boundaries of the politically possible as a fundamental part of their project. Some advocates maintained their pragmatic focus on working within the confines of existing policy priorities and power relations, viewing their project as a process of incremental achievements, even as others insisted that the appropriate role was to stake utopian ethical claims.

Although these groups were publicly recognized for their human rights knowledge, lobbying and advocacy required multiple forms of expertise. Advocacy required mastery of the Washington system that mapped legislative action, power, and leverage. "We had to know their schedule, know when bills were coming up," one researcher-turned-advocate told me, "what was happening in the committees, how to get into the hearings, when we testified how to be prepared, and what day." In some cases, pushing these pressure points involved political horse trading rather than providing details of abuses; one congressional staffer recalled the importance of knowing who was motivated to make political deals—what he called "playing real politics"—to securing votes on human rights legislation. Getting a road project in a member of Congress's district authorized or facilitating the passage of specific agricultural subsidies would ensure votes. As this advocate told me, "If you are lobbying by saying, come meet this priest and some nuns, do the right thing, you are losing from the start."

However, efforts to promote human rights in Colombia through lobbying and advocacy in support of particular pieces of legislation were controversial among human rights activists and advocates. Some argued that the translation of human rights claims into policy "asks" betrayed their broader goals, erasing their origins in radical critiques of empire or pacifist political projects as they were rearticulated as support for technocratic programs. Support for the Leahy Law and the human rights conditions written later into Plan Colombia suggested that, should specific requirements be met, human rights groups would endorse military aid to Colombia. A number of pacifist and progressive organizations rejected this premise: they categorically rejected military aid as immoral and counter to their political principles. They argued that the focus on these piecemeal policies distracted from the larger goals of ending military aid, transforming the U.S. role in the world, promoting social justice, and acting in solidarity with victims of human rights abuses. For some of these activists, participation in policymaking was wasteful, politically dishonest, and undemocratic. They critiqued lobbying strategies as compromising their political goals for the sake of access and power. Such activists insisted that a complete cutoff of U.S. military aid was the only appropriate policy position; they rejected efforts to ensure compliance with human rights standards or "improving the balance" between military and humanitarian assistance.

Making Leahy

The creation of the Leahy amendment demonstrates how alliances between activists, policymakers, and advocates make human rights legislation possible. It was one of the most important pieces of contemporary national human rights legislation, and its passage played a central role in U.S.-Colombia relations during this period. According to U.S. Embassy officials, during the initial years of Plan Colombia implementation the Colombia vetting program was the largest in the world. Names of soldiers and officers to be trained are run against a human rights database and checked with information from Colombian government agencies, NGO reports, and media sources. As of 2008, more than 30,000 names had been vetted, in contrast to the vetting program in Saudi Arabia, which only included approximately 300 names at that point. The amendment was written in direct response to concerns about the possible misuse of U.S. military aid by Colombian security forces. The central players in its design were AI activists working with congressional staffers, including Tim Rieser, the long-term Leahy (D-VT) staffer on the Appropriations Committee who had a long history of NGO collaboration. The process of execution, however, demonstrated the limits of working within the dominant policy logic of militarization.

The first generation of human rights legislation was written into the Foreign Assistance Acts in the 1970s and was generally known as 502B. This subsection of the 1974 Foreign Assistance Act prohibited the United States from supplying security assistance to governments that grossly violated human rights. Later modifications to the law included an optional presidential waiver.[17] Section 116 of the 1976 Foreign Assistance Act required that human rights conditions be considered in the provision of economic assistance as well. 502B was never applied, however. In the words of former AI Washington director, Steve Rickard, "502B is extreme; it puts everything that the U.S. wants to do on one side of the table, and human rights on the other." Carlos Salinas, then advocacy director for Latin America at Amnesty International USA, had worked previously with congressional allies to promote the use of Section 502B to cut off aid to abusive Latin American militaries, but these efforts never progressed beyond briefly freezing aid already in the pipeline. "We were giving military assistance to people with terrible track records [through counternarcotics programs], and we couldn't cut off the aid because the overall mission was seen as too important, the aid was seen as so important," he said. "If we tried to rule out aid to countries, it would never go anywhere. They weren't going to cut off aid to Colombia." Pentagon representatives and other supporters of military aid argued that cutting off all military aid to a country because of specific abuses carried out by particular units was unfairly punishing an entire institution for the deeds of a few bad apples.

AI decided to work within this logic, "going after the few bad apples," Salinas told me. "The innovation was to require research on specific units." According to Rickard, the language in the Leahy amendment was actually written by Senator Paul Sarbanes' (D-MD) staffer Diana Ohlbaum, who emailed him ideas about crafting legislative language to address human rights violations committed by units receiving U.S. assistance for counternarcotics efforts.

AI reporting on Colombia also played an important role in raising the issue of U.S. counternarcotics assistance going to abusive units. In 1994, it published a report focusing on abuses by the Colombian military and national police titled "Colombia: Political Violence: Myth and Reality." It detailed a number of dramatic cases, including the case of a Swiss nun who had been allegedly killed in a combat operation, and tied those cases to specific Colombian units. AI activists requested information from the State Department on possible U.S. assistance tied to units listed in the report. AI never received an official response, but leaked internal U.S. government documents reported that thirteen of the fourteen military units were receiving U.S. assistance.[18] "There is now no doubt that the U.S. provided guns and ammunition to Colombian military units with a track record of killing innocent civilians not involved in any way with the drug trade," Amnesty announced in a November 2, 1996, press release.[19] The leaked documents, released by AI, spurred public debate over the issue of misuse of U.S. counternarcotics funding. On November 25, 1996, the New York Times also published an editorial supporting the amendment.

Carlos Salinas, AI's advocacy director for Latin America, combined a confrontational personal style with savvy policy strategizing around linking grassroots activists to legislative campaigns. He also had a long history of personal interest in Colombia, having studied there in the mid-1980s as an exchange student. As he described it, the Leahy amendment "happened accidentally." After Paul Coverdell, a Republican senator from Georgia, advocated increasing military counterdrug assistance, Salinas prepared an AI brief on human rights abuses committed during counternarcotics operations funded by the United States. When Coverdell did not respond to this report, Salinas began working with Georgia-based AI activists, consulting frequently with them as they increased constituency pressure on Coverdell. Coverdell responded by approaching Salinas, who told me, "That gave the space for Tim [Rieser] to do something."

Policymaking relies on bureaucratic positioning and privilege. As the senior staff member on the Senate Appropriations committee representing the majority, Reiser was able to place the language in the bill without there being open debate on the floor; this was an example of how congressional staffers' knowledge of and positioning within the legislative process allow them to insert policy prescriptions without reaching institutional consensus. Rieser added the amendment into the bill during the conference session, the closed-door negotiations to reconcile House and Senate versions of legislation. "There were a lot of people who would have fought it, if they had known about it," one former staffer said, "but Tim put it through quietly, under the radar."

Some supporters of militarized counternarcotics assistance remained concerned that the measure would result in cutting off assistance to the Colombian police or other security forces they viewed as deserving of U.S. assistance. According to the *Congressional Record*, in 1997 hearings Representatives Gilman and Burton and Speaker of the House Dennis Hastert all attacked the measure. Senator Leahy sent letters to national security advisor Sandy Berger and Representatives Hastert and Gilman in 1998, assuring them that the law would not be used to improperly withhold aid from the CNP. In addition to Leahy's formal assurances about the effect of the Leahy amendment, Carlos Salinas also recalled bringing constituency pressure on Representative Gilman to support the measure: "I was working with activists, and they would call several times a day. They would talk to Gilman's office and then report to me, and then I would send them back with the rebuttal...An hour later, the chief of staff called Steve [Rickard, his boss at AI], and that is when things changed."

Bureaucratic Vulnerability and Human Rights
Policy Implementation

Human rights policy production is not only the expression of ideal norms but also one of a series of competing narratives produced about what those norms are and how they should be realized. The Leahy Law was one claim to what U.S. values signified in action: that the United States does not support abusive foreign military units.[20] Through NGO alliances with critically positioned congressional staff, Leahy was written into law. Yet this claim was by no means a consensus position. For the majority of military aid supporters, human rights was not an accepted norm, but a threat to their policy visions.

The debates over creation and implementation of the Leahy Law highlight the role of bureaucratic vulnerability in policymaking. Anthropological considerations of bureaucratic practice have emphasized the power of officials over citizens, resulting in their "indifference" and arbitrary attention to citizen needs.[21] Analyzing relationships among officials within a range of governmental agencies reveals how competition between them produces fear of the loss of political power, prestige, and control. Officials are enmeshed in disputes over always scarce resources and jurisdiction; frequently they focus on protecting their own vulnerable and besieged institutions. For example, Michael Barnett's insightful analysis of the failure of the United Nations and the State Department to respond to the unfolding genocide in Rwanda highlights the importance of perceptions of bureaucratic vulnerability in institutional action (or inaction). During debates over the appropriate policy response, officials within these state human rights agencies implicitly argued that "genocide was acceptable if the alternative was to harm the future of the UN."[22] Tolerating abuses in the present was prioritized over possible future institutional weakness. Similarly the creation and implementation of Leahy exposed how human rights legislation incites fears of bureaucratic vulnerability among officials within militarized agencies. Throughout the process, officials jockeyed for institutional power: some viewed human rights concerns as a possible threat to their political agendas, whereas others pushed for more expansive implementation. The dominant interpretation resulted in an assessment framework that allowed for compliance with the legislation while permitting uninterrupted military aid delivery.

In this case, foreign policy production generated concerns about bureaucratic vulnerability between U.S. and Colombian bureaucracies, as well as within other Colombian institutions. Imposing new conditions for the delivery of foreign assistance, the Leahy amendment (and later law) involved intense negotiation with foreign governmental agencies, many of which viewed human rights concerns within the context of their national interagency power relations and as part of U.S. efforts to unilaterally impose its agenda. With passage of the Leahy Law, delivery of military assistance required the signing of formal agreements— end-use monitoring agreements (EUMs)—stipulating how the foreign government would meet the requirements of the Leahy Law. Previously, the United States had accepted a biannual "good faith certification" from the Colombians, simply stating that they had met all the U.S. requirements for the legal transfer of funds.[23] Efforts to negotiate an EUM that would satisfy all parties demonstrated the contrasting political agendas between and among U.S. and Colombian government agencies and revealed the weakness of Colombian civilian power structures compared to military institutions.

Efforts to finalize the EUM occurred during the worst modern crisis of U.S.-Colombian relations. As mentioned earlier, in 1996 the United States revoked President Ernesto Samper's visa and decertified Colombia following revelations (publicly released by the DEA) that he had accepted campaign contributions from the Cali Cartel.[24] Colombian military officers chafed under the perception of the corruption of national civilian political leaders.[25] U.S. assistance at the time went primarily to the Colombian National Police, which enjoyed a stellar reputation among their congressional Republican supporters, particularly because of the charismatic leadership of General Rosso José Serrano. The military felt marginalized from the exclusively counternarcotics-focused assistance packages and maligned by accusations of corruption and incompetence made by many of their U.S. counterparts. Despite a history of close U.S.-Colombia military relations dating from the Korean War, Colombian military officers generally viewed human rights concerns as politically motivated slander, even those coming from U.S. officials.[26] Operating under an informal agreement known as the Lleras pact, they were also long accustomed to the authority to design and implement national security policy largely independent of any civilian oversight.[27]

During an initial discussion with the U.S. ambassador on April 28, 1997, President Ernesto Samper agreed to "intercede" with the military to reach an end-use monitoring agreement. One of the major points of contention remained the repercussions for individuals accused of human rights abuses. The United States proposed that they be removed from active duty and placed on "administrative" leave, whereas Colombian officials argued that "there is no way under Colombian law for an individual who has merely been accused to be removed from a unit." President Samper noted, "Such things are not as easy in the military as they are with the National Police." He also related concerns expressed by the military that these requirements would release a "floodgate of accusations against the military." The U.S. ambassador disagreed, noting that the Ministry of Defense would control the process of transferring accused individuals. The ambassador concluded with a warning: "In the end, if the military cannot accept the Leahy Law requirements, the equipment will go just to the police."[28] On April 30, the Colombian Air Force and Navy signed EUM agreements, but the Army refused. The embassy reported receiving a letter from Armed Forces commander Harold Bedoya, "objecting in the strongest terms" to the agreement. The embassy also reported that it rejected requests from the Colombian Ministry of Defense to keep any possible agreement secret and for additional equipment.

The debates over the Colombian military's acceptance of the Leahy provisions must be understood in the context of their broader objections to civilian oversight by Colombian governmental agencies, including the delegitimized president, as well as their view that the United States was displaying both hypocrisy and left-wing bias in its demands. In a section of a State Department cable reporting on conversations between the U.S. ambassador and the Colombian minister of defense titled "Human Rights: Much Later, Please," the minister of defense requested that the United States support peace efforts by "laying off the subject of human rights," because it "was making it tougher on the military, whose cooperation he needed to achieve peace . . . [the Minister] needed the support of the generals, and if he pushed human rights, he would not be able to do his job as minister."[29] The cable also revealed that the Colombian Defense Ministry had requested a U.S. visa for a colonel linked to death squad activity. The Colombian military high command had nominated him for a position at the Inter-American Defense College, a graduate school for military officers and government officials operating under the control of the Organization of American States and the Inter-American Defense Board, and housed in donated buildings in Fort McNair, Virginia. The Defense Ministry had been warned by the U.S. Embassy that the United States would not grant the colonel a visa, and the cable includes this comment: "The idea of trying to send to the U.S. an officer about whom the ambassador has complained for more than a year for tolerating or promoting death squads shows the insensitivity to U.S. human rights concerns of top Colombian Army commanders."

Colombian officials were not the only ones opposed to the inclusion of human rights issues in foreign policy: some U.S. officials also believed that enforcement of the Leahy requirements made the U.S. military vulnerable to pressure from civilian agencies, to reduced budgets and material supplies, and to an erosion of mission control. Some also argued that such requirements weakened U.S. allies involved in complex conflicts. In one of the most telling examples, declassified embassy cables revealed that during a May 1997 trip to Colombia, while the Leahy EUM agreement was being negotiated, Speaker of the House Dennis Hastert explicitly expressed his rejection of the human rights conditions in meetings with Colombian officials. He told Colombian military officials that he would work to "remove conditions on assistance" and complained about the previous years of "leftist" influence in the U.S. Congress that "used human rights as an excuse to aid the left in other countries." Hastert promised to promote counternarcotics assistance and recommended that Colombian officials should "bypass the U.S. executive branch and communicate directly with Congress."[30]

Negotiations over the EUM agreement came to a head in a series of frustrating talks during the summer of 1997. A 1997 cable reporting on a meeting between the U.S. Ambassador and his staff with Defense Minister Gilberto Echeverri, military forces commander Harold Bedoya, and Bedoya's legal counsel documented the stalemate. Colombian military lawyers objected to the phrase "credible allegation," arguing instead an individual could be held accountable (including the imposition of any kind of sanction, such as removal from a unit) only after a completed judicial process with a finding of guilt or innocence. The lawyers maintained that the concept of credible allegation "was not admissible under Colombian law."[31] During this and subsequent discussions, the U.S. ambassador argued,

"Gross violations of human rights" is a very high standard which is well defined in U.S. and Colombian law. Many accusations like those the military regularly received would not qualify under that standard, and more than a lawsuit was required to have such accusations form a basis for USG action. The USG was not setting a trap for the Colombians, but rather urging their acceptance of an agreement which met their stated conditions while upholding U.S. law.

Army Commander General Harold Bedoya in turn complained of State Department bias against the Colombian Army. The cable reporting on the meeting concluded, "The Colombians were only willing to promise that Colombian law would be carried out in the same unsatisfactory manner as in the past." The cable concluded with a final recommendation from U.S. officials: deliver all the aid to the police as soon as possible.[32] Despite their frustrations with the Colombian army, throughout the process U.S. officials made clear their commitment to the ongoing delivery of U.S. military equipment, training, and funding to Colombian institutions.

At this point, events were transformed by the internal dynamics of Colombian politics. General Bedoya was forced to resign after a showdown with the president over proposed negotiations with the guerrillas in July 1997. His replacement, General José Bonnet, signed the EUM agreement on July 30, 1997, despite voicing many of the same concerns as his predecessor.

Leahy Vetting

The debates over implementation of Leahy reveal the degree to which policy domains are unstable and dynamic and their state effects emerge through measurement and assessment—which themselves are profoundly shaped by cultural frameworks and political claims.[33] In this case, the assessments focused on the contested meanings of critical words: "unit," "effective measures," and "credible." The debates over the meanings of these categories reveal how the underlying agendas and power structures are shifted but not transformed through such policy interventions. Policy opens up realms of political life to intervention and surveillance; in particular, human rights policy is intended to make transgovernmental relations and exchanges legible to human rights scrutiny. The law sets out implementation as a transparent and self-evident process of information management, a central technocratic endeavor of modern governance. However, although claiming to increase transparency, the categories used to engender this legibility are not themselves transparent.[34] The forms of auditing and assessment serve to contain and manage bureaucratic vulnerability. As written, Leahy codified human rights concerns as privileged over military aid. As applied, the dominant logic of militarization prevailed.

All accounts of even the apparently simple first step of gathering the allegations of human rights abuses—before assessing their credibility—reveal that the assumptions of transparency were a fiction. Centralized information management systems do not exist in Colombia. "If we want to know how many outstanding cases there are against the [paramilitary group] the *Águilas Negras*, we don't just walk across the street to the prosecutor (*fiscalía*) and ask, we have to call every region, every city, all the specialized prosecutors' offices and ask them to go through their files," one embassy official involved with the vetting program told me in 2008. In addition, many crimes are not registered as allegations. Lack of investigative capacity and threats and violent attacks against witnesses and prosecutors have prevented many cases involving abuses by military units from even entering the legal system.[35] Many victims of abuses rightly concluded that by coming forward with complaints they risked additional violence; many of those who did come forward had their cases dismissed. In a 1998 conversation with the U.S. ambassador, Colombian minister of defense Lloreda concluded, "A culture of impunity prevails in Colombia," calling the civilian judicial system "woefully ineffective" and noting "a lack of confidence in the military judiciary." He "discounted the likelihood of improving the current situation in the short term for cultural reasons," including the fact that many military officers think long-term incarceration for any crime seems "unfair."[36]

Who produces allegations plays a central role in their assessment. Here as in other realms, institutional positioning and hierarchy played a central role in establishing credibility. U.S. officials charged with the vetting program continue to question the credibility of the NGOs,[37] in part because they do not satisfy embassy standards of evidence. Officials frequently classify the oral testimony of local populations and NGO reporting as vague, lacking the required corroborating accounts or identification of specific units involved in events, or as politically motivated. Colombian government officials also accuse NGOs of ties to the Colombian guerrillas.

An imagined military "unit" is not easily transferrable into the logic of accountability that the authors of the Leahy Law attempted to establish. Military personnel are organized into a range of military "units"—patrol, platoon, company, battalion, brigade, division—ranging in size from six people to thousands. These administrative divisions are used as the receptacles for assistance, equipment and training, as well as operational deployment, with missions assigned by geographic location. Yet these units are administrative fictions, set in a permanent hierarchy and relatively stable organizational structure, but with their membership in constant flux. Through the rotation of personnel due to injuries and command promotions, the specific individuals within the structure are difficult, often impossible, to trace. Human rights activists critical of the Leahy provision used this administrative instability to argue against the vetting process or as evidence that the Leahy language was inadequate, urging that systematic institutional reform be the prerequisite for eligibility for U.S. funding and support.

In defining the standard for vetting, the State Department settled on vetting the smallest "unit" possible. According to a 1999 General Accounting Office (GAO) report, "In a May 8, 1999 cable to all overseas embassies, the State Department defined the unit to be trained as the unit to be vetted. Thus, for individual training, the individual will be vetted. For unit-level training, the unit itself will be vetted." According to this interpretation, individual soldiers from abusive units could participate in training as long as they were not linked by name to a credible allegation.[38] The focus on units also erased the ways in which military equipment and training are fungible, as people and goods circulate freely within military networks. Any aid sent to military institutions benefits the entire force; anyone trained benefits the entire military institution. Individuals from abusive units, after receiving training, simply returned to their abusive units, which then benefited from their new expertise. There was no tracking of their location or performance post-training. U.S. assistance to vetted units allowed the Colombian military to devote more assistance to abusive units. Significant forms of U.S. assistance, such as expertise and intelligence, are nonmaterial, such that they cannot be restricted but circulate freely throughout the units, vetted and unvetted alike.

The architects of the law intended to address the issue of systematic impunity by ensuring that allegations resulted in criminal trials, the "effective measures" that the government had to take to address the allegations. However, in some of the cables describing the vetting process, embassy officials appear to endorse the view that simply preventing accused soldiers from participating in U.S.-supported units meets the standard. The author of an April 1999 cable wrote, "One particular problem has been that 'dirty' individuals have been moved into 'clean' units during the annual personnel rotation cycles, requiring us to suspend assistance to the unit." The embassy advises that the Colombian Ministry of Defense "take full advantage" of the database to "review the transfer lists and makes sure people are 'clean' before their transfer orders are cut."[39] A July 1999

GAO report describes the Defense Department's (DOD) policy guidance as "adjusting the planned activity or participants." According to the DOD guidelines, this would constitute the necessary "corrective action to address situations where there is credible information of gross human rights violations by a member of a unit."[40] Thus simply removing an individual for the duration of the training would meet the legal requirements. During interviews, embassy personnel told me that the Leahy vetting process did result in senior officials being forced out of the military because they could not get the training required for promotion. However, there are no public records available documenting such cases nor any evidence of systematic pressure brought to bear in following up the cases of individuals found to have credible allegations against them.

By focusing on abuses tied to individual soldiers within specific units, Leahy assessment ignored evolving forms of political violence in Colombia. During this period, human rights groups tracked a decline in the direct participation of military forces in abuses, whereas the number of such attacks attributed to paramilitary forces rose dramatically as political violence was privatized (explored in the following chapter). Military supporters, including officials in the U.S. military and the Clinton administration, claimed that this reduction in direct military participation was the result of genuine reform within the military. Critics instead pointed to the evidence of collaboration between military and paramilitary forces, arguing that the military had not reformed, but had replaced direct action with collusion. Paramilitary forces also resorted to new modalities of violence, designed to allow perpetrators to escape the scrutiny of international human rights reporting. Other emergent forms of violence were particularly difficult to link to individual soldiers or even particular units, such as the practice of "false positives," in which young men were disappeared from their homes and presented in distant states as guerrillas killed in combat.[41]

Clean Units

Leahy did shift U.S. military aid delivery, but not in the ways that the architects of the law intended. Finding overwhelming evidence that many Colombian military units had been involved in human rights abuses, U.S. officials quickly realized that, given the widespread allegations of military misconduct, it was practically impossible to find Colombian military units that could pass the Leahy vetting requirements. Rather than suspend aid, U.S. officials devised a new mechanism for aid delivery: the creation of new, "clean" units. Made up of vetted individuals, these units would be eligible for all U.S. assistance and training; as new units with no existing record, they would be instantly cleared.

In March 1998, the first unit to be vetted and cleared for U.S. assistance was the Eastern Specified Command (CEO), and it proved an inspiration for the creation of new units. As noted in a March 1998 U.S. embassy cable to Washington, the unit "didn't really exist": as a unified military command converted into an army command in 1996 for "contingencies in the border area," it was not a fully constituted military unit, but was rather an administrative designation with only a "minimal number of full time troops." Instead, "battalions from other units are 'op-conned' to the CEO."[42] Although the CEO was recommended for immediate aid, the vetting process exposed problems with all the other units proposed for U.S. assistance.[43]

By October, the proposal to create a "clean" counternarcotics battalion was supported by the Colombian military and the Samper administration. According to a 1998 U.S. embassy cable, the "unit to be designated would probably be relatively new and 'clean' of significant human rights problems." The Colombians viewed the creation of these new units as a concession to U.S. pressure, asking "in return" for U.S. funding for equipment; military officers also reported "understanding" that making such units focused on counternarcotics would "maximize ready access to US intelligence."[44] After outlining the logistical and financial requirements of such a battalion, the issue of Leahy and vetting led the embassy to propose a "Breakthrough toward staring out with 'clean' units?" To meet all the human rights objectives, the embassy intended to pursue with the Ministry of Defense the "possibility of standing up 'clean' new units comprised of pre-screened troops," concluding that "in the context of a major boost in designated assistance (e.g. counternarcotics battalion) the colar [Colombian army] might be willing to consider such a move." A State Department cable dated the next day describing a meeting between the U.S. ambassador and the Colombian minister of defense reported that, after pointing out problems with existing units proposed for U.S. assistance, the ambassador "raised the possibility of standing up new, clean units."[45]

Policymakers involved in the design of the Plan Colombia package emphasized the importance of creating new units that could receive the massive influx of assistance. Similarly, officials with SouthCom reported that the Leahy requirements were "why we did not use an existing battalion." As one such official told me,

We went down there, with Special Forces trainers, and figured out how to make things work with the State Department vetting. We made sure that none were from other units, that they were individuals that were new to the military, that they were brand new with no possibilities of problems.

Conclusion

Policymaking as a political field encompasses a range of actors beyond the state, exemplified by the alliances between nongovernmental activists and congressional staff that produced legislation such as the Leahy Law. Human rights activists' engagement with policymaking required participation in a contested process of professionalization. These advocates built on the previous generation of activism focusing on U.S. policy toward Central America to produce new forms of expertise and credibility. By moving human rights work into a lobbying culture organized around "the ask," they developed new institutional orientations toward the articulation of specific requests for action, in part so that politicians can claim the results as an example of their political power and leverage. In many ways, this is a much more complicated and controversial process than investigating violence, because embedded within "the ask" are profound moral, ethical, and political claims about the possibilities of political action. Nowhere is this controversy more evident than in efforts to assess the impact of the Leahy Law.

Leahy operated within the logic of the existing policy narrative, not challenging the militarization of counternarcotics policy or the official assessment of the Colombian military as being afflicted with a "few bad apples." It did not address systemic issues of abuse, corruption, and violence. The new strategy of aid delivery—through the creation of new, "clean" units—did not engender the institutional military reform and legal sanction of officers who committed abuses that the law's designers' intended. The distinction between new "clean" and existing abusive units proved nearly impossible to maintain, particularly given the U.S. focus on improved military operational integration and coordination. Joint campaigns between vetted and unvetted units eroded these distinctions on the ground. The new "clean" counternarcotics units operated in joint campaigns with local units, including those facing allegations of abuse, as part of the United States' "Push into Southern Colombia" strategy.

The focus on monitoring implementation shifted the terms of the debate and political action to efforts to support the legislation itself. Rather than articulating larger policy critiques, mobilizing grassroots action, or arguing over the causes and consequences of political violence, advocates found themselves attempting to protect the legislation from critics within other government agencies. They also were expected to work to support implementation by monitoring compliance and providing their own assessments and reporting. Some critics of efforts to shape legislation focused on the institutional and political cost of monitoring, whereas others argued that vetting practices silenced larger debates over the causes and consequences of political violence. Some grassroots activists viewed the lobbying practiced by professional human rights NGOs as inherently undemocratic and nontransparent. The focus on what one termed "inside baseball," including policymakers' schedules, the construction of personal relationships, and the backroom deals facilitating legislation, excluded activists who lived outside of Washington or who did not have these forms of expert knowledge.

The contested process of defining the categories for assessment and evaluation allowed existing policy priorities to dominate, in this case militarization and the ongoing delivery of military aid. Human rights policy was subjugated to the institutional interests of the state in its own self-presentation as democratic and participatory, without shifting the ideological parameters of militarization that were the foundation of the policy. Implementation of the Leahy Law demonstrates the ways in which such policymaking generates not new norms but bureaucratic vulnerability among officials operating within distinct institutional agendas. Human rights legislation also contributes to the transformation of violence, as actors attempt to avoid surveillance and scrutiny. This perhaps most troubling legacy of human rights policymaking is explored in the next chapter.

At the same time, the Leahy Law continues to be critiqued by supporters of military aid. In 2013, the *New York Times* reported that the Leahy Law was "drawing unusual fire from some top military commanders who say it undermines their ability to train the troops to fight militants and drug traffickers."[46] General John F. Kelly, then head of SouthCom, described the law as a "complication." The article went on to note that 1,766 individuals and units from 46 countries were denied assistance in 2011. However, this is less than 1 percent of units nominated for U.S. aid. For these and other supporters of U.S. military aid flows to abusive militaries in Africa and the Middle East, the Leahy Law continues to generate bureaucratic vulnerability for U.S. military forces.

Activists continued to debate how to make human rights' utopian claims meaningful in specific contexts. During interviews, former AI staffers described the limited success of previous efforts to suspend military aid to abusive governments through human rights conditions. According to Steve Rickard, such conditions nearly led to aid being cut off to Guatemala, but the government chose to reject aid before such measures could be implemented; according to Carlos Salinas, aid to Colombia and Peru was frozen in the early 1990s because of human rights concerns. The Leahy Law has resulted in aid being suspended to foreign military forces in Colombia, Jamaica, Turkey, and elsewhere. In the context of sometimes bitter disputes over what human rights policymaking accomplished, Leahy Law supporters argued passionately that these efforts resulted in progress in specific cases, improving the real lives of actual people, and kept human rights within the policymaking landscape of possibilities.

Part II

Putumayo on the Eve of Plan Colombia

Figure 3   Paramilitary graffiti left on a local house in Putumayo, 1999. The wall reads: "Here we are, miserable communists, A.U.C. [United Self Defense Forces of Colombia]."

Photograph by Nancy Sánchez, used by permission.

Chapter 3
Paramilitary Proxies

[The paramilitary commanders] assembled [the residents] into two groups above the main square and across from the rudimentary health center. Then, one by one, they killed the men by crushing their heads with heavy stones and a sledgehammer. When it was over, 24 men lay dead in pools of blood. Two more were found later in shallow graves. As the troops left, they set fire to the village . . . More than two dozen residents interviewed in their burned-out homes and temporary shelters said they believe the Colombian military helped carry out the massacre. In dozens of interviews, conducted in small groups and individually over three days, survivors said military aircraft undertook surveillance of the village in the days preceding the massacre and in the hour immediately following it. The military, according to these accounts, provided safe passage to the paramilitary column and effectively sealed off the area by conducting what villagers described as a mock daylong battle with leftist guerrillas who dominate the area.

"Chronicle of a Massacre Foretold,"
Scott Wilson, *Washington Post*, January 28, 2001

A CENTRAL ISSUE for U.S. policymakers in considering U.S. policy toward Colombia was categorizing and accounting for Colombian paramilitary violence in the context of escalating military aid. Escalating violence was a policy problem: massacres, assassinations, and threats were highly visible factors in Colombian instability. At the same time, paramilitaries were also a policy solution, because this same brutal violence served a critical counterinsurgency function. Here, I examine the emergence of Colombia's paramilitary armies in the late 1990s as a form of proxy violence for the state. This violence pushed guerrillas into more remote regions, breaking their supply chains and facilitating military occupation of small rural towns, while allowing the state security forces to meet the human rights requirements of U.S. assistance.

The official policy—denial of the state's role in supporting this violence—performed multiple state effects. For U.S. policymakers required to certify the professionalism and accountability of the Colombian security forces, Colombian official denials fit neatly into the narrative of the absent state, positing the Colombian government as simply absent rather than aligned with paramilitary forces. For rural residents of Colombia living under paramilitary dominion and witness to the pervasive links between these forces and the military, however, these denials circulated as a form of state terror. In organized forums and informal encounters, military officers insisted that they were unaware of paramilitary violence and incapable of monitoring the region. They insisted that residents and civilian officials were responsible for providing intelligence to the state about armed actors and illegal violence. These demands exposed local residents to multiple forms of retaliatory violence—committed by state agents themselves should residents report official complicity with abuses, or by other armed actors if residents aligned with the state denounced their actions.

Although the contemporary neoliberal state is frequently described as in retreat, anthropologists have documented the multiple ways in which state presence is reconfigured through proxies, which are assigned some state functions but are not subject to the same oversight or citizen-state dynamics as the state.[1] Such proxies include NGOs and foundations that, in the process of providing health, humanitarian, education, and other welfare services in lieu of the state, exert profound state effects.[2] Here, I focus on another critical proxy: paramilitary forces used as the foundation of counterinsurgency efforts, operating outside the law but unofficially sanctioned by the state. These forces must be understood in the context of the privatization of state security functions through the use of mercenaries, private guards, and other military entrepreneurs.[3] Government investigators, journalists, and human rights activists have extensively documented the paramilitary forces' brutal tactics and the close ties between local officials and paramilitary commanders. These forces took up the work of the state in several areas: by acting not only in lieu of the state (exercising governance by restricting local movement, mandating appropriate behavior, and adjudicating conflicts) but also, more importantly, by acting in concert with the state, in close and deliberate alliance with military and police forces to carry out counterinsurgency campaigns. These operations constituted necropolitics by proxy, as Colombian paramilitaries did the work of the state in deciding who would live or die.[4]

Although a monopoly on the use of force is one hallmark of the Weberian model of the modern state, scholars of contemporary state formation in Latin

America have documented the multiple ways in which contemporary governance has coexisted with the failure to consolidate such control.[5] Military entrepreneurs—violence professionals who enter and exit state service while pursuing personal economic projects—have a long history in Colombia and are central to this contradictory dynamic.[6] Paramilitary commanders were only the most recent iteration, working at the juncture of counterinsurgency efforts and illegal enterprise. Their economic and counterinsurgency projects were linked in critical ways, as drug traffickers became the owners of massive tracts of land and were targeted for guerrilla violence and extortion. These complex relationships constituted an important contemporary example of what Deleuze and Guattari characterize as the "war machine."[7] Although much remains to be written, academic, human rights, and journalistic research has begun to reveal the entanglements between local paramilitary commanders, regional businesses and multinational corporations, political elites, politicians, and military command structures.[8] In this chapter, I focus on the state–paramilitary dynamic in the period immediately prior to and during the initial implementation of Plan Colombia. During that period, the paramilitaries allowed the state to present a two-sided mask: modern and accountable to its international sponsors, and terrorizing and authoritarian for rural residents viewed as criminal guerrilla supporters.

Pursuing counterinsurgency through proxy forces was a strategic imperative for the Colombian security forces during this period because of the contradictions between their military mandates to address the increasing military strength of the FARC and the institutional demands of the human rights era. Government security officers supported brutal paramilitary counterinsurgency operations not in spite of their claims to be transparent, accountable, and professional, but because of the contradictory demands of their local military mission and their international entanglements that required transparency, accountability, and professionalism. The Colombian central command needed to represent themselves as professional and modern partners to their U.S. funders and to comply with human rights regulations written into foreign assistance legislation such as the Leahy Law. Over the past three decades, an increasingly consolidated human rights regime championed by significant sectors of the U.S. government and written into the legislation regulating the dispersal of U.S. military aid has produced demands for transparency and professional military practices in which excessive violence has been officially considered as uncivilized, unprofessional, and unmodern. Demonstrating their worthiness to their U.S. patrons (particularly those congressional representatives supportive of human rights legislation) required evidence of these forces' transparency and rejection of extralegal violence. Paramilitary proxies allowed the military forces plausible deniability.

Colombia was one of many regions depicted during this period by U.S. analysts as "ungoverned spaces" characterized by an absent state.[9] This label indicated the lack of appropriate state institutional presence, generally conceived of as the state's repressive and policing functions, and the subsequent production of threats to both precarious regional nation-state formations as well as the United States. U.S. foreign policy experts during the mid-1990s mobilized the discursive production of the absent and failing state to advocate for largely militarized forms of intervention. However, the designation of "absent and failing state" was the product of particular constellations of Washington policy knowledge production, rather than an analytical category illuminating regional dynamics in the areas so described. By describing violence as the product of an "absent state," U.S. analysts misidentified and obscured the contemporary state practices of privatized and extrastate forms of political violence operating alongside public denial and strategies of concealment. One powerful form of state presence within this declared absence was the deployment of paramilitary proxies.

At the same time, official denials of paramilitary violence and of state complicity with it, proclaimed in meetings with local residents and civilian government representatives, constituted a form of state terror intended to intimidate residents into silence.[10] Denial and concealment have been central tactics in the deployment of state terror in Latin America, most notably in the practice of "disappearances," in which state agents capture and, in some cases, torture and kill those perceived to be enemies of the state.[11] State terror operates on multiple registers in these cases: the cognitive dissonance generated by the denial of well-known social facts, the explicit disavowal of the state's obligation to protect its citizens, the family's lack of knowledge of the fate of beloved family members, and the ongoing violent persecution of those seeking to reveal these crimes and achieve justice. In Colombia, military officers produced and performed denials of official responsibility in state-citizen encounters including local security council meetings with local officials, and in public meetings convened in small town central plazas. Military commanders positioned community leaders as violence experts, demanding they publicly reveal paramilitary activities. Residents were required to sign official documents listing any complaints or affirming regional peace, which were then archived in military files.

Paramilitaries as Counterinsurgency Proxies

Legally constituted "peasant self-defense groups" represent a classic use of "indigenous irregulars," long a central strategy in counterinsurgency doctrine.[12] By employing local residents, military commanders gain a strategic advantage over their elusive guerrilla enemies, benefiting from the local knowledge of terrain and community dynamics.[13] A 2008 Rand Counterinsurgency Study titled "Doctrine of Eternal Recurrence: The U.S. Military and Counterinsurgency Doctrine: 1960–1970 and 2003–2006" concluded that U.S. counterinsurgency doctrine since the early 1960s has remained remarkably consistent, including an emphasis on the civilian population, the importance of integration of military forces with civilian authorities, and the focus on small-unit operations and intelligence gathering. Throughout the long decades of the Cold War and into the present, such forces have operated in Latin America beyond the authority of legally recognized military operations to conduct death-squad–style assassinations and attacks.[14]

Violence and counterterror are central tactics in counterinsurgency operations, frequently described as part of "psychological operations" (psyops). During the Cold War, death squad operations targeting opposition leadership and suspected guerrilla sympathizers were part of the National Security Doctrine promoted by the United States.[15] One of the principal architects of U.S. psyops and civic action doctrine (which promotes military involvement in civilian development efforts) in the 1950s and early 1960s, General Edward Lansdale advocated a broad range of strategies including threats and mutilation of enemy corpses.[16] In 1984, a CIA Spanish-language manual was distributed to U.S.-sponsored Contra fighters for use against the Nicaraguan Sandinista government. Titled "Psychological Operations in Guerrilla Warfare," the manual advocated assassination. After it was leaked to U.S. journalists, congressional hearings absolved the CIA of any institutional wrongdoing.[17] In 1997, additional manuals were made public that refer to using torture and other practices that were technically illegal for U.S. forces; these manuals had been used until the early 1990s for training Latin American military forces at the School of the Americas.[18] In a 1985 year-end report, a U.S. officer who spent a year working with the Colombian Army as part of an official military exchange referred to these manuals as part of the U.S. material being incorporated into Colombian psyops manuals.

In Colombia, U.S. military intelligence teams suggested the use of indigenous irregulars and military proxies repeatedly during Cold War advising missions and training. The U.S. Army Special Warfare Center's report following a two-month research mission in 1962 advocated the secret training of civilian and military personnel to "develop underground civil and military structure" and that the Colombians begin "paramilitary, sabotage and/or terrorist activities against known communist proponents."[19] In the early 1960s, as part of its counterguerrilla strategy the Colombian army organized "civilian self-defense units (*autodefensa*) and directed them to relieve army units of some patrolling and local garrisoning."[20] The legal basis for state sponsorship of paramilitary organizations was Law 48, approved by the Colombian Congress in 1968, allowing the government to "mobilize the population in activities and tasks" to restore public order.[21] According to human rights groups and government investigators, during the first phase of paramilitary activity, there was considerable overlap between the civilians legally trained by local military forces in the 1970s and illegal paramilitary death squads such as the American Anti-Communist Alliance (AAA), active in the Magdalena Valley Region.

At the same time, the Colombian military pursued a low-intensity counterinsurgency strategy.[22] On the advice of U.S. military analysts, the Colombians focused on containment of the guerrilla threat to remote rural areas, rather than costly large-scale military operations intended to eliminate them. During the 1970s, U.S. military attention was largely directed elsewhere, and the Colombian military was left to its own devices. The Colombian military focused on enhancing administrative perks and privileges, developing an extensive bureaucratic apparatus that remains in place to this day. For example, the Colombian military has a very high logistical-to-combat soldier ratio of 6:1, compared to the international average of 3:1. Thus, as Nazih Richani reports, a career in the military was seen as providing a relatively safe and stable livelihood: "the low-intensity conflict has allowed the military to develop an institutional setup that was relatively comfortable within the context of a civil war."[23] Despite the ongoing insurgency, Colombia had the smallest military and the smallest military budget as a percentage of GDP of comparable countries in the region, a fact that would not change until Plan Colombia.[24]

The Role of the Drug Trade

In the 1980s money from the drug trade allowed paramilitary forces to evolve from small groups linked to local military commanders into private armies. The fusion of counterinsurgency ideology and illegal narcotics revenue produced one of the most lethal fighting forces in Latin America. As the owners of vast haciendas, drug traffickers were natural allies of the military in counterinsurgency efforts. Traffickers needed protection from the guerrillas, whose primary fundraising techniques involved *boleteo* (extortion), protection or *vacunas* ("vaccination" against guerrilla attack), and, increasingly, kidnapping the rural elite. Drug traffickers, business leaders, and local military commanders began to work together in regional groups that were generically known as paramilitary forces to target guerrillas and their perceived supporters. In many regions, paramilitary death squads became known as Masetos, after the group MAS (*Muerte a Secuestradores*, Death to Kidnappers), which was organized by drug traffickers, business leaders, and military officers following the 1981 kidnapping by the M-19 guerrillas of Martha Nieves Ochoa, daughter of Medellín Cartel leader Fabio Ochoa Sr. In 1983, the Procuraduría (Office of the Inspector General) found that fifty-nine active duty military officers were involved in MAS.[25] The loosely structured MAS grew throughout the decade, although there was little coordination between localized death squads. Rather, drug traffickers developed regional strongholds: Henry Pérez and Gonzalo Rodríguez Gacha operated in the Middle Magdalena valley; the Eastern Plains region was split between Rodríguez Gacha and emerald baron Victor Carranza; Fidel Castaño controlled Córdoba and northern Antioquia; and Pablo Escobar founded a Medellín-based group of young assassins for hire, known as *sicarios*.

Regional elites and their allies unleashed these drug-trafficking–funded paramilitary death squads to suppress democratizing reforms. Until these efforts, most political officials were appointed (elected presidents appointed governors, who appointed mayors) and a decades-long power sharing agreement between the two major political parties known as the National Front (instituted in 1958 and official phased out in 1974, but with long lasting effects) further restricted political life. New laws passed in the late 1980s attempted to decentralize political power and increase opportunities for participation.[26] The popular election of mayors (beginning in 1986) and governors (beginning in 1991) initially generated significant opportunities for other political parties. The Patriotic Union (UP) was the most successful and the most controversial because of its origin in frustrated peace talks with the FARC in the early 1980s. Many on the right, including traditional party leaders and landowners, decried the UP's possible ongoing guerrilla ties and were vehemently opposed to any power sharing, economic reforms, or land redistribution projects. Paramilitary assassins, working in many cases with military intelligence officers, killed thousands of UP members, in what survivors called a political genocide.[27] In many regions, the economic elite and traditional politicians enthusiastically supported paramilitary forces, viewing them as safeguarding their business and political interests.

During this period, the extravagant violence of the drug trade dominated many facets of Colombian society, as signified by the saying *"plata o plomo"*— silver or lead—meaning "take the bribe or take a bullet." The Cali Cartel emerged as the Medellín Cartel's main rival; their violent competition culminated in the creation of the PEPES (People Persecuted by Pablo Escobar), a shadowy group dedicated to attacking the Medellín Cartel's businesses and associates, as well as allegedly supplying the DEA with information about its adversaries. A group of drug lords opposed to extradition treaties pushed by the U.S. government declared war on the Colombian government and used what became known as "narcoterrorism" to cow officials into denying extradition attempts. They killed hundreds of judges, police investigators, and public figures, including three presidential candidates for the 1989 elections.

Paramilitary expansion in the 1990s resulted in part from changes in the structure of the narcotics trafficking industry. As the heads of the Medellín and Cali cartels were killed or jailed in the early 1990s, a new generation of regional traffickers and warlords emerged, working with paramilitary traffickers who had come up through the cartel hierarchy and the PEPES. A national network of newly legalized peasant "defense cooperatives" also contributed to the growing strength of paramilitary forces. After being briefly outlawed in 1989, in the early 1990s "indigenous irregulars" were once again incorporated into the military's counterinsurgency strategy through a new legal structure for rural defense forces, known as the "Convivir" (the term's literal meaning is "coexistence," but it glosses a much wider sense of living together and tolerance). Officially launched in 1994, Convivir groups were enthusiastically supported by Alvaro Uribe during his tenure as governor of Antioquia (1995–97). Many groups served as front organizations for paramilitary groups. The Convivir–paramilitary nexus was a lynchpin in counterguerrilla operations and the provision of security for elites. In only one example, documents from the widely publicized lawsuit involving Chiquita Banana's payments to paramilitary forces reveal that, between 1997 and 2003, some of these payments passed through a Santa Marta-based Convivir directly to paramilitaries operating in the region. Company officials met with high-ranking paramilitary representatives in the home of a prominent Medellin businessman; the company's defense in the lawsuit included the fact that such payments were a common business practice and were widely known.[28]

The Human Rights Era and the Paramilitary Solution

Beginning in the late 1990s, U.S. policymakers began pressuring the Colombian military to conform to human rights standards. Most prominently, the Leahy Law, passed in 1997, prohibited foreign military units facing credible allegations of abuses from receiving U.S. military assistance (see Chapter 2). The United States encouraged Colombian military compliance by linking human rights vetting with travel visas and training opportunities. Elite training in the United States was not only critical for career advancement but was also considered a reward. Colombian military officers were routinely treated to a trip to Disney World during their U.S. training, for example.[29]

The Colombian military decried U.S. human rights standards as discrimination, claiming such efforts created serious impediments to their counterinsurgency efforts. During interviews with Colombian military officers in 2001 and 2002, they explained to me that military personnel have no recourse against these unfair allegations, so officers would avoid any combat operations in order to avoid being demoted, jailed, or fired because of baseless, politically motivated charges of misconduct. They bitterly pointed to the cases of officers denied visas to the United States and Germany, their careers stagnating from the loss of training opportunities and bad press. This fear even had a medical diagnosis; it became known as the *Procuraduría* Syndrome, after the oversight agency created by the 1991 Constitution to investigate allegations of official misconduct. Military officers complained of being *empapelado*, literally papered over by complaints and investigations of allegations of misconduct.

During this period, many Colombians viewed their country as in crisis. As noted above, the administration of President Ernesto Samper (1992–96) was thrust into political chaos after evidence was leaked immediately following the election that he had accepted campaign contributions from the Cali Cartel. For the first time in a century, the country experienced negative economic growth:

a record low of -4.5 percent in 1999. Unemployment almost doubled and the number of people living in poverty rose to 55 percent. Beginning in 1996, guerrilla attacks against garrisons resulted in high levels of military casualties and growing predictions that the Colombian military was inadequate to the task of civil defense (see Chapter 1).

By far the most important indicator of the crisis for many middle- and upperclass Colombians, however, was the fear of escalating attacks by the guerrillas. In addition to its escalating combat operations, the FARC was responsible for the dramatic rise in kidnappings, which became a major industry in which criminal bands would sell their hostages to the guerrillas. For first time, the elite felt directly affected by the war, which had been long restricted to remote rural communities. Being targeted for kidnapping and unable to safely traverse the country's roads brought the war home. One Colombian who had worked in the Foreign Service during this period compared the country to Afghanistan. "The FARC was going to take over the country," he emotionally proclaimed, while the callous elite fled to Miami. As I heard from other elite Colombians, as well as from U.S. officials in Bogotá, FARC strength was symbolized by its presence in La Calera, a small town about a fifteen-minute drive from the Bogotá city limits over the eastern mountain range, where many wealthy residents had country homes or spent the weekend horseback riding and enjoying leisurely barbeques. "The FARC took over La Calera. La Calera! That is Bogotá!" he exclaimed, concluding, "The state was unraveling. A FARC takeover was likely."

Widely reviled as corrupt and incompetent, the military was now in the crosshairs of Bogotá elites for failing to contain this mounting guerrilla threat. For many, the expanded paramilitaries appeared to be the solution. During interviews with wealthy residents of Monteria, a paramilitary stronghold, I heard many times how the paramilitaries had saved the region from the relentless guerrilla attack. "When the paramilitaries called, the ranchers really responded. People took up the cause," one bank executive told me. "Each farm had its own group, defending it . . . The paramilitaries saved us from drowning."

The same year that the Leahy Law was passed by the U.S. Congress, paramilitary leaders announced the creation of new national coordinating body, the United Self-Defense Forces of Colombia (AUC). Initiating a new, expanded counterinsurgency strategy, the AUC issued a statement announcing an offensive military campaign into new regions. Paramilitary gunmen targeted civilians and presumed guerrilla sympathizers in guerrilla strongholds, pushing them into remote rural areas and breaking their supply networks. Newly created "mobile squads"—elite training and combat units—carried out these operations, which included numerous massacres and assassinations targeting the civilian population in these areas. Paramilitary commanders set up bases and occupied small towns, with local military commanders providing close coordination and logistical support for these operations. According to Colombian government statistics, the AUC committed more than 900 massacres between 1997 and 2002.

This violence was conducted with the active support of the Colombian military. In typical Colombian black humor, the paramilitaries became known as the "armed branch of the army." While soldiers were at home in the barracks or occupying small towns after they had been "pacified," the paramilitaries were fighting the counterinsurgency war, primarily by targeting civilians. Throughout the country, survivors described military forces scouting the region prior to paramilitary attacks and then blocking escape routes. Military officers would tell villages that paramilitaries were on their way, referencing the spectacularly brutal violence such groups employed, including public acts of torture committed with acid, machetes, and chain saws. In some cases, paramilitary and military forces carried out joint patrols. Military officers and paramilitary commanders were frequently seen drinking and socializing together in small towns throughout the country.[30]

Human Rights Watch's 2001 report, *The Sixth Division: Military-Paramilitary Ties and U.S. Policy in Colombia*, referred to the common view that paramilitary forces in Colombia operated as a "sixth division" of the Army, which was then divided into five regional commands.[31] The report contained "extensive, detailed, and consistent evidence" showing that the brigades in different regions of the country "maintained a close alliance with the paramilitaries, resulting in extrajudicial executions, forced disappearances, and death threats." State prosecutors and investigators gathered hundreds of thousands of pages of testimony and case files documenting the connections between paramilitary forces and military units, the vast majority of which were archived with no charges brought. The few dissident officers who publicly complained of this malfeasance were relieved of their commissions and often investigated themselves on trumped-up charges.

Paramilitary Public Relations

The paramilitary leadership had a clear interest in presenting themselves as an autonomous political force. Gaining state recognition as a political force offered significant benefits, including possible reduced sentences for the leadership, amnesties for the troops, and reincorporation into legal civilian life. Through media campaigns, including an extensive web presence, paramilitary leaders attempted to transform perceptions of their organizational structure and behavior, denying both their brutality and their links to the state. In 1999, the paramilitaries launched Colombialibre.org, a website that by 2001 rivaled official Colombian government sites for sophistication, graphics, and content (the guerrillas' websites, in contrast, languished until 2003 with only occasional flashing updates). One of the first documents posted on the site included "proposals for structural reforms for the construction of a new Colombia." The site included diagrams outlining the AUC's alleged command structure, communiqués and open letters issued by paramilitary leaders, and documents outlining the history and evolution of paramilitary forces. AUC commanders circulated a photocopied text titled "The Constitutional Statutes and Disciplinary Regime," which was described as having been adopted at the AUC's second national conference in May 1998; the text claimed the organization had developed a highly regimented military command structure to incorporate regional groups, along with having hymns, uniforms, and insignias particular to each region.

Beginning in 1997, charismatic spokesman Carlos Castaño became the new face of the Colombian paramilitaries as the AUC was launched into public life. Castaño had come up through the ranks of the Medellín trafficking organization and then stepped in to lead the Córdoba and Urabá Peasant Self-Defense Forces after the 1994 murder (either in a guerrilla attack or by Carlos) of their leader, his brother Fidel. He then began a new era of politically astute maneuvering, including launching a media offensive on behalf of the paramilitaries. In his first major interview in 1997, Castaño announced he was "tired of fighting and ready to sit down at the negotiating table." His proposals for reforms required for peace were published by the Colombian newsmagazine *Cambio 16* in May 1998, along with responses from the guerrilla leadership.[32] In March 2000, Castaño appeared wearing a sweater and slacks in his first on-camera interview in a prime-time television special on the *Caracol* network. In that interview he admitted that he often cried when thinking of the tragedies caused by the fighting in Colombia and that his troops should have "operated with more prudence." In addition to subsequent, nearly weekly appearances in the Colombian press, Castaño was featured on the cover of the international edition of *Time* on November 27, 2000 (under the headline, "King of the Jungle"), and profiled in the *Washington Post* on March 12, 2001 (under the title, "Colombia's Other Army").

That same year, Castaño approved the release of *My Confession*, a fawning biography resulting from a series of interviews with a Colombian journalist; the book became a Colombian best seller. Regional paramilitary leaders also began appearing frequently in the Colombian press during this period.

These leaders used their knowledge of human rights norms and international humanitarian law standards to escape international scrutiny and to give the appearance of reforming. In the 1990s, the International Committee of the Red Cross (ICRC) negotiated an expanded mandate allowing it to meet directly with illegal armed groups. Then head of the ICRC Pierre Gassman was one of the first international officials to meet with Castaño. Beginning in 1997, the ICRC provided training in international humanitarian law to paramilitary commanders and their troops throughout Colombia. In part as a result of these training workshops, the AUC wrote the concept of respect for international humanitarian law into its policy documents, and its leaders claimed during interviews that they would respect human rights standards.

Paramilitary commanders also altered their modalities of violence so as to avoid high-profile incidents such as massacres and mass displacements. One small-town councilman told me of being summoned by a local paramilitary commander, who informed him that they had learned how to avoid human rights criticism, but that they would continue to kill anyone who opposed them. Because a massacre is defined as four or more individuals killed in a single act (at the same time and in the same place), paramilitary groups would scatter the bodies of those they killed in different places or hold them for different lengths of time. Human rights groups responded by creating a new category for such deaths: multiple homicides. However, such a term did not have the emotional impact of "massacre," nor was the category tallied in their statistics. In their public statements, paramilitary leaders—and some government spokespeople—pointed to the decline in the number of massacres as progress, while ignoring the fact that the total number of violent homicides remained the same. Similarly, in areas where paramilitary forces once forcibly displaced inhabitants to consolidate their control, they now prevented people from traveling from the region (called "confinement" by human rights groups). Difficult to quantify and assess, such measures allowed paramilitary groups to avoid public scrutiny from human rights groups.

These paramilitary public relations efforts were ultimately successful, and they began discussions with the government in the early 2000s. The talks ended in a series of agreements providing benefits to paramilitaries participating in demobilization programs, including subsidies, job training programs, and shorter (or no) jail terms for many crimes.[33] The AUC's public relations campaign was a key factor in public acceptance of the demobilization program. Through interviews, websites, and other documents, paramilitary leaders articulated a new version of Colombian history, in which they were both the victims in the Colombian conflict, sacrificing security and domestic life to defend the nation, and the victors, able to defeat the guerrillas in areas where the military had merely maintained an uneasy stalemate or ceded control entirely. In this narrative, paramilitary forces emerged as an independent force ready to step into the vacuum left by an absent state. For many Colombians, including many in the rural elite and the urban middle class, this narrative resonated with their direct experience (as well as projected fears) of guerrilla violence and of the failure of the state to provide security. The paramilitaries' extreme brutality, support from military officers and other state agents, use of drug trafficking to finance their operations, and the role of other financial interests in determining their priorities were elided from public debate.

The Absent State and Washington Paramilitary Narratives

Military officers' and paramilitary commanders' denials of the state role in paramilitary violence included claims that the state would have acted against paramilitary violence, but did not have the capacity to do so. State weakness, failure, and absence were described as the causal factor in all forms of violence in Colombia, including that of the paramilitaries. This lack of state capacity mapped neatly onto a new category emerging in Washington during this period to label areas of concern: absent and failing states. In the mid-1990s, political scientist I. William Zartman popularized the idea of a "failed state" in his work on Africa, and the label soon circulated widely in the Washington punditry and think-tank circuit. According to this view, in a process facilitated by insufficient state institutions, warlords seeking control and driven by the criminal pursuit of profit had replaced the ideological divergence that characterized the Cold War.[34] This label reflected a postdevelopment paradigm, in which states are no longer viewed as on an upward trajectory (as the binary "developed" and "developing" categories suggest), but rather are considered to have missed the opportunity for such progress and are instead more likely to be declining into anarchy. In policy debates, there was considerable ambiguity between "failed" states and "absent" ones: in many cases, states were categorized as failing be-

cause of their absence. State absence was a precondition for failure in many regions, because of the lack of infrastructure, the weak revenue base, and the presence of social divides (such as geographic, ethnic, or religious differences). This
calculus positioned strengthening the state as the natural solution: if states fail
because they are absent, then, of course, building state presence creates state
success. In practice, building state presence signified expanding its military apparatus. In the logic of militarization, such forces were perfectly positioned to
take advantage of international investment in the state without a messy analysis of what qualities of the state were being reinforced. Such models also obscured the multiple other factors contributing to protracted conflicts and state
inadequacies in many regions, including the role of globalization, power inequalities, and existing economic relationships.[35]

For U.S. analysts, Colombia soon became one of many countries considered
through this framework. In interviews, senior Defense Department officials described their view at the time of Colombia as a country that was "sliding off
the table." One told me, "We were in danger of losing Colombia." The National
Defense University's Institute for National Strategic Studies published a policy
brief concluding that Colombia risked "becoming either a 'narcostate' or disin-
tegrating."[36] Influential political scientist Robert Rotberg, then a program director at the Harvard Kennedy School of Government, classified Colombia as an
"at risk of failing" state, alongside Cote d'Ivoire, Iraq, North Korea, and Indonesia.[37] Senator Mike DeWine (R-OH) claimed at a 1999 Heritage Foundation conference that "the balkanization of Colombia into ministates that are politically
and socially unstable is the most significant threat in the region. Colombia is
becoming the problem of the Balkans in the Americas."[38] Academics as well heralded the "erosion and partial collapse of the state" as a means of understanding
Colombia's crisis.[39] This collapse was seen as a regional security threat for Latin
America, endangering the neighboring states of Ecuador, Peru, Venezuela, and
Panama in a possible domino scenario.

The dominant policy narrative in Washington minimized the role of paramilitary groups, portraying the Colombian conflict as the guerrillas against the
government. If mentioned at all, paramilitary groups were described as a localized reaction of the middle class to guerrilla violence in the absence of the state.
"Our view was that they emerged from the vacuum of power; the government
had no capacity to fill their own territory," Ambassador James Mack, the coordinator of the Plan Colombia Interagency Task Force, told me. "So first, there was

the FARC and other smaller guerrilla groups. Then the AUC rises up to satisfy the felt need for security." Policymakers often dismissed human rights concerns by claiming that paramilitary groups were the same as the guerrillas in that they were both responses to local grievances with no relationship to the state beyond minor local alliances in remote regions. This version of paramilitary history ignored the two central factors that were critical in paramilitary expansion in the 1990s: their connection to the drug trade, particularly through a generation of leaders schooled in the Medellín Cartel, and the historic role of the state, particularly the military, in establishing and supporting the paramilitary groups. This narrative also dismissed the paramilitaries as a significant policy issue by positing that they would simply fade away once the guerrillas were defeated (or, presumably, negotiated with), and state authority reinstated.

Military analysts such as David Spencer played an important role in articulating a narrative of paramilitary history that portrayed the paramilitaries as independent of state support and as sympathetic opponents of the guerrillas. Like many critics of U.S. policy, he had been schooled in policy debates in Central America in the 1980s; he had supported military assistance and worked as a consultant for the Salvadoran Department of Defense. Currently a professor of national security studies at the National Defense University, during the initial Plan Colombia debates and design (1999–2001) he worked for the Center for Naval Analysis on studies including analyses of the Colombian counternarcotics brigades and the Marine Corps; until 2003, he also worked as a policy advisor for U.S. agencies, including the CIA, Department of Justice, and SouthCom.

In 2001, Spencer wrote a study, *Colombian Paramilitaries: Criminals or Political Force?*, published by the Center for Strategic Studies of the U.S. Army War College. It focuses on the emerging political claims of the paramilitaries, while minimizing the history of legal paramilitary incorporation in counterinsurgency doctrine and operations, as well as their pervasive, illegal violence and links with military officials. He describes the paramilitaries as simply the logical result of guerrilla violence:

The core of their intense violence is the pent-up anger and frustration of important sectors of the rural population at guerrillas who have terrorized the countryside for 30-plus years. This has been exacerbated by a state that has been unable to provide more than fleeting relief from insurgent violence. The atrocities of the paramilitaries are not acts of abnormal men, but rather the acts of normal men subjected to and victimized by unremitting violence, who see the disappearance of the guerrillas as the only sure solution to their plight.[40]

In the report Spencer uncritically accepts Colombian military statistics and reports. For example, he cites Colombian officers' inability to recall any counternarcotics operations against paramilitaries as evidence that "the guerillas seem to be more heavily involved in drug trafficking."[41] He consistently minimizes paramilitary attacks by ignoring their high civilian death toll. He describes the Mapiripán massacre as a "bold strike at the heart of FARC-controlled territory. The people killed were not chosen randomly, but were deliberately targeted for their involvement with the FARC."[42] Although the area was, according to paramilitary pronouncements, chosen for its strategic importance to the FARC, the attack was carried out on unarmed residents and did not involve combat with the FARC. Spencer also does not mention the desperate efforts of the local judge to call military forces to protect the town, the dismemberment of living victims in the town's slaughterhouse over the course of several days, and the widespread allegations that military commanders in the region provided logistical support to the paramilitaries.[43]

For the "mainstream" think tanks, in the 1990s paramilitary groups were only a marginal concern. Groups such as the Inter-American Dialogue and the Council on Foreign Relations, prominent supporters of U.S. military assistance to Colombia, rarely featured paramilitary groups in their policy briefs and lobbying efforts. The Council on Foreign Relations' website entries on Colombia were typical. Its Americas program produced widely circulated reports on Colombia policy, the result of a task force convened in 1999. Yet in its backgrounder titled "FARC, ELN, AUC," the webpage devotes only two sentences to the AUC, with the remainder of the document explaining the history, development, and "terrorist attacks" committed by the FARC and the National Liberation Army (ELN).[44]

An analysis of human rights reporting by the U.S. State Department and the UN High Commissioner for Human Rights Office in Colombia offers an opportunity to trace the differences in the United States and the United Nations' accounting for paramilitary violence and their institutional positioning.[45] A comparison of the 2002 State Department Colombia Country Human Rights report and the UN High Commissioner for Human Rights yearly report reveals that the United States consistently minimized paramilitary strength and activities. In covering the human rights situation of a close ally and partner, the 2002 State

Department report emphasizes government pledges to reform while meticulously avoiding language describing military institutional collusion or support to paramilitary forces. The report avoids drawing conclusions about the pervasiveness of close relations between the regular armed forces and paramilitary forces, referring only to individual ties, while stressing progress in severing these relationships. Any criticism is presented alongside praise, with emphasis placed on high-level rhetorical commitments to rights-respecting policies rather than examining ongoing paramilitary violence. These descriptions of progress in reining in the paramilitaries contrast dramatically with the findings of the annual report on the same period prepared by the office of the UN High Commissioner for Human Rights in Colombia. The UN report highlights government inaction in the face of evidence of paramilitary operations; it describes the ubiquity of abusive paramilitary groups and the evidence that the military persistently provided a shield for them. It also cites cases in which the regular security forces went into areas in advance of paramilitary forces and "where local inhabitants recognized members of the military forces among paramilitary contingents."

In interviews, senior State and Defense department officials told me that the United States devoted few intelligence resources to following paramilitary groups. Then undersecretary of state Thomas Pickering, who was charged by President Clinton with chairing the interagency task force that developed Plan Colombia, admitted that it was more difficult to obtain significant intelligence on the paramilitaries than on the guerrillas. In part this was because of biased intelligence sharing: the United States could benefit from Colombian intelligence gathered against the guerrillas, but did not receive information about paramilitary forces. Given the extensive evidence of widespread military collusion with paramilitary forces, that the Colombian military did not provide intelligence to their U.S. allies on these groups is not surprising. According to Pickering, the "bulk of our technological collection was focused on the guerrillas for historical reasons, *maybe political reasons.*" [emphasis added]

Similarly, counternarcotics and counterinsurgency intelligence officials reported focusing on the guerrillas, while they waited for convincing evidence of paramilitary abuses and links with official sources from nongovernmental groups. Brian Sheridan is a former CIA agent who rose through the ranks as a Clinton appointee to the position of assistant secretary of defense for special operations/ low intensity conflict. He was one of the active architects of Plan Colombia and was deeply involved with the Colombia debates. He reported that both a focus on the guerrillas and minimal active intelligence gathering on the paramilitaries drove the policy debates. "The intel guys, DIA [Defense Intelligence Agency] [were] focused on counterinsurgency," he told me. Tracking "every attack, every movement, all the weapons," he went on to say, they were completely focused on the FARC's military expansion. He naturalized the shift in U.S. interest from Pablo Escobar and the Medellín Cartel in the early 1990s to the FARC. When I asked him about DIA reporting on the paramilitaries, he responded that it relied on NGOs to provide evidence of paramilitary activity. "When human rights groups would come to me, WOLA, Human Rights Watch, I would say, show me some evidence, something that I can sink my teeth into. Apart from that, I am inclined to adopt a more conventional view and see them as isolated cases." Although he had earlier said that that the DIA was "concerned" about paramilitary activity, he concluded with the oft-repeated military point that, because the paramilitaries were not attacking the Colombian military, they understandably were not a primary concern for the state. "When you talk to the Colombian military guys out in the middle of nowhere, they say, well, this [guerrilla] guy is trying to kill me and this [paramilitary] guy isn't, so guess which guy I am going after. And you can't fault that logic. So my position was, absent the evidence, I am not going to go contrary to the national interest."

U.S. military personnel and civilian advisors told me that paramilitaries were providing security that the Colombian military could not, tacitly accepting the argument that such forces were state proxies. Because paramilitary forces were fighting the guerrillas, they could be considered allies of the state forces, I was told. "A lot of the attitude was that the AUC was a counterweight to the FARC, they were providing security in areas where the military can't," according to a former senior SouthCom official active on Plan Colombia. "That is the rationale that people use, that kind of attitude, of rationale, swirls around very much in these kinds of issues."

Denial as State Terror

The Colombian official state policy regarding paramilitary forces was denial. In press conferences, private meetings, and policy documents, Colombian government officials denied the existence of pervasive links between paramilitary groups and the security forces. These denials acted as the papier-mâché covering over of a public secret.[46] In one example, in its annual report released in

February 2001 the Office of the United Nations High Commissioner for Human Rights in Colombia reported,

It is common knowledge that a paramilitary roadblock stands at the entrance to the settlement of "El Placer," only fifteen minutes away from La Hormiga (Putumayo), where a Twenty-Fourth Brigade army battalion is stationed. Eight months after the Office reported to the authorities that it had seen it, the roadblock was still there. *The military authorities denied its existence in writing.* This Office also observed that paramilitaries were still operating at the Villa Sandra estate between Puerto Asís and Santa Ana in the same department, a few minutes from the base of the Twenty-Fourth Brigade. [emphasis added][47]

The Colombian military performed these denials during their meetings with U.S. officials, and I heard many during my work as a policy advocate in Washington. I also heard these denials in meetings held in Colombia, including to a delegation to Colombia in February 2000 that included two members of Congress and six congressional staff.[48] During two day trips outside of Bogotá— one to a "Peace Community" in San José de Apartadó, Urabá, and the other to examine illicit narcotics issues in Puerto Asís, Putumayo—we met with local military commanders. In each region, the military commanders greeted us with a carefully honed message about human rights, offering a defensive message about their role as "true human rights defenders" and proclaiming that they had no relation with the *autodefensas,* as they called the paramilitaries. Seated in wide circles in chairs at times almost shouting distance apart, we listened to the stiff, formal speeches of military commanders describing the complexity of threats in their region, their respect for human rights, and their categorical denial of any allegations of complicity with paramilitary forces.

In Puerto Asís, the largest city in Putumayo, the U.S. ambassador joined the delegation for a day with a large entourage, and so for security reasons we were confined to a large school auditorium, surrounded by pacing security officials with bomb-sniffing dogs. The military commanders had to come to us. Putumayo had been a FARC stronghold for a long time, but the paramilitaries had gone on a major offensive several years before, establishing almost total control in the small town centers in the region over the course of three years as the U.S.-funded counternarcotics battalions began their operations. The military officers, slumped like the rest of us in uncomfortable student desks, blamed allegations of abuse on the drug traffickers, who stood to profit if U.S. operations failed. "There is distortion, slander, damage to the image of the work that we are doing," the commander told us in a stilted speech on their work in the region. "That is natural because it is in the interest of those who oppose the process begun by the state government." They insisted that legal standards were followed: "we follow a process, if there is a death in combat, with the *fiscal* (the prosecutors charged with investigating crimes)." They were anxious that we appreciate their efforts, describing in detail combat operations against the paramilitary—whom they also called "*antisociales*"—and guerrilla forces. "Last year, aggressive operations against the paramilitaries, killed nine *antisociales*, captured twelve, and turned them in to the *Fiscalía* (Attorney General's office); we also captured weapons." Having heard accusations that the army was favorably disposed to the paramilitaries, the commander explained, "The reasons we appear to focus on the guerrillas is proportional analysis; they have more troops. Also, the guerrillas fight the army, while the *autodefensas* avoid combat with the army." Emphatically, he declared that they had "no relation, couldn't even think of it" with the paramilitaries.

Colombian official denials of military complicity with paramilitary forces performed multiple state effects. To the international community, such claims were presented as evidence of state innocence: overpowered by illegal armed agents, with minimal resources and little support, state agents seek to fulfill their duties, but simply are unable to do so. State complicity in paramilitary violence was visible to local residents while concealed from U.S. patrons through the deployment of proxies and the power of their stated denials. In meetings with local residents, state officials claimed that they were unaware of this violence, positioning local residents as tainted by their knowledge of illegal groups. Facing demands that they collaborate with official requests for information, rural residents were required to deny their daily experiences of violent repression sanctioned by the state or face brutal retribution. Many rural residents, civilian officials, and priests—immersed in the daily evidence of the enmeshment of security forces and paramilitary groups—experienced such demands as a form of state terror.

Local security council meetings (*los concejos de seguridad*) convened at the departmental level and including all the civilian and military authorities of a given region were key sites for these encounters between and with state representatives. Called in times of crisis, these ephemeral bodies provided the opportunity for registering complaints and demanding state redress; in practice, the majority resulted in state denials of paramilitary collusion and demands for information from local residents. These meetings also resulted in subsequent violence, when those denouncing paramilitary-state collaborations were targeted. Although these spaces were unavailable to me as an anthropologist, local civilian officials and priests who participated in these encounters frequently recounted them to me. They were also recorded in official military records, in documents that were photocopied and circulated by military officers as part of their human rights files.

In a 2001 interview, a military officer provided me a thick stack of papers, his "human rights file" with one such document at the bottom. This file contained material derived from an "urgent action"—a widely circulated complaint by a Bogotá-based NGO of increasing paramilitary links with local military officers, which is included in the file. The next page lists the minutes from a *concejo de seguridad* called to address the situation in one of the small towns mentioned in the urgent action. The first statement in the minutes records a request from the local priest that in this *concejo* no explanations of the events (presumably involving the paramilitaries) be given. After a blank line, military commanders, local officials, and community representatives discuss the possibility of the construction of a military base, further support for military operations, and the need for local support. One military commander is noted as asking if the community has denounced the events involving illegal armed groups, stating that it is "important that the community collaborates and denounces." The priest in turn defends the inhabitants and asks who will provide security for people who provide such testimony (*denuncias*). A local official confirms that no *denuncias* have been provided. In the next document in the file, a report on the meeting submitted by the army official present, there is no mention of the priest's concerns.

One priest in Putumayo recalled the last *concejo* he participated in, held in late 1998 shortly after the paramilitaries had begun taking over the town where he worked. He described his intervention as "attempting to shock, trying to touch on the [sensitive] issues so that they would start to react." The case involved six local townspeople who had been presented by the army as guerrillas killed in combat, while the priest knew them as community members who had been seen alive, detained, and taken away in a truck by the military. The priest learned of the events from family members and a friend who witnessed the detention; the priest confirmed their accounts with a visit to the morgue to inspect the bodies. At the *concejo* he confronted the colonel because of "the pain and my outrage."

Angrily rejecting the officer's congratulations for his role in the community, the priest denounced the military for their work with the paramilitary groups and their role in the deaths of the six residents. The colonel responded by threatening to sue him for slander, to which the priest responded, "Go ahead and do it, I know you killed those men." The priest concluded his story, saying, "It was a big risk for me. Because they would know that I knew many things."

After this encounter, the priest decided to make public his knowledge of military complicity with paramilitary forces. He carefully planned the funeral mass, inviting the national media to attend. Echoing Salvadoran Archbishop Oscar Romero, whose painted portrait and photo hang prominently in his office, in his sermon the priest called on the president to sanction the guilty officers, saying, "You need to look at see what your army is doing, that you need to purge these forces."[49] Following the mass, his life changed. Men in camouflage visited the parish, threatening notes were left on his doorstep, and he could only venture out into the neighborhood in the company of colleagues—in his case, a Franciscan Mother Superior. After seeking advice from human rights groups, he decided to make the threats public and was forced to leave the region. He concluded the story of his departure from the region by reflecting that what was occurring was widely known by all: "There was no doubt that the army and the police were working with the paramilitaries, they were in complete union, *total sintonía.*"

Official claims of ignorance and demands for additional information came in other forms as well, including memos that circulated among government offices. Many local ombudsmen (*personeros*) and other civilian officials described a fear of reprisals when they received requests for official reports from other government agencies, as well as their frustration that they were unable to fulfill their mandate of assisting endangered and victimized residents. In one small town, the *personero* described the local government prosecutor as "playing hot potato" (*se tira la pelota*) with the issue. "She would send memos (*oficios*) saying that there were reports of paramilitary activity in the area, and we should certify what criminal acts were being committed," he told me in a cramped, airless office on the second floor of the mayor's building. He described her actions as a "great irresponsibility," endangering them all. "The situation of the public order is known by all the institutions here," he went on. "Yet they all pretend, during a *concejo de seguridad*, that if someone talks about the presence of the paramilitaries it is the latest news flash."

I interviewed many local officials, including mayors, town council representatives, and *personeros*, who described public meetings convened by military officers during the period of the paramilitary takeover of small towns and villages. During these meetings, military officers demanded that townspeople and
officials who had expressed concern about escalating paramilitary violence publicly present the details of their concerns. One typical account described a
meeting called by the local military commander two weeks after a paramilitary
incursion into the town had resulted in deaths, the theft of farm animals and
other property, and the destruction of several rope bridges linking rural hamlets to the town. In this account, the mayor described how the captain convened
the meeting to discuss "rumors, because of the complaints that had been presented [by a human rights NGO] about the situation in town, the failure of the
military to do anything." In the presence of the town business owners and traders, the captain told them that

he had heard reports that people were being pressured, threatened by the paramilitaries. The Captain said he wanted to verify this. He said if anyone there had been the object
of threats, like the NGO had said, they could publicly register a public complaint, iden-
tifying themselves with their name, their identity document, address, and place of business. About ten people spoke, but everyone agreed, that there was no problem, that
nothing was happening. Because they were afraid to give a public *denuncia*. So the people
said that they had never seen paramilitaries, they had never been called to a meeting by
them, never threatened. The Captain took notes, then wrote the minutes of the meetings and made everyone sign them. These would be presented as proof against the *denuncia* presented by the NGO. The Captain said that everything that was happening, it
was all the fault of the people in the town. The Captain said that they couldn't act, because of the failure of the people to complain, that the subversives would kill people in
the middle of the street and no one had seen anything. He asked that if anyone had seen
the *autodefensas* in the town, that people denounce it . . . He said, it seemed like they [the
people who complained] were defending the guerrillas, or were supported by them.
There were 200 people there, more or less, with the Captain and some soldiers, and
the police were there for a while. That same day, the urgent action from the NGO had
arrived by fax, about the paramilitary entrance into the town.

It is no wonder that officials and community leaders who confronted the
paramilitary–military nexus were the exception rather than the rule. Their experience demonstrated the ways in which state power was expressed, not in
support of efforts to ensure the safety of local populations, but to deny and to

threaten those willing to register complaints. I heard numerous accounts of such encounters during the early years of the paramilitary arrival in Putumayo.

Another such story came from the wife of one mayor's assistant. She described his struggle to fulfill his official obligations and her conclusion that silence was rewarded, after he was forced to flee for his life. In her account, the close relationship between the security forces and the paramilitaries was painfully clear. "There was a civic-military brigade that was practically the installation of the AUC; they came with the entire military deployment." After the brigade and the AUC settled into town, a military officer asked her husband if there had been any strange movements in the town. "And my husband, believing that he was doing the right thing, said that people were worried, they were afraid because there were some strange guys that were going around armed, in cars and were driving all over, and were already living in one of the hotels." The military officer and the presumed paramilitaries were staying in the same hotel and were seen eating meals and drinking together.

She described her husband's response—an attempt to protect the local population and communicate their concerns as part of his official obligations—as "sinning because of naiveté." He imagined that the military officer was asking in good faith for him to report on conditions in the town, rather than realizing the implications of the evidence before his eyes: that the military forces were working together with paramilitary forces. The military officer's request for information was merely a performance of his obligation to gather intelligence to protect the town; his true purpose was to gather intelligence on the civilian officials in an effort to gauge the deputy mayor's response.

The deputy mayor was then called to meet with the AUC commander and was told that he had a limited time to "settle his accounts." He fled the region, fearing for his life. His wife concluded,

He should have seen but not said anything to [the military officer]. What does this reveal? That there are agreements, there are things that they do and people shouldn't speak about it. No one should say anything or they are the ones who are accused, *señalado*. And that is what happened.

Conclusion

Then assistant secretary of defense for special operations/low intensity conflict (SOLIC) Brian Sheridan typified the way in which guerrilla and paramilitary violence were collapsed into a single category of chaos produced by the lack of state security infrastructure. "Putumayo is a poster child for why you need Plan Colombia," he told the *St. Petersburg Times* in the fall of 2000. "The FARC and the paramilitaries are running roughshod all over the Putumayo right now, killing each other, blockading roads, holding villages hostage . . . and the military and the police are nowhere to be found." This vision of Colombia fit neatly into U.S. assumptions about how state absence absolved the state of responsibility for violence and the possibilities of its redemption through U.S. nation-building efforts. These assumptions mischaracterized the role of the Colombian state in this violence: it was not absent, but instead actively supported paramilitary forces as its counterinsurgency proxies.

That Colombian paramilitary proxies were in part the product of human rights pressure on the security forces complicates the rosy vision of human rights. As Lori Allen points out in her penetrating analysis of the human rights industry in Palestine, such human rights projects become "a performance for the international community" in which state agencies " 'do human rights' in order to get foreign goodies, and demonstrate 'stateness' through the illusion of complying with codes of conduct expected of states." Although the rhetoric of rights employs lofty claims, in practice it is "window dressing hung to prettify and obscure."[50] In this case, what was obscured was the state's role in deadly paramilitary violence.

State denials of their complicity in this violence were performed in multiple arenas. To their U.S. patrons, such claims served to authenticate their worthiness as aspiring modern, professional military forces. These denials were also reinforced by claims from paramilitary public relations efforts positioning their forces as independent, as well as military analysts' sympathetic descriptions of these forces. As a form of state terror, these denials suppressed residents and local officials' efforts to seek redress for the violence they confronted on a daily basis. These local strategies are the subject of the next chapter.

Chapter 4

Living Under Many Laws

PUTUMAYANS FREQUENTLY DESCRIBED THEIR EXPERIENCE in the late 1990s and early 2000s as "living under many laws." Civilian state officials and local residents understood themselves to be subject to the machinations of distant, powerful forces that shaped both daily life and the political possibilities in their region. Putumayo was home to multiple state-like actors, each with opposing visions of how political life was to be organized and with conflicting institutional orders as well as conflicting claims about who was to govern, according to what legitimating principles, and toward what ends. Conditions in the Putumayo region of Colombia challenged virtually every aspect of the standard narrative of the relations between state, society, territory, citizenship, and rights.[1] The normative ideal of modern state-society relations assumes territorial control via a state apparatus capable of guaranteeing citizens' rights and the rule of law when threatened by illegal activities, by armed actors undermining the state's monopoly of force, or by interference from other nation-states. In Putumayo, however, it was not the national state apparatus that attempted to safeguard the rights of citizens but rather a criminalized population of smallholding *cocaleros* (coca farmers), who sought to establish the liberal freedoms and the rule of law and who strived to develop the economy. In so doing, they sought support for their cause from a complex and evolving network of regional, national, and transnational NGOs; elements of regional, national, and foreign governments (including the United States); religious organizations; and, at times, illegal armed actors.

Throughout the years of Plan Colombia, Putumayo became a "shadow zone" in which the official and the covert, the legal and illegal converged. At the same time, residents were forced to navigate extreme violence.[2] The militarization of daily life was expressed in constant encounters with violent actors, checkpoints, detentions, surveillance, coercion, and incidents of harassment, rape, and torture. The unbearable circumstances endured by residents have been most clearly documented in the book-length report by the Center for Historical Memory documenting the history of the FARC and the later paramilitary occupation of the small hamlet of El Placer.[3]

At the same time, residents articulated political alternatives through demands for what I call an "aspirational" state. These inhabitants understood the state "as both a verb and a noun, as a state and a statement, as an aspiration made real in varying proportions" through their own political projects.[4] This aspirational critique of the politics of the present focused on the qualities of the state, its affective ties to its citizens, and daily practices of governance in an ideal form: caring, responsive, generous, and abundant, rather than distant, repressive, and extortive. These fantasies channeled oppositional imaginaries during the height of the violence. In these extreme circumstances, the magic of the state was revealed not through ongoing encounters, but rather conjured through these possible futures. The aspirational state described by these officials and activists drew on the conceptual categories of modern liberal democratic citizen-state relations, while at the same time resonating with historic ties of authoritarian paternalistic clientelism. This chapter explores the limitations and possibilities of local actions and how claims to jurisdiction and territorial control shift over time, particularly at the "fuzzy boundaries" of state action, where state agents and local inhabitants become entangled in competing claims.[5]

As a frontier region, Putumayo has been simultaneously remote and marginal, and deeply implicated in national and transnational projects. The region is lowland jungle with a small population of indigenous groups and poor *colonos* (settlers); it was made into a department in 1991. As such, it lacks an entrenched political and economic elite on the scale of those in urban areas or regions with longer histories of settlement, and local political culture reflects an ethos of colonization, exploration and creation. Waves of colonization resulted in part from land policies: the area was designated as *tierras baldías*—empty, ownerless lands that were free for settlers—the only requirements to claim it being a machete and a tolerance of back-breaking rural labor. The region played a central role as one of the "escape valves" to accommodate the escalating demands for land generated by Colombia's extreme inequality and repeated waves of violence to dispossess small farmers from their holdings.[6] At the same time, Putumayo has been deeply enmeshed in transnational economic and political processes, including Catholic missionary efforts; quinine, fur, rubber, and oil exploitation; and the cultivation of coca paste for the illegal drug trade on the international market.[7] Beginning in the 1970s, the wild profits generated by dramatically expanded coca cultivation brought thousands of small farmers into the region, who built villages and began organizing to secure state services such as roads, schools, and health centers.[8]

Understanding this history is crucial for understanding both how Putumayo became a centerpiece for U.S. intervention in the decade that followed and the unintended consequences of this project. The illegal coca trade was legitimized by the refusal of the central state to respond to demands for political recognition and investment in services, and the resources of this illegal commerce created paradoxical opportunities for the creation of local political organization. Despite being subjected to ongoing criminalization and marginalization by the central state, local residents continued their efforts to make themselves visible as legitimate political actors and participants in policymaking. These residents' analysis of the impact of national and transnational policies and their encounters with the growing number of local illegal armed actors shaped their ongoing efforts to take control of their own political destinies.

Stigmatized as violent criminals intent on personal enrichment through the drug trade, *Putumayenses* are considered throughout Colombia as excluded from citizenship and rights claims because of their assumed criminality.[9] Yet these residents attempted to fully inhabit citizenship rights, if only through their claims on the state. They articulated demands for citizenship organized around peasant identities and justified their criminal practices as necessary through their critique of the state, charging the state with responsibility for failing to provide security, services, and market infrastructure. Anthropologists working in other marginal and criminalized regions have documented similar dynamics, in which local populations articulate their "longing for the state" as Diana Bocarejo describes in the case of coca growers in northern Colombia, feel the presence of the "phantom state" as Daniel Goldstein found in urban Bolivia, and experience state violence as constituting law even while violating it as Richard Kernaghan writes about Peru.[10] I explain these developments by locating them within a subterranean history of the region, one that focuses on the weak and incipient efforts of popular organizations to define new forms of citizen-state relations. I attend to the alternative visions of just rule that have been generated by everyday encounters between the general populace and the violent efforts of those who claim the right to govern them. This approach tracks the dispersed institutional and social networks through which claims to legitimacy are described and consolidated; it explores the roles that state and nonstate institutions alike play in the mundane processes of governance.[11]

Making Coca Farmers

The first settlers to arrive in the region were fleeing violence and seeking land, propelled there by historic patterns of Colombian land tenure characterized by both extreme land inequality and repeated waves of violence to dispossess small farmers from their holdings. At the same time, responding in part to pressure from large landowners, government policy focused on promoting the colonization of unsettled land rather than on land redistribution. Much of the brutal conflict of the 1940s and 1950s, known simply as *La Violencia*, centered on efforts to gain control over land. Agrarian elites frequently employed mercenaries to consolidate their landholdings. The development of commercial agriculture accelerated violent displacement during this period, especially in Tolima and neighboring Cauca.[12] Lauchlin Currie, an American development expert who spent his career as an advisor to the World Bank and the Colombian government, defined "traditional peasant production" as a major "obstacle" to national development.[13] The resulting national development policies supported the expansion of large agribusiness and accelerated urbanization. As a result, thousands of colonos arrived in Putumayo during the 1960s and 1970s to raise subsistence food crops.

Liberal efforts to expand peasant landholdings have been thwarted at every turn in Colombian history, especially in the last fifty years. President Carlos Lleras Restrepo (1966–70) created the National Association of Users of State Agricultural Services (ANUC) to channel peasant agrarian aspirations through official political structures, as part of his reformist platform and in response to growing land pressures. While actively promoting peasant land occupation, ANUC was significantly weakened by internal ideological divisions, violent repression, and subsequent government retrenchment by the administration of Conservative Misael Pastrana Borrero (1970–74). By 1970, "96% of the new titles granted were for public lands and areas of recent colonization."[14] In 1972, the Pact of Chicoral formalized the "agrarian counterreform," setting strict restrictions on land expropriation from massive holdings and increasing government support for agribusiness.[15] In the 1980s, drug traffickers' accumulation of vast swaths of land contributed to rural displacement in what became known as the "reverse agrarian reform." According to one estimate, as many as six million hectares changed hands between 1985 and 1995.[16] In comparison, during twenty-five years of state-sponsored agrarian reform, only approximately 900,000 hectares of land were redistributed. In the 1980s, the World Bank found Colombia to have one of the worst ratios of land inequality in the world.[17] As property sizes grew, land was used less for agricultural production and more for cattle ranching and pastureland (and money laundering), requiring less labor and further exacerbating the economic pressure on rural populations.[18]

Colombia has a low road-to-area ratio compared with other Latin American countries, particularly along its agricultural frontier. Limited market access and transportation costs make the production costs of many food crops too high to sell beyond regional markets, and even those markets are out of reach for many remote producers. Throughout the end of the twentieth century, a single unpaved road connected the municipal center of Putumayo with secondary and tertiary roads that were in bad condition, and river transport was prohibitively expensive.

Coca cultivation, like coca chewing, is not native to the Putumayo region and southern Colombia; the plant was brought from other regions as a cash crop. Peasants could carry out the initial refining process to make coca paste, an easily transported, high-profit-margin product with a guaranteed market. Families needed cash to pay for school fees and basic supplies, but had little access to financial and technical assistance.[19] For the peasants of Putumayo, coca seemed like a godsend.

Coca farmers viewed their work as part of the agricultural economy, not as transnational crime. In their stories I heard during my fieldwork, they compared cultivating coca not to smuggling or other criminal traffic, but to the growing of corn, wheat, and plantains, citing these crops' harvest cycles and sale prices. As one such farmer told me, "I wasn't afraid to work with something that was illegal because this was common, everyone was working in this. It was normal." Even while producing a cash crop for the transnational illegal drug trade, local farmers maintained their peasant production practices, employing family labor in a variety of tasks. Many small farmers planted coca on their plots; others worked as sharecroppers in larger plantation-style farms in lower Putumayo. Migrant laborers worked as coca harvesters, known as *raspachines*, from the verb to *raspar*, which means to strip or to pull, referring to the action of stripping the leaves from the small branches without damaging the plants. Many residents used small coca plots to supplement their income from growing legal food crops or from working in salaried positions. Coca harvesters and farmers, although relatively prosperous compared to those dedicated solely to subsistence food crops, lived a life that was a far cry from the urban extravagance of traffickers in Medellín and Cali.

Producing coca paste, also known as base, is the initial refining stage in making cocaine, and the peasant families who grew the coca were able to complete the process at home. On industrial plantations, contract workers carried out a larger scale version of the same process. Using a modified weed cutter, the farmers (or, in the case of plantation production, contract workers) shredded the leaves, mixed them with cement powder, and then soaked them in barrels of gasoline. They added hydrochloric acid to the liquid squeezed from this mixture to crystallize the alkaloid. They sold the resulting powder, coca base, to middlemen in southern Colombia for about $700 per kilo.[20] As was common in other arenas of agricultural production, the *traquetos*, or middlemen, who brought rural products to their urban consumers made the majority of the profits. These intermediaries purchased the coca paste produced by Putumayo's small farmers and sold it to traffickers in the Medellín and Cali family-based trafficking empires that came to control a billion-dollar cocaine industry. The coca economy became the central economic engine of the region, financing a range of secondary businesses, including restaurants, retail stores, and transportation services.

Paradoxically, U.S. efforts to break up the major trafficking organizations and sever their ties to coca-growing areas in Peru and Bolivia contributed to Putumayo's coca boom. Initially the Coast Guard, Customs agencies, and the DEA focused on interdiction, interrupting shipments abroad. Then, beginning in 1989 with the implementation of the Andean Strategy, U.S. funds, equipment, logistical support, and personnel played a leading role in counternarcotics operations in Colombia. Colombian police working hand in glove with U.S. agencies killed off Pablo Escobar in 1993; most of the heads of the Cali Cartel were either captured or surrendered by the end of the following year.[21] Their replacements vertically integrated the trafficking organizations, seeking more Colombian sources for their coca paste.[22] At the same time, the United States began targeting the flights that brought coca paste from Peru and Bolivia into Colombia. Through the Air Bridge Denial Program, the United States provided equipment and intelligence to help the Peruvian and Bolivian authorities shoot down the planes. U.S. officials pointed to the significant declines in Peruvian coca prices as their primary achievement; critics, however, argued that prices in

Peru fell because all the buyers had left for Colombia.[23] Little data is available on the number of flights or how much cocaine was transported via plane compared to other routes, new transport technologies, or the increase in corruption.[24] What is clear is that, as coca production declined in Peru and Bolivia, coca farming in Putumayo skyrocketed.

This abbreviated history of Putumayo charts the ways in which U.S. and Colombian national policies played a determining role in creating the conditions for Putumayo coca cultivation. U.S. counternarcotics policy generated new trafficking and production routes, in large part as the result of changes in enforcement strategies. The interdiction of coca grown in Peru and Bolivia encouraged the vertical integration of the Colombia narcotics industry, bringing cultivation into new areas of southern Colombia. At the same time, Colombian land policies and economic development strategies privileged large landowners and commercial agriculture, while encouraging invasive settlement of ownerless lands, the tierras baldías. Despite the resulting mass colonization, limited access to markets, credit, and other sustaining support for small-scale production prevented peasant farmers from producing agricultural goods beyond the subsistence level. Coca emerged as a market-driven solution to these structural challenges. As the population grew and local knowledge of coca cultivation and processing spread throughout the region, an alternative vision and practice of (illegal) economic development took root. The production and trafficking of illegal products occurred not in spite of official policies, but in large measure because of them; this trade was not separate from the regional agricultural economy but central to it.

The FARC's Law

The 32nd Front of the FARC settled in Putumayo in the early to mid-1980s, when the FARC was still a marginal group with a minimal national presence. Putumayo was logistically important because of its shared border with Ecuador, Peru, and Brazil. The FARC encountered minimal state resistance and found a ready base of social support in the growing population of colonos, many of whom had lived under guerrilla leadership in other rural areas. FARC commanders came to control much of the social and economic life of the region, maintaining a strong militia presence in hamlets and town centers and regularly patrolling rural areas. They used their military power to mediate disputes and enforce local contracts, as well as to organize community improvement projects. "People depended a lot on them," one priest told me. "There would be lines of people taking their problems to the commander, [everything from marital] infidelity and conflict in the communities; the guerrillas took on the role of the state. They were the judges." Another described how residents during this period viewed them with "admiration and affection."

From the time of the FARC's arrival in the 1980s, and extending in some areas to the present, local officials in Putumayo have been expected to meet with FARC commanders to resolve disputes and to answer for violations of FARC-established regulations. Small-town officials were called to such encounters and instructed to provide the guerrillas with information on state projects and budgets. Numerous local state officials described these "commissions," in which a delegation including representatives from the local government and frequently local priests as well would travel to FARC camps to present their governance plans to local commanders and in some cases to request clemency for those facing FARC punishment—especially those slated to be killed.

FARC efforts to regulate local life were clearly evident during my first trip to the region in 1999. The local activists who helped organize the trip requested permission from the regional commander for our travel by boat down the Putumayo River, from Puerto Asís to Puerto Leguizamo, and we only proceeded after given clearance. We did not stop in particular hamlets where local commanders were known to be mercurial. On the road from Puerto Asís to Mocoa, we passed a large, slightly tattered poster attached to the wall of a concrete community building. It was titled "Sanctions and Fines: Norms for living in a dignified and honest community." Signed by the 32nd Front of the Southern Block, the poster listed nineteen regulations and the corresponding fines and punishments for violations, ranging from 200,000 to 2 million pesos (approximately US$100 to US$1,000). The crimes ranged from gossiping (US$100 fine) to the more serious violations of bringing unknown people into the region (US$1,000), selling a farm without consulting with the FARC, or traveling in a vehicle after 6 p.m., which also could result in confiscation of the car.[25] Local commanders enforced community rules, ensured participation in collective work brigades, and punished those who failed to comply with fines, additional work assignments, and, after three warnings, banishment or death.

In general, the FARC was and is an extremely hierarchical, closed organization. Officially, decision making is restricted to members and occurs through nested vertical structures. FARC commanders describe the smallest military unit

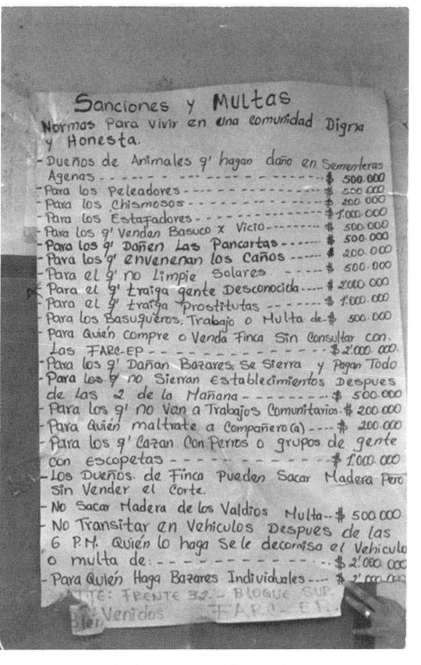

Figure 4 FARC poster detailing community regulations and sanctions, 1999.
Photograph by Winifred Tate.

as a political cell that meets every two weeks for collective decision making and analysis.[26] Each front of several hundred troops holds a yearly general assembly to resolve disciplinary issues, discuss any communiqués from the Secretariat (the organization's seven-member, highest ranking body), and choose representatives for the Guerrilla National Conference.[27] Ostensibly held every four years (depending on security conditions), this conference makes all major policy decisions. Internal regulations are laid out within the disciplinary code, which is enforced by a disciplinary body.

Within this rigid structure, local commanders have varying degrees of autonomy. In their meetings with local commanders, residents and officials could in some cases intervene in FARC adjudication of community disputes, request the release of or clemency for those judged guilty of misdeeds, and ask commanders to change established practices. In one example, local schoolteachers lobbied local commanders not to occupy school buildings or intervene in school classrooms. One teacher described her repeated encounters with guerrillas in her role as a rural schoolteacher attempting to defend her right to decide the curriculum. "They would come into the school and take over the social studies class; they would have their lesson," she recalled. "I would get so mad and yell at them to get out of there. They took me for two days, up there talking with them. I was laughing [in the meeting], I already have enough teachers, I don't need any extras." She made her case to them by explaining her role as a teacher: "I have my job, and you have yours, and we have to know where the lines are." She also appealed to their family obligations: "they are parents, they understand that you have to keep the kids safe, the school safe."

During the years of undisputed FARC domination in Putumayo from the early 1980s until the late 1990s, priests carried out what they called "pastoral dialogues" with the guerrillas, which included traveling to their camps to conduct mass and baptisms and meeting with commanders and troops to instruct them about their conduct.[28] "We took advantage of the fact that when the priest arrived for the Mass, everyone had to go and listen to him," one priest said, and so moral instruction was provided through the sermon.[29] Conducting mass provided an opportunity for tacit rebukes. Another priest described leading a memorial mass for teachers killed by the FARC. In other cases, priests intervened when their parishioners were detained or accused by the FARC of crimes or infractions. The diocese also maintained a fund to provide support for people attempting to escape FARC rule by fleeing the region. Local priests viewed guerrillas as both part of their broad religious community—as rural youth to be accorded the rights and obligations of ministry and pastoral care—and as authorities with whom they engaged in delicate mediation and advocacy efforts on behalf of their parishioners. Many rural priests knew that their parishioners had family connections to the FARC, including many parents whose children became FARC members. "In general we had good relations with the guerrillas," one priest recalled, citing as one reason that the FARC at the time was the uncontested power in the region. "There weren't as many human rights violations as there were later, because the territory wasn't under dispute."

For much of the 1980s, the experience of the residents of Putumayo who were forced to deal with FARC governance differed little in practice from the political experience of rural residents of much of Colombia. In the winner-take-all political system established by the 1886 Constitution, the president appointed governors, who in turn appointed mayors. Elected legislative assemblies were subject to strict review by national politicians. This political system fostered strong patron-client relationships among politicians and communities, encouraged backroom dealing and the use of violence to resolve political disputes, and consolidated the power of local strongmen. Political exclusion was further cemented by the National Front agreement, in place from 1958–74 (although its effects lingered thereafter), which prohibited third parties and put in place an alternating power-sharing system between the two traditional parties as a means to end the partisan violence of the 1950s. Given profound economic inequality and a constrained political system, few rural peasants had the opportunity for autonomous political participation until this system was transformed by a series of political reforms beginning in the late 1980s. These reforms led to the popular election of mayors and governors, the creation of new institutional channels for local participation, and the decentralization of resources from the central state to the municipalities. Up until that time, and in many regions continuing despite these reforms, the political experience of most rural Colombians, although formally operating within a democracy, was characterized by greatly restricted political access, reliance on personalized networks and public appeals, and frequent violence.

Creating the Local State in Putumayo

Local residents worked to enact their utopian visions of the state in a process of "longing for the state," as described by Colombian anthropologist Diana Bocarejo in the case of other coca-growing regions.[30] Even while engaged in illegal activity, local residents pushed for greater recognition from the state and the creation of administrative structures that would allow them to participate in political life. Paradoxically, the coca boom facilitated this process by bringing in new people and resources to the region. During the 1980s, Putumayo had one of the country's highest rates of internal colonization. From 1973 to 2005, the coca-growing region of Lower Putumayo experienced a 725 percent growth in population, while Middle Putumayo grew 89 percent and the Upper region grew 137 percent.[31] The resulting new communities were largely self-built and financed. Local farmers subsidized state budgets by contributing labor, but unlike other rural farmers, coca's high profit margin allowed them to also make substantial cash contributions to local governance projects. Collective work brigades built roads and schools; relatively flush coca farmers paid construction costs and even supplemented teacher salaries in some remote regions. I even heard stories—unconfirmed but repeated by trusted sources—that local traquetos (coca paste middlemen) contributed land and money to build the police station in one municipal center. At the same time, residents continued to press for state services, in many cases through strikes and protests organized by unions and civic committees. In the early 1980s, the teachers' union, Asociación de Educadores del Putumayo (ASEP), together with other sectors, conducted strikes to demand the construction of water, electricity, and sewer systems in Puerto Asís, the region's largest town. In 1984, peasants again gathered in Puerto Asís to protest the lack of rural public services, including credit availability, market assistance, roads, and education.

The Catholic Church, in particular a loose cohort of "native son" priests, played a critical role in developing a vision of peasant autonomy and political participation. Born and raised in the region, these priests worked to connect Putumayo farmers in remote hamlets to national and transnational networks promoting grassroots education, sustainable development, and human rights. Father Alcides Jiménez, a parish priest in the region from 1977 until his assassination in 1998, led this process. In his community work, Jiménez emphasized the transformative power of collective participation, using the resources of the church to support educational and community initiatives throughout the region. With minimal funding, mostly from Catholic-affiliated European development NGOs, he offered workshops in community leadership, sustainable development, and health and wellness, which led to substantial networks of health and rural

development promoters throughout the department. Parish leaders also established a community radio network that broadcast both locally produced news
and distance learning programs to this day. Jiménez also created special leadership and training courses for local women. His rural development program *Mujeres, Caminos y Futuro* (Women, Paths, and Future) enhanced the ability of
women to serve as the leading voices against coca cultivation, able to convince
their husbands to plant food and cash crops to improve their families' situation.
Small loan funds and cooperatives for women grew out of this program. In 1987,
women active in the parish founded ASMUM, the Municipal Women's Association, whose representatives traveled to national and international conferences
on feminism and development. All these efforts generated new political subjectivities, based on a Catholic-flavored vision of social justice and collective work,
while establishing institutional networks that channeled new relationships
and political practices.

Putumayans also benefited from national transformations in Colombian political institutions that opened new administrative avenues to recognition by
the central state. Law 11 of 1986, which provided for the direct election of mayors, also created mechanisms for community participation in local decisions, including the creation of local administrative boards.[32] These committees were
legally recognized and frequently required the participation of both civil society and local officials, providing an important space for state-resident encounters. Throughout the country, President Virgilio Barco's (1986–90) national development strategy known as the National Rehabilitation Plan mandated the
creation of joint government-civil society municipal councils. Through their participation on these local bodies, leaders learned to negotiate with officials and
gained access to government services and training courses.

Efforts to promote "territorial organization" (*ordenamiento territorial*) also
generated new political spaces. Many of the new communities in Putumayo organized pro-municipal committees to lobby for legal recognition as a municipality, which would allow them to gain access to resources from the central state
and establish local political offices, such as mayors and assemblies.[33] This complex and nebulous process involved negotiating with government representatives, as well as local FARC commanders, and moving through stages of increasing state recognition—beginning with the designation of "*inspección de policía*,"
until reaching the goal of being designated a municipality. This process was
another critical mechanism for the participation of local people in state

formation. These efforts to generate relationships with the central state profoundly influenced later local apprehensions of the state.[34]

The opportunity to vote for local political offices generated new third-party movements throughout the country, and Putumayo was no exception. In the late 1980s, local activists with the Grassroots Civic Movement of Putumayo (*Movimiento Cívico-Popular del Putumayo*) traveled throughout the region to campaign for office and register voters. The generally high levels of voting during this period reflected local interest in political participation. This political opening was short-lived, however. Newly arrived paramilitary forces in the region soon began targeting these activists and opposition candidates.

First-Generation Paramilitaries: *Los Masetos* in Putumayo

Paramilitary forces linked to major drug traffickers arrived in the region in the late 1980s, challenging both FARC dominance and autonomous peasant organizing. Large drug traffickers began buying land in Putumayo to establish what was known as "industrial" coca paste production on large plantations. The most famous trafficker was Medellín Cartel founder Gonzalo Rodríguez Gacha (called *"el Mejicano"* because of his love of all things Mexican), rumored at the time to be Colombia's largest landowner. In 1987, Rodríguez Gacha established a major base of drug trafficking and paramilitary operations in a farm known as *El Azul* two hours west of Puerto Asís.[35] Revoking their initial agreement with the FARC, paramilitaries attacked their guerrilla "protectors" and declared war.[36] Working with the state security forces to attack leftists and suspected civilian supporters of the guerrillas, Rodríguez Gacha sponsored a bloody campaign against the FARC throughout the country, during which he primarily targeted the Patriotic Union, a political party born of the frustrated peace talks between the FARC and the government in 1984. He and other paramilitaries brought in Israeli and British mercenaries to train their forces and provided them with advanced military equipment. By his own count, he killed more than four hundred supporters of the Patriotic Union. In Putumayo he directed the Masetos' death squad operations that worked closely with local police and military officers to carry out so-called social cleansing killings of drug addicts, alcoholics, and debtors, as well as anyone suspected of having guerrilla ties.

By the late 1980s, the Masetos were forced out of the region by a combination of FARC military operations and political pressure from local residents. *El Azul* was the site of one of the few decisive military battles between the FARC and the paramilitaries. After an attack in 1988 that was successfully repelled by Rodríguez Gacha's forces, the guerrillas returned in 1989 and managed to kill an estimated eighty paramilitary troops. Residents in Puerto Asís organized a march to protest the escalation in paramilitary violence and killings. The protest march and the subsequent departure of the Masetos were critical moments in popular memory of local resistance to paramilitaries.[37] The expulsion of Rodríguez Gacha and his paramilitary forces and the public rejection of their security force allies contributed to the consolidation of FARC power in the region, including its efforts to regulate the local cocaine industry.[38]

In response to the ongoing violence by the Masetos and other paramilitary death squads, newly created national human rights networks began documenting these attacks in the region.[39] In Putumayo as in the rest of the country, violence became a central factor in political life. The Bogotá-based Jesuit progressive think tank CINEP paid the salary of a staff advisor for the region's first municipal human rights committee, one of a growing number of local human rights committees sponsored by Bogotá-based NGOs.[40] Working along with community activists and local priests, the committee documented human rights abuses and participated in national forums. Although it was forced to disband because of increasing paramilitary persecution in the mid-1990s, committee advisor Nancy Sánchez continued to work with the state health service and became a critical link between Bogotá and international NGOs and local communities.[41] These new spaces for negotiation between the state and civic groups transformed local political culture and were central to the organizing efforts of the 1990s and 2000s.

Fumigation and the Limits of the Local State

Putumayans' inability to influence policy was nowhere more evident than in the case of fumigation, the aerial spraying of chemical herbicides over vast swaths of territory to kill illegal coca plants. These U.S.-funded efforts began in the neighboring state of Guaviare in 1994 and extended throughout Putumayo beginning in 1997. By 1998 more than 100,000 hectares had been sprayed with a mix of glyphosate and various adhesive chemicals. Such operations were only carried out in Colombia; all U.S.–sponsored eradication efforts in other countries were limited to ground-based initiatives to remove the plants manually and, in some cases, to voluntary crop substitution. U.S. and Colombian national officials argued that fumigation was required in Colombia because of the lack of security in the region. The FARC violently opposed the operations, firing on the planes and in some cases succeeding in shooting them down. Putumayo residents also unanimously rejected fumigation. The failure of the central government to address their concerns and implement their proposals led to increasing disenchantment with the central state, as growing paramilitary violence forced activists underground or into the ranks of the FARC.

After the first rounds of fumigation, Putumayans employed a range of tactics, including street protests, lobbying, and crafting written policy plans, to draw attention to their rejection of fumigation policy and their alternative proposals. Many of the leaders of these efforts emerged from the ongoing efforts to organize alternative political networks. They had been trained in political practices in the peasant movement promoted by Father Jiménez and his Catholic colleagues, as well as in the Movimiento Civico-Popular del Putumayo. In November 1994, a mass protest took place in downtown Puerto Asís, coordinated to coincide with local officials' testimony at congressional hearings being held in Bogotá on fumigation that had begun that year in neighboring Guvaire. From December 20 to January 5 of that year, a "general strike" paralyzed travel and public life in three municipalities. As a result, the national government agreed to meet with local leaders in Bogotá in February 1995. At that meeting, Putumayo representatives presented a proposal for gradual crop substitution in the region as an alternative counternarcotics policy. Local activists then presented their concerns to the president during his August 1995 visit to Puerto Asís. Frustration with the lack of results of these lobbying efforts led to the 1996 cocalero protest marches, during which thousands of striking farmers closed down the regions' roads and occupied town centers for more than three months. "Coca growing peasants have exhausted all possible means searching for the path to dialogue, but given the use of force, mass protest remains the only alternative against these erroneous policies," wrote civic movement leaders in one of their public communiqués.[42]

The cocalero marches, as they became known, were a flashpoint for Putumayo disenchantment with national policies and policymaking venues. The president deployed the military to stop the marches, and many marchers were wounded and several killed. March committees, established by the civic movement leaders, called on the government to respond to the protests not with violence but by appointing state officials empowered to negotiate with march leaders. Working groups within the march committees were established to design alternative policy strategies; after further clashes, government representatives joined these groups to discuss issues put forth by the marchers. According to former NGO staff who worked closely with the civic leaders, these groups put together a platform of demands that was largely based on the local government's petitions to the central government to increase funding for public services, including electricity, health care services, and transportation infrastructure. Putumayo at the time had no paved roads and lacked any public electricity.

The discussions between march leaders and the central government representatives broke down over one issue: national counternarcotics policy, specifically, what to do about coca. The cocaleros were not demanding legalization, but rather an end to forced eradication (including fumigation) and the implementation of gradual, voluntary crop substitution with substantial government support. In turn, the government's position was "zero tolerance," according to one of the NGO staff participating in the process. After a week of intense debate, it became clear that no agreement on the issue would be forthcoming, and the representatives signed what became known as the Orito Accords, which promised increased government services but produced no new policy guidelines on the issue of coca.

The implementation of even these limited accords demonstrated the difficulty of policymaking in the region. Local state officials objected to the process as a form of "parallel government," claiming that the central state should have been negotiating with them, the legitimately elected officials, instead of the self-proclaimed leaders of the civic movement. They also objected to the management of the projects that resulted from the negotiations. Fearing corruption and clientelism in the administration of the projects, the central government channeled the funds through a Bogotá-based NGO, CINEP. Local state officials argued that their agencies should have received those funds instead. Finally, participants in the process alleged that a FARC infiltrator in the civic movement had worked to torpedo the process. They pointed to the final document presented by the civic movement as evidence. Rather than submitting the farmers' concrete proposals for negotiation, the statement presented the FARC's ideological arguments about class struggle. Rumors that the document's author had been extremely well paid from the project fund generated further tensions among the march's leaders, who had sacrificed months of work with no remuneration.

Despite these failures, specific projects in the region were funded as a result of the accords, including electricity in the main towns and expanded hospital services in the region. However, the road projects never materialized, and the opportunity to design and implement pilot projects in crop substitution was lost. Following the Orito Accords, paramilitary groups sparked a major escalation of violence in the region. This was graphically demonstrated when one of the NGO workers supporting the accords' development and implementation reviewed documents with me, describing the violent deaths of the civic leaders who were signatories on the Orito declarations. These leaders had been the AUC paramilitaries' first targets in the region.

Escalating Violence and the Dream of Putumayo Without Coca

Jorge Devia was elected governor of Putumayo in 1997; his campaign slogan "*Putumayo Sin Coca*" (Putumayo Without Coca) reflected not only an awareness of the political liabilities of the region's reputation but also the growing local ambivalence toward the coca economy. Recalling this time, many reflected with wonder on the opportunities and material rewards that coca farming offered, but spoke with sorrow of the many dangers that accompanied the illegal trade. Residents told me of how the coca trade had transformed the region into a vibrant economy, bringing riches, people, and movement into a remote rural area—but they also recalled the violence, conflict, and mistrust generated by the illegal trade. One local teacher interviewed in 2008 described the town as during the boom as "*una belleza*, [a beautiful thing] with so much business you couldn't tell if it was Saturday, Sunday, Tuesday or Wednesday," unlike in other rural areas with their single weekly market day. But, she went on, you could always hear a lot of gunfire. She had been "invited" to work in the coca trade and heard tales of a friend's new life in Miami after traveling there as a "mule" carrying cocaine on an international flight. Despite recognizing that her students earned more working the coca harvest then she did as a teacher, she refused to become involved because of her father's strict respect for the law and because she was "too afraid."

Residents reflected on the multiple ways in which the coca economy distorted local economic, social, and affective relationships as the coca boom created wealth and the strength of traffickers and illegal armed actors in the region grew. Fatima, president of the Women's Alliance of Putumayo and a supervisor for the Department of Education, recalled the coca bonanza as the promise of prosperity unrealized, resulting in weakened social relationships. She called the increase in domestic violence and male drunkenness resulting from the coca trade "total social decomposition."

One woman who had worked as a community leader and in local government described the disordered world of the coca bonanza as "the world in reverse." Peasant farmers no longer raised sustenance food crops, instead dedicating all their land to coca and traveling to town not to sell their produce, but to buy food imported from other regions. The high wages and wealth offered by coca cultivation splintered the traditional kinship-based, shared work of peasant agriculture, because local farmers were no longer interested in growing less lucrative food crops. The relatively high wages for raspachines meant that few were willing to perform other kinds of necessary but lower paying agricultural labor, such as weeding, clearing land, or applying pesticides. The money made in the coca trade was often spent on ostentatious purchases: fancy clothes, cars, and elaborate houses bought with those proceeds that now stand empty on the edges of town.

The changing dynamics of the conflict transformed the political visions of local inhabitants during the late 1990s as the two illegal armed groups fought for control of the region and the profits of the coca trade. Local FARC commanders became increasingly abusive in their treatment of the population as suspicion and paranoia grew about possible betrayals. Residents and civilian state officials found themselves caught in the crossfire, without even minimal space to advocate for local autonomy. The FARC's Southern Bloc became one of the most powerful in the country, operating with multiple fronts and able to mobilize thousands of combatants, as well as urban militias based in small towns.[43] As paramilitary forces steadily gained control over urban centers, FARC commanders became increasingly paranoid and draconian, heightening the danger for any who challenged their abuses. Deeply concerned about infiltration and betrayal, the guerrillas viewed any attempts to establish autonomous organizations with great suspicion. In response to the threat to their monopoly of the region, the FARC imposed greater regulations on daily life, with devastating effects for local inhabitants. One such restriction was the curfew, which outlawed travel after 6 p.m. unless authorized by the local commander. In one case, one woman told me how her husband was killed in front of her and their children: "they told him to put down the box he was carrying, and they shot him right there, they shot him eight times." His crime: taking a sick child to the hospital past the curfew without permission.

In response to the growing guerrilla abuses, the unfulfilled promises resulting from the protest marches, and the fear of escalating paramilitary violence,

Father Alcides viewed community organizing as the central safeguard for increasingly victimized residents. He attempted to organize a Catholic peace promoters network, *Red de Formadores de Paz*, and marshaled resources from the Catholic Church's Social Ministries programs to help leaders organize as peace communities. At the time, national Catholic institutions, including CINEP, were promoting "active neutrality," a conflict-resolution strategy in which communities rejected the presence of any armed actors in the regions.[44] Father Alcides participated in workshops in which activists working with Colombia's most famous peace community, San José de Apartadó, described how they had become organized in 1997. Putumayans began debating international humanitarian law (also known as the rules of war) and considering how communities could develop greater autonomy. Although they were unsuccessful in gaining central government support for these programs, these community forums were able to exert pressure that resulted in the creation of the office of the regional *personero*, a human rights ombudsman linked to the National Ombudsman's Office. Father Alcides' organizing efforts also resulted in a growing resistance to abusive practices by the guerrillas. When the local guerrilla commanders attempted to pressure communities to come out for another large-scale protest march in 1997, Father Alcides urged them to resist. Following his counsel, many peasants refused to participate, arguing that the previous marches had led to increased violence and poverty without any gain for the communities involved.

On September 11, 1998, two FARC gunmen killed Father Jiménez while he was officiating at a mass celebrating the end of Peace Week. An elderly parishioner, Ester Martinez, was also killed as she attempted to shield him. The attack was widely viewed as retaliation for his encouragement of autonomous community organizing. One participant in the workshops he organized recalled his work promoting such independent groups as "more dangerous than being a human rights defender [who were also widely targeted]. In this rural area, [he was] giving workshops that people shouldn't go into the war, that they shouldn't use arms. . . . The FARC was mad because they thought that he was taking people away from them, that he was too critical of them. And he was very much against coca." Following his death, the networks and projects he nurtured fell dormant, as residents feared further retaliation.

Living with Paramilitary Law

The mass arrival of the paramilitary group, the United Self-Defense Forces of Colombia (AUC), marked a decisive change in the region. Members of the AUC's Southern Bloc arrived in 1997 (see Chapter 3), carrying out intelligence operations and selective assassinations. On January 9, 1999, they announced their intention to stay and to conquer with a spectacular public display of violence: 150 paramilitaries occupied the small hamlet of El Tigre, killing at least 28 people and disappearing 14; many were dismembered and their bodies thrown into the river. During the following years, paramilitary commanders terrorized the region in order to consolidate their social and territorial control.

Paramilitary commanders exercised governance in small town centers, using violence and brutality but also regulating public space, individual comportment, and interpersonal relationships. They informed residents of these rules in large public meetings, frequently held in the public plaza. One priest described the rules for daily life, *normas de convivencia* (literally, norms for coexistence), as being primarily aimed at organizing violence, such as regulating who could carry weapons. "People could go into the bars with their guns," he recalled, "but if anyone got drunk and started to shoot in the air, he was immediately assassinated." The commanders ordered communities to clean the streets and display specific Christmas decorations. They intervened in local disputes, regulating domestic violence and punishing thieves. I heard stories from many local residents about how commanders charged local businesses "taxes," called extortion by others, as well as kickbacks on all government contracts. One priest also described constant interrogation at public paramilitary roadblocks and the ruthless elimination of all community leadership. "They weren't interested in social organization. On the contrary, they wanted to destroy all the social networks that existed, all the visible leaders, even the religious leaders," he told me. "Any kind of leadership, even in sports, cultural groups, religious leadership, was assassinated. The important thing for them was that everyone be silenced, *callado*, and that they work in drug trafficking and that they sell the coca to them, nobody else."

Like the guerrillas, paramilitary commanders called local officials to meetings, forcing them to attend with implicit threats of violence (and sometimes overt attacks). Local officials were required to submit budgets and development plans, as well as pay kickbacks. "[The paramilitaries] walked around in army uniforms. They called us to a meeting and all the council representatives went," according to one assemblyman in La Dorada. "They said, you have to work this and that way . . . To work especially for them, and anything bad we saw we had to help them camouflage it, because supposedly they were the state and they were working for a good cause, supposedly against the guerrillas." Although consistently brutal, paramilitary governance varied over time and according to the whims of individual commanders. Within the region, inhabitants spoke of differences among commanders and modified their approaches to them accordingly. The handsome *Blanco* was described as a "soft touch," who once cried when confronted about the murder of a mother in front of her children by troops under his command (residents did not, however, describe a reduction in violence following this emotional encounter). *Orejas* ("Ears"), famous for his pathological violence and so nicknamed because of his necklace of human ears, and *Tyson* (named for Mike Tyson), who demanded birthday gifts and attendance at his parties, were to be avoided at all costs.

The idiosyncrasies of local commanders opened up an extremely limited space for local residents, primarily women and priests, to attempt to lobby for the release of detained friends and family members or for the opportunity to retrieve their bodies for burial. I heard many stories in which women mobilized their caretaker roles as mothers, wives, and daughters to carry out humanitarian missions, intervening with local commanders to plead for the release of family members and neighbors. One local teacher described such women as "defenders of life," recalling that

when they took a father, or a teacher or any young person, immediately all the women got organized and we talked to everyone and it was always the women who went to *reclamar* to the people who took them. . . . Some have been given back alive, some, others given back dead, but we went for the bodies.

These efforts were not always successful and exposed women to more violence, particularly sexual abuse. I heard accounts of women being held hostage for hours or even days and enduring multiple rapes after attempting to advocate for the release of their husbands. But however paradoxically, mobilizing existing gender ideologies and exclusions became a central tactic for women attempting to intervene and protect their families. Men constituted the vast majority of the forces involved in the violence as well as its victims.[45] In contrast, women in the region were viewed as inherently apolitical, imagined as part of the domestic sphere and exclusively focused on family welfare. This view of women's roles allowed them greater mobility to move between and among communities. One anthropologist who conducted fieldwork in the region reported that "threatened peasants would send their wives to do errands because the paramilitaries wouldn't kill them, figuring the men made the decisions."[46]

Unlike the guerrillas, the majority of paramilitaries were from distant communities, not embedded in local kinship networks, and they employed much more brutal methods. Local priests recalled paramilitaries as largely impervious to the clergy's claims to authority. Priests told me of fruitless efforts to intervene on behalf of threatened parishioners and lay religious leaders. One recounted protesting the detention of two catechists; the paramilitary commander assassinated the crying men in front of him. Another priest recalled his frustrated efforts to negotiate with a commander for the return of the dead for burial. "[The paramilitaries wouldn't return the bodies because] it was a way to demonstrate that the person that they killed was a delinquent, was an enemy," the priest told me "and that they could do what they liked with him. It was the best way for them to express their rage, their anger." He described their forces as "more terrifying... [They were] more bitter, rougher, harder... more brutal, more bloodthirsty, and less trusting." He attributed this difference in part to their origins as urban forces linked to the state, who could face legal consequences should they be discovered, thereby requiring the bodies to be destroyed or hidden, rather than being made available for burial.

Father Campo Elías de la Cruz, who had served as a novice under Father Jiménez and was the most outspoken of this cohort, developed what he called a "prophetic voice," explicitly linking his religious vocation with what he viewed as a moral duty to denounce military complicity with paramilitary violence in the region. Even as he recognized that ministering to the security forces remained part of his sacramental duties, he described his growing awareness of their role in the violence. "I knew that my work as a priest was to be there for everyone, for the soldiers too," he told me. But in traveling to a local military base for his religious duties,

I realized what was going on, I knew that there were things going on that weren't right. On that short stretch of road between [the military base of] Santa Ana and Puerto Asís, so many bodies appearing there and it was such a short piece of road, right there near the base. I would talk about these things in the mass, and the colonel didn't like it...

Because I knew that the security forces weren't doing the right thing, *no estaba haciendo bien*, and I would say it.[47]

Father de la Cruz accompanied a 1998 peasant march to Bogotá in which they occupied government buildings to demand government action against the paramilitary forces. March leaders participated in a meeting with then-president Ernesto Samper during which they denounced the government's support of paramilitary forces; many of the leaders were killed on their return to Putumayo.

During this period, paramilitary counterinsurgency operations targeted civilians in the region, while allowing paramilitary leaders to protect their business interests and solidify their alliance with state security forces. The arrival of the paramilitaries and their confrontation with the guerrillas created new dilemmas for local residents, now confronted with opposing military forces, contradictory governance demands, and brutal violence. In the face of disputed and rapidly shifting boundaries of territorial control, widespread suspicion of local residents, and brutal retaliation by armed actors, organized political activity in the region was overwhelmed by violence.

Conclusion

The market logics of the illegal drug trade—the incredibly high profit margins driven by demand abroad—created opportunities for a range of social actors in Putumayo. For local residents, coca crops paid for their immediate family needs and allowed them to organize new settlements, build roads, and construct schools. These settlements in turn made demands on the state for administrative recognition through the creation of new municipalities and for expanded services.

At the same time, illegal armed actors also viewed drug trade profits as critical elements in their military expansion. Both guerrillas and paramilitaries, despite their different relationship to the state and political objectives, capitalized on the money generated through the coca trade. Guerrillas funded their military growth through a deepening reliance on the drug trade at the cost of political support as their efforts to police their business interests resulted in growing abuses against the population. At the end of the 1990s, paramilitaries moved into the region from their largely northern strongholds, pursuing the vertical integration of the drug trade linking their established trafficking routes to controlled production, as well as expanding their counterinsurgency operations.

The presence of multiple projects of rule vying openly with one another meant that Putumayenses found themselves confronted with an array of institutional orders, each of which presented itself as the locus of authority. No one group developed complete control over the area; all were deeply implicated in policing the shifting boundaries of territorial and institutional control and producing competing norms and policies. The situation in Putumayo thus inverted much of the standard narrative concerning state–society relations: "criminals" sought to establish the rule of law, while the state subverted it. Instead of viewing nonstate armed actors as a threat to sovereignty, state offices actively encouraged and supported Colombia's paramilitary groups. The latter, however, worked with the offices of government not to protect and safeguard the rights of citizens, but instead to brutalize the population. Indeed, rather than establish broad conditions of social peace across the national territory, the military and its ferocious allies waged war on the civilian population, who were seen as an internal enemy rather than a national citizenry.

Local residents were frequently described as criminals, willfully retreating from the state and ensconced in a region characterized by state absence. Although undeniably driven by the profits of the illegal coca trade, local residents rejected public officials' categorization of them as outlaws. Rather than criminals seeking to avoid the law, the huge number of migrants to the region considered themselves to be farmers seeking a better life. While resisting punitive state sanctions, at the same time they organized to expand access to state services and increase the state infrastructure in the region. Putumayan residents and local state officials called on the state to respond to their concerns and incorporate their collective demands into policymaking. Peasant farmers in the region used a range of tactics to encourage state presence in the region, including protests demanding additional state services, the formation of committees lobbying for recognition as municipalities with rights to central state resources and the ability to elect local officials, and subsidizing state services such as education with money from coca crops. Space for political mobilization was increasingly limited, however, by repressive governmental responses, such as fumigation, and the growing power of illegal armed groups. Despite these multiple challenges, this history demonstrates that criminalized coca farmers did not seek to elude the state; they sought to create a place in it.

Part III

What We Talk About
When We Talk About Plan Colombia

Figure 5 Child playing pool in Putumayo, 1999.

Photograph by Winifred Tate.

Chapter 5

Origin Stories

MUCH OF THE DEBATE over the Plan Colombia aid package at the time it was proposed centered on the "real" intentions of policymakers—whether the package was intended to fight drugs (through support for counternarcotics efforts)—or guerrillas (through support for counterinsurgency operations). I argue that it was precisely this strategic ambiguity that enabled the range of institutional alliances to coalesce in support of military aid. In this chapter, I excavate the multiple origin stories for the package involving both the technical details of production—such as the language in which it was written—and the political stakes in these debates over who could take credit and who got the blame. My project is not to establish a single definitive account, but to present the multitude of ways in which ongoing policy debates become sites for distinct political claims through the articulation of origin stories. The officials I interviewed described Plan Colombia as emerging from a range of policy priorities: a domestic counternarcotics policy intended to address the Clinton administration's moral crisis, a peace policy to support negotiations with the guerrilla forces, a counterinsurgency policy that would strengthen the security forces, and an economic development policy to spur development in remote regions. These origin stories were produced by actors within distinct institutional positions and revealed a range of bureaucratic logics, marshaled to support a predominantly military aid package presented as a broad political consensus. This story was produced as "Plan Colombia," described in U.S. official documents and statements as the Colombian government's "integrated strategy to meet the most pressing challenges confronting Colombia today—promoting the peace process, combating the narcotics industry, reviving the Colombian economy, and strengthening the democratic pillars of Colombian society."[1]

David Mosse argues that policies do not set practices of implementation, but rather the inverse: policies are produced through the practice of implementing programs.[2] He further claims that ethnography allows researchers to escape a common analytical dichotomy: the instrumental view of policy as rational problem solving or the critical view that sees official policy as a rationalizing discourse concealing the hidden purposes of bureaucratic power whose failure is self-evident. Neither approach captures what can be understood ethnographically: that policy primarily functions to mobilize and maintain political support; that is, to legitimize existing practice rather than originating it.[3] Policy ideas are less important for what they say than for how they bring together different actors and the alliances, coalitions, and relationships they allow. Here, I argue that it is the multiplicity of policy narratives, produced by and bringing together a range of institutional and individual interests in particular configurations and alliances, that allows programs and material funding to move forward in particular designs.

This strategic ambiguity does not encompass all political visions, however. In the case, of Plan Colombia, policy narratives had to conform to the central organizing logics of U.S. foreign policy. Militarization was a central organizing principle that appeared in all of these origin stories. Increased military aid enabling the expansion of the already growing military programs, such as the counternarcotics battalions established in 1998, was widely promoted as a policy solution to this range of distinct issues. Alternative narratives and ways of characterizing problems leading to distinct policy formulation were excluded and dismissed.

Policy origin stories are, at their heart, narratives of how particular social worlds and events are made into problems that must be resolved through policy interventions, what Susan Greenhalgh calls the process of policy problematization. Origin stories reveal the ways in which "framings" are central in policymaking, examining the availability of certain narratives to explain problems and naturalize particular policies as inevitable and reasonable. Theories of frame alignment, which examine how the representations of events and issues mobilize support for specific kinds of policies, are important analytical tools for understanding the work of social movement organizations.[4] Policy origin stories function as "naming, blaming, and claiming" processes, in which particular situations are categorized as problems, responsibility established, and action mobilized.[5] In these narratives, policy functions to galvanize and maintain political support, legitimating existing practices rather than orienting new institutional regimes.[6] The real political value of these stories is how they bring together different actors and produce relationships defined through alliances, coalitions, and consensus.

Plan Colombia brings to life one Washington cliché: success has many fathers. Multiple senior officials claimed to have the cocktail napkin on which they sketched the first outline of the package—on a flight home after a fact-finding mission to Colombia, in a back office at the Colombian Embassy, or in a Washington cubicle. These origin stories inject agency, both individual and institutional, into policy accounts that are often produced in the passive voice—as a generalized product of amorphous political forces. They highlight the actions of specific people and particular bureaucratic configurations in the production of policies and programs. Origin stories reveal the multiple institutional agendas and cultural logics used to shape policy, with varying degrees of success, providing a small window into the disputes within closed sites of policy formation. These narratives can reveal the institutional agendas, interests, and relationships that are absent from official public policy accounts. Origin stories signal hierarchies of power and control: who are the most important actors, what institutional mandates prevail, what time scales are used to determine the beginning of the problem. Does Plan Colombia emerge from peasant entanglements with development programs or with the Clinton administration's perceived moral failings? With the growing strength of the FARC guerrillas or the institutional positioning of the congressional drug warriors? Origin stories are one way in which policymakers use the past to make political claims on the present. Each of these stories allows the teller to establish a particular institutional and ideological genealogy of Plan Colombia and, in doing so, to both open political terrain for specific material practices of implementation and lay the groundwork for defining the definitive evaluation frameworks.

Origin Story I—The Clinton Administration's Drug Crisis

At the 1992 Republican National Convention, conservative pundit Pat Buchanan claimed, "There is a religious war going on in our country for the soul of America." He defined it as a "culture war, as critical to the kind of nation we will one day be as was the Cold War itself." Although the Republicans failed to win the presidency—Bill Clinton defeated George Bush Sr., taking office in 1993— the fault lines of the so-called culture wars came to define his presidency. After the 1994 "Republican Revolution," in which that party came to dominate both the House of Representatives and the Senate, the Clinton administration was on the defensive. Republican attacks against the administration exploded with the January 1998 revelation of Clinton's sexual relationship with former White House intern Monica Lewinsky. Special Prosecutor Kenneth Starr, who had been charged in 1994 with investigating improper real estate and banking deals in the so-called Whitewater case, expanded his probe into allegations of sexual misconduct by the president involving Paula Jones and then Lewinsky. The scandal dominated Washington political life for much of the year, involving allegations of oral sex in the Oval Office, a dress tested by the FBI for traces of semen, and secretly taped confessions by Lewinsky, which all culminated in the failed impeachment trial in late 1998.

That same year, the House Republican Conference published an issue brief titled "The Drug Problem in America," which stated, "The Administration's response and inattention to this growing national crisis, and the resulting explosion of drug use across the nation, is frightening." The report went on to urge the administration to adopt a focus on source countries by increasing military aid to foreign governments for counternarcotics operations. The fact that according to the Office of National Drug Control Policy's (ONDCP) own figures drug use was declining did nothing to stop the Republican onslaught on the drug issue. Democrats were particularly worried by polls reporting their vulnerability on this issue.[7]

Clinton officials were desperate to salvage the administration's legacy, as well as to counteract ongoing political attacks, channeled through accusations of Clinton's immoral conduct and ideology. According to Rand Beers, then assistant secretary of state for international narcotics and law enforcement, Plan Colombia was born directly from the Democrats' concern that the Republicans would propose a grander plan and then would accuse them of being soft on drugs. Sitting in a windowless conference room at the National Security Archive, Beers told me that he and General Charles Wilhelm, then head of SouthCom, had been invited to a meeting in the summer of 1999 organized by recently appointed Speaker of the House Dennis Hastert to talk to the Republican House drug caucus. At this meeting Porter Goss, chair of that caucus, handed Beers their proposal for a several hundred million dollar supplemental budget for Colombia, with another sizable funding request intended for the fall. When Beers reported on this meeting to other members of the Clinton administration, he told them, "You have to get out in front. I talked to Barry McCaffrey, and we walked from his office to the White House to propose Plan Colombia."

In Beers' recounting, senior advisor to the National Security Council Sandy Berger then convened a meeting to discuss Colombia outside "the normal interagency channels." Because of institutional protocol, as head of SouthCom, General Wilhelm would have had to make public any interagency meeting about Colombia attended by "principals" (referring to anyone with a diplomatic rank of assistant secretary of state or above), most likely resulting in the Joint Chiefs of Staff (the military equivalent) attending the meeting themselves. So the meeting was announced as an ad hoc discussion—not a meeting requiring a particular bureaucratic rank—focusing not on Colombia but on the future of Howard Air Force base in Panama and the U.S. departure from Panama. "That was how they had to play it to get Wilhelm there," Beers told me. Wilhelm's participation was important because he could marshal the bureaucratic and material resources of SouthCom—and was motivated to do so by his interest in the region—in contrast to the Joint Chiefs who would have been more concerned about administrative overreach within the armed forces. At this meeting Beers described his prescription for administrative action. "I said we have to get out in front of this," he recalled. "We have to propose a full blown program for Colombia, the entire Andean region. It has to be serious, it needs a billion [dollars] at the lowest level of the program." He was instructed by Berger to "come back with a plan." According to Beers, the administration was primarily motivated by fear of a Republican victory on the drug issue. "The Republican proposal was what I needed, a political scare for the administration," Beers told me. "So I sold the program. Nobody knew this was coming, but it was an opportunity to say, they are going to get out in front of us again if we don't do it first." The importance of partisan motivation was underscored by Beers' conclusion to the story. He ended his Plan Colombia origin story by questioning why the Republican drug caucus had given him a copy of their proposal. His only explanation was that, because of his military background, "everyone thought I was a Republican."

Origin Story II—The Colombians in Plan Colombia I: Pastrana's Plans

In 1998 U.S. policymakers had gained a new Colombian ally: newly elected Colombian president Andrés Pastrana. In contrast to his predecessor, Ernesto Samper, whom U.S. officials treated as a pariah because of evidence leaked by the DEA immediately following his election that he had accepted campaign contributions from the Cali Cartel, Pastrana was seen as a potential ally, someone U.S. officials could work with. A member of Colombia's historic political elite (the son and grandson of former presidents), Pastrana was a newscaster who rose to prominence after surviving a week-long kidnapping by the Medellín Cartel and then served as the first elected mayor of Bogotá. The primary issue during the 1997–98 presidential campaign was ending guerrilla violence, and both major presidential candidates campaigned on peace platforms, advocating a negotiated settlement to the conflict. A significant pro-peace constituency had gathered force during the mid-1990s, with NGOs galvanizing marches, symbolic votes for peace, and other public actions designed to demonstrate political support for negotiations. Pastrana seized the momentum before the second round of voting, announcing his plans for peace in a major speech and sending his advisor Victor G. Ricardo to a secret (and illegal) meeting with the FARC leadership. During the meeting, Ricardo gave his watch to senior commander Manuel Marulanda; in a 2010 interview he told me that he intended it as a gesture symbolizing the Pastrana administration's willingness to take all the necessary time for peace. The watch—now on Marulanda's wrist and with Pastrana's campaign slogan clearly visible—appeared prominently in the widely circulated photo taken as proof that the meeting had taken place. Although Ricardo claimed he did not foresee the impact of his gift, many interpreted it as Marulanda's endorsement of Pastrana. In the final vote, he defeated Horacio Serpa by a 2 percent margin. Pastrana began talks with the guerrillas immediately following his inauguration.

During the campaign and in the months following the election, Pastrana discussed his hopes for massive foreign assistance to the country—a "Marshall Plan" for Colombia—as a central component of the peace process. The Marshall Plan, officially the European Recovery Program but nicknamed for its champion, Secretary of State George Marshall, provided billions of dollars in aid from the United States for postconflict reconstruction in Europe following the devastation of World War II. By invoking this "plan," Pastrana was discursively positioning Colombia as the appropriate recipient of massive international assistance. In this logic, the international community—in this case, the primarily Western countries that are the primary consumers of illegal narcotics— had to assume moral and financial responsibility for the effects of Colombia's conflict. Narcotics trafficking was a "motor" of the conflict because armed groups used drug profits to finance their military operations, thus implicating consumers.

This funding was to be provided not in a future postconflict moment, but in the present as a contribution to conflict resolution.

This proposed Colombian "Marshall plan" never materialized, not even as a written plan, much less in funded programs, but existed merely as a talking point in a series of speeches and meetings that were held with U.S., European Union, and Latin American officials as he sought support for the negotiations. When I inquired about the possible contradictions among announced plans and attempted to trace their bureaucratic lives, I was frequently met with polite derision. Numerous Colombian officials and military officers told me that, as an anthropologist, I should understand that Colombia had an oral tradition of policymaking, in which little was written down and programs were produced through multiple bureaucracies; therefore any effort to establish a final, comprehensive analysis was a waste of time.

However, this "plan" played a critical role, existing not as concrete initiatives in the present but as possible futures. Simply invoking one plan created political space for the counteroffer of other plans. In this sense, the plan discussed in Pastrana's speeches should be understood as an advocacy strategy, as "the ask" in meetings with other governments: not as an existing governmental policy, but as an initial salvo in an effort to gain specific measures and material aid from another government and its agencies. Within Colombia, invoking this plan engendered a possible future state that could be realized with international funding, transforming not only the transnational relationships between Colombia and these foreign powers but also the commitment of the central state to remote rural regions. A prime example was point fifteen of Pastrana's Tequendama speech, a major campaign event during the month before the second round of voting, which called on "developed countries" to fund "extensive investment in social issues, in the agricultural sector and in regional infrastructure, to offer our peasants alternatives different from illicit crops."[8] In addition to his efforts to convince Colombian audiences, he took this message to the foreign officials whom he hoped would provide funds after the election; these officials included U.S. government representatives. In a September 1998 embassy cable, Mark Schneider, director of Latin America programs for USAID, reported the president describing "plan Pastrana," which he expected would incorporate funding from a variety of sources toward the costs of peace and investment in the areas most affected by the war and illicit cultivation.[9]

Within Colombia, Pastrana presented his call for a Marshall Plan for Colombia in a speech in December 1998 in Puerto Wilches; it is the first time he used the name "Plan Colombia." The location of the speech was indicative of Pastrana's intended emphasis: the region was not a drug-producing or trafficking area, but was deeply affected by the conflict because of the presence of FARC and ELN guerrillas and paramilitary forces. The region was also the center of a large development project, *Programa de desarrollo y paz del Magdalena Medio*, run by a well-known Jesuit priest, Father Francisco de Roux. The project had gained international renown, bringing together funding and project expertise from the European Union, businesses, foundations, and NGOs, and was held up as a model for similar programs throughout the country. Pastrana also offered an invitation to the guerrillas: "the insurgency must take part actively in all decisions of Plan Colombia." The speech made minimal reference to the issue of illegal narcotics, discussing them mainly in terms of ecological devastation and as an issue to be discussed in future negotiations.

Pastrana was using public discussion of the plan to fulfill two of his expected mandates: to produce a plan to support peace talks with the guerrillas and to generate an administration-specific economic development project. Earlier presidents had announced their primary goals through such plans; for example, Belisario Betancur's National Rehabilitation Plan and Ernesto Samper's *Salto Social* (literally, the social jump, an antipoverty initiative). Thus it was expected that Pastrana's peace plan would be incorporated into the National Development Plan (NDP), titled "Change to Build Peace 1998–2002." Both the NDP and the peace plan discussed on the campaign trail focused on development and sustainability models rather than on law enforcement or a militarized security approach. The NDP declared that the two primary issues facing Colombia were the conflict and the faltering economy. However, the NDP plan and the campaign peace proposals had different emphases, which could be explained by a lack of institutional coordination and the competition between bureaucratic fiefdoms: the "plan" presented by Pastrana at Puerto Wilches originated with the High Commissioner for Peace's office, whereas the National Planning Bureau designed the National Development Plan, with little contact between the two offices. Unlike Pastrana's campaign presentations, the NDP plan targeted coca growing. Its section titled "Strategies Toward Zones Affected by Violence Conflict" listed crop substitution and alternative development in coca cultivation regions, attention to forcibly displaced persons, and a focus on the most violent regions as priorities. Another major difference was that the NDP plan did not invite guerrilla participation. Rather, the emphasis was on participation by the civilian population in local governance initiatives to increase state services in rural areas.[10]

Neither plan got off the ground. According to several former Colombian officials I interviewed, there was interest at the InterAmerican Bank in the High Commissioner for Peace's version of a proposal that would involve the guerrillas in administering a major development initiative, but funding never materialized. The National Development Plan was voted on by Congress and passed into law on July 29, 1999, but was later declared unconstitutional by the Colombian Supreme Court. No new national development plan was ever presented. However, circulating the proposals performed important national and international work for the administration. Pastrana's plans fulfilled domestic expectations of voters. The plan conceptualized by the High Commissioner for Peace was produced as part of the standard peace process narratives, as rhetorical strategies for imagining the public transformations that could be achieved under possible but remote future conditions. At the same time, the international circulation of these rhetorical proposals served as a hook on which U.S. policymakers could hang their own designs.

Origin Story III—Support for Peace

The U.S. State Department publicly proclaimed its interest in supporting the Colombian peace process initiated by Pastrana with the FARC. Many of those involved in Plan Colombia discussions had played a role in U.S. diplomatic efforts in El Salvador during the 1980s, when the United States had supported the government in its fight against Marxist insurgents and ultimately assisted in brokering a peace deal between the two in the early 1990s. Although some Foreign Service officers were critical of the ongoing U.S. assistance to abusive military forces during that period, most recalled U.S. policy in El Salvador as a triumph of conflict resolution efforts. Peter Romero, who at the time of Plan Colombia was the acting head of the Andean Section at the State Department, recalled with relish his work as a political officer in the U.S. Embassy in El Salvador; this was despite the low prestige within the State Department of postings to Latin America, which Romero said was described as the *cucaracha* (cockroach) circuit by foreign service officers posted in Europe.

According to Romero's then deputy, Phil Chicola, Plan Colombia grew out of the State Department's interest in supporting peace and its concern over the multiple plans emerging from Colombia. Following an official visit to Colombia to assess the peace process, Chicola recalled that he and Romero were appalled at the lack of coordination among the different Colombian agencies involved. "We were briefed by everybody," he told me during a phone interview from his posting at the U.S. consulate in Vancouver. "There was no common thread at the time. The army, police, civilians were all going their own way." On the return flight to Miami, Chicola described a discussion with Romero in which they realized that "the Colombians have great plans but nobody seems to be talking to each other." This conversation, he claimed, "was the genesis for Plan Colombia."

The peace process itself had gotten off to a rocky start. Guerrilla elder statesman Manuel Marulanda failed to appear at its much publicized launch, leaving an empty chair widely viewed as demonstrating the guerrillas' lack of commitment to the process. Government initiatives to raise money for special "peace projects" were hobbled by bureaucratic ineptitude and allegations of corruption. Pastrana's most controversial decision was to withdraw government troops from a wide swath of south Colombia that journalists frequently compared to the size of Switzerland or Maryland. The remote area was sparsely populated and had been under de facto guerrilla control for decades.[11] Despite being widely known as the *despeje* (demilitarized zone), heavily armed guerrillas patrolled regularly and some civilian government officials remained in that area. Critics, including Colombian military officers, called the region *Farclandia* and described it as an affront to Colombian national sovereignty and a needless concession that would be abused by the guerrillas. In a symbolic vote, the U.S. Congress passed an amendment condemning the zone.

Congressional critics, including high-ranking Republicans, actively opposed State Department support for the peace process. After Romero's approval of a secret 1998 meeting between Chicola and FARC leaders was leaked to the press, members of the Senate used their power in the appointment process to prevent Romero's confirmation, effectively ending his Foreign Service career. In March 1999, U.S. support for the process was further eroded by the murder by FARC of three U.S. activists—Terence Freitas, Ingrid Washinawatok, and Lahe'ena'e Gay—who were visiting Arauca in support of the Uwa indigenous people and their protests of Occidental Petroleum oil exploration. Despite the published pleas of Freitas's mother in favor of peace efforts, U.S. officials prohibited future meetings with the FARC until those responsible for the murders were handed over to Colombian justice, which they would not do. U.S. officials refused to participate in any public events or any diplomatic efforts to form a "group of friends" of governments supporting the process. During this period, Marulanda also reneged on promises to allow independent inspections in the despeje. According to Beers, by June 1999, the new consensus within the State Department was "to encourage Pastrana to step back from the policies he was ineffectively pursuing with the FARC and the peace talks."

Many Plan Colombia supporters understood increasing military aid as providing support for peace. Rather than engaging in diplomatic efforts to encourage negotiations and to secure material resources for postconflict demobilization and reconstruction, they emphasized escalating the conflict as a path to eventually ending it. According to this logic, building up the security forces at the same time as peace talks were being held would be a win-win for the Colombian government and its U.S. allies. A more powerful military would motivate the guerrillas to begin dialogue because of their fear of defeat. Should the talks succeed, the Colombian government would negotiate the final settlement from a position of strength—meaning it would need to make fewer concessions. Should the talks fail, the military would be poised to increase combat operations and pursue a military victory. Either way, the Colombians would develop a larger, more professional military, which was seen as an undisputed positive in the logics of militarization.

Origin Story IV—Bureaucracies in Motion

Making policy real by moving into the implementation phase required bureaucratic action, generated through the commitment of strategically located individuals who could activate specific institutional channels. For the U.S. government to move beyond rhetorical commitments to material programs required particular constellations of bureaucratic action. Lower ranking State Department officials claimed to have carried out an educational effort targeting senior officials, in which they convened "Colombia 101 in small groups" to prepare them to respond to anticipated calls for specific proposals from "higher-ups." Bureaucratic commitment to the process came in the form of the Plan Colombia Interagency Task Force, which was charged with creating Plan Colombia. Undersecretary of State Thomas Pickering was named as chair; his high rank meant that the group had decision-making power rather than simply offering recommendations. To create the group, Secretary of State Madeline Albright used an administrative mechanism known as an executive committee—ExCom for short—a bureaucratic form that was established by a Clinton executive order (and later abolished by George W. Bush). One mid-level State Department official described the group as a bureaucratic "halfway house" established at the assistant secretary level (the next higher levels are the deputies and the principal)—high enough to make decisions but low enough to focus.[12]

Assistant Secretary for International Law Enforcement and Narcotics Rand Beers chaired the majority of the Task Force meetings, which he and others viewed as meaning that drugs were the priority. Member agencies included State Department bureaus (International Narcotics and Law Enforcement, Western Hemisphere Area), the Agency for International Development, the Department of Justice (DOJ), the Defense Department, and the Central Intelligence Agency; additional agencies participated as needed. The meetings were intended to "hash out all the issues regarding implementation;" disagreements were "sent up the food chain," meaning a meeting chaired by Pickering of the ExCom itself. The Task Force included three bilateral working groups: counternarcotics and security, socioeconomic issues, and justice reform and law enforcement. Each group combined work on general coordination issues with a focus on southern Colombia.[13] Expenses, including staff, were paid for by a $1.5 million line item placed in the Plan Colombia budget by Tim Rieser, the aide to Senator Leahy (D-VT) who had also been instrumental in crafting the Leahy Law and had remained closely involved in Colombia funding through his position on the Senate Appropriations Committee. This money funded meeting preparation and follow-up, as well as the salary of four staff responsible for vetting the Colombian military personnel participating in Plan Colombia programs, as required by the Leahy Law.

Throughout 1998, weekly Task Force meetings and periodic delegations to Colombia and meetings in Washington signaled growing institutional focus on Colombia as a policy problem. Beers traveled with a delegation of officials in early 1998; their trip included visits to three military bases operated by the U.S. for counternarcotics operations known as forward operating locations, as well as other sites of U.S.-sponsored eradication efforts.[14] In February and March, the State Department bureau of International Narcotics and Law Enforcement (INL) hosted working-level interagency meetings to discuss Colombia's counternarcotics programs.[15] Declassified notes from a June 11 interagency working group (IWG) meeting on Colombia concluded that there would be a "principals" (meaning higher ranked officials with decision-making power) meeting on Colombia, requiring an updated engagement strategy paper from the State Department's Andean Region Area as well as talking points about the new Colombian president.[16] (This meeting was held the next month and chaired by a higher ranking official, Ambassador James Dobbins of the National Security Council.) The discussion included military aid, human rights, and plans for INL and AID to prepare "a paper for the next IWG on a plan for a pilot alternative development project in Colombia," the first proposal of its kind.[17] The Andean Region Area was also directed "to prepare a comprehensive list of various USG programs currently being funded in Colombia," proposals for the following year, and a "prioritized list of currently unfunded proposals," indicating an anticipation of additional funding.[18] The notes went on to outline what came to be major administration arguments in favor of increased U.S. military aid:

DOD strongly supports providing Colombian security forces unrestricted intelligence information concerning narcotraffickers [bullet point excised] since CNP cannot operate in FARC-controlled coca cultivation areas without Colombian military support, our successes against the drug traffickers hinges on the operational effectiveness of that military, especially the Colombian army. A modernized, more professional military could more capably support counternarcotics efforts and the pp [peace process].

A new military-military cooperation agreement signed during the December 1998 Defense Ministerial—a meeting of U.S. and Latin American military and civilian officials to discuss issues involving the armed forces—set the stage for increasing U.S. military assistance to Colombia. In addition to a broad public pledge to improve the relationship, the U.S. military established a series of Bilateral Working Groups on topics including counternarcotics, professionalization, and human rights. According to one SouthCom official, "The bilateral working group came out of the defense ministerial, when we were hoping for a large package. We didn't anticipate it, but we were hoping . . . We talked to the Colombian Army, Navy, Air Force, asking what they needed, but not promising anything." U.S. assistance was instrumental in establishing the U.S.-supported Colombian Joint Task Force South (JFT-S), designed to increase Colombian military and police cooperation, including a new joint intelligence center run out of an expanded military base, Tres Esquinas, in Caquetá. Wilhelm began sending piecemeal funding from existing budget lines for the JFT-S operations, including the counternarcotics battalion pilot project: its mandate was to focus on "attacking narco targets systematically, in a way that also hits the guerrillas center of gravity; their narco financing; and maximizing US support." The first of the new, vetted Colombian army counternarcotics battalions became operational by the end of 1998.

Political commitment to Plan Colombia shifted in a principals' meeting in the summer of 1999, according to Assistant Secretary of Defense for Special Operations and Low Intensity Conflict Brian Sheridan. "That was the meeting where it penetrated, with [National Security advisor] Berger, [Secretary of State] Albright, and others that we were losing Colombia. Things changed direction in that meeting." One important shift involved getting the budgeting infrastructure on board. "We had OMB [Office of Management and Budget] support. They were directed to support things," Sheridan continued. "That was the first time that everything was aligned. Before, OMB says no, no money, everyone would have been fighting over things. But after that, the principals got to go off and do other things." These accounts stress the critical importance of the involvement of specific channels of bureaucratic machinery to producing policy, in particular, the role of officials empowered to move decisions forward.

Barry McCaffrey, a retired army general, former commander of SouthCom and Clinton's drug czar, was a vocal and enthusiastic proponent of military aid despite having no budget authority in his position as director of the Office of National Drug Control Policy. On July 16, 1999, he gave a press conference recommending one billion dollars in "emergency drug supplemental assistance" for South America, including $570 million for Colombia, most of it in the form of military aid. McCaffrey also said that differentiating between antidrug and anti-insurgency efforts was counterproductive. At the end of the month, during a visit to Colombia, McCaffrey again stated his support for increasing military aid to the area and proposed that the United States should "reevaluate" its policy toward Colombia. An embassy cable describing the visit reported Beers' telling the Colombian Ministry of Defense and Armed Forces leadership "that Colombian issues in Washington were heating up, and that it was time to being planning strategic solutions," including making requests for helicopters for the new counternarcotics battalion. The cable reported that "Beers explained that any new assistance packages would be tied to GOC [government of Colombia] movement against illicit coca fields in Putumayo and expanding aerial interdiction into southern Colombia."[19]

In August, SouthCom completed its counternarcotics plan, describing the threat, its mission, and objectives and laying out the required resources.[20] That same month, McCaffrey and Undersecretary of State Thomas Pickering traveled to Colombia to meet with Colombian officials. News reports of the visit described their warnings to Pastrana that the United States might withdraw its support if he continued to make "concessions" to the guerrillas, but that aid might be "sharply increased" if he presented a "comprehensive plan to strengthen the military, halt the nation's economic free fall and fight drug trafficking."[21] At around the same time, the Colombian ambassador to the United States, Luis Alberto Moreno, had begun conversations with members of Congress with the aim of promoting increased U.S. involvement with Colombia; he also met with Undersecretary Pickering. As Moreno told me,

[US officials] said to Pastrana, you have to come up with a plan, this was the first week of August [1999], so that we can get it going. Pastrana said that he wanted to come up with something big, something that would last until the end of this administration. Pickering said, ok, lets do something big. They said you need to get the plan together and we need to deliver it to Congress by mid September.

One origin story describes the production of numbers before narrative. At an interagency meeting in Pickering's office, according to one senior USAID official, the Colombian government faxed a single page titled "Plan Colombia" that was "literally just one page, just numbers—just a one-page budget. The total on that page was 8 billion dollars." This official strongly questioned why Colombia was going to get the additional money when it was unable to meet its existing commitments. He described his incredulous reaction as a product of his naïveté about the process: "I was the kid on the block," he told me. The other officials admonished him for his ignorance and then explained to him that Colombia would count World Bank loans, existing expenditures, and other funding as their commitment to Plan Colombia in the publicized budget.

U.S. officials also frequently announced in press conferences and meetings with NGOs that they were planning to meet with European governments and agencies to seek additional funding for the "soft side" of aid: development, human rights, and other nonmilitary programs. Donor meetings were scheduled in London and Madrid with the aim of convincing European governments and foundations to fund pieces of what was to become Plan Colombia.

Origins Story V—The Colombians in Plan Colombia II:
Moreno in Washington

Critics of Plan Colombia frequently focus on language as shorthand to indicate that the plan was a U.S. intervention with little Colombian participation, arguing that the proposal was written in English, reflecting its gringo origins. As the Colombia analyst at WOLA, I repeated this talking point myself in interviews. During one elevator encounter with a State Department official, he chided me for focusing on the plan's having been written in English, but with a wink essentially acknowledged that to do so was correct. Some U.S. officials openly admitted that the U.S. devised the plan. "It was striking; the U.S. drafted just about every word of it," one former State Department official told me. "The Colombians commented on it, but I was surprised at the extent of the US drafting... Everyone felt a little embarrassed about it."

In my later interviews, Colombian senior officials turned this discussion on its head by insisting that the plan *had* indeed been written in English—but by Colombians. According to Colombian ambassador Moreno, the plan itself was written over two weeks at the Colombian Embassy in Washington because "it needed to address U.S. constituencies." He claimed to have submitted the plan to the State Department before showing it to Colombia's foreign minister or even President Pastrana. Similarly, political scientist and Colombian government official Eduardo Pizarro claims that then-U.S. Ambassador Kamman told him at a conference that the document had been written in English by Colombians because of time pressure. His proof: the grammatical glitches in the document that revealed the author as a non-native English speaker.[22] Jaime Ruiz, a high school friend of Pastrana's who became one of his closest advisors and was tapped to be the Colombia coordinator of Plan Colombia, claimed to have authored the plan in a mix of Spanish and English. He described his Plan Colombia as *recogiendo,* gathering up the agreements that were in the works between the U.S. and Colombian militaries.

A former Colombian cabinet minister described the Colombians' role in Plan Colombia as that of "puppet masters," insisting that their role was to convince the gringos to give them what they had desired all along—and what they wanted was military assistance. International relations scholar Arlene Tickner describes this relationship as "intervention by invitation."[23] Pastrana began the military's expansion in 1999. These efforts included increasing combat operations, transferring units from urban garrisons to field encampments, and replacing conscripts with professional soldiers. New military programs improved the army's mobility and intelligence-gathering capacity, which quickly succeeded in garnering U.S. support. Colombian officials lobbied for U.S. money and equipment for these efforts during U.S. diplomatic delegations to Colombia as well as Colombian official visits to Washington. During a 1999 visit to Washington, Colombian Defense Minister Luis Ramírez and Armed Forces Chief of Staff General Fernando Tapias requested $500 million in counternarcotics and counterinsurgency aid. Plan Colombia, some Colombian officials argue, was simply these politicians' cagy way of getting the gringos to pay for their military expansion. In this view, the convergence of counternarcotics interests (the gringos) and counterinsurgency funding (the Colombians) played right into Colombian hands through the logic of militarization.

Getting what they wanted from the gringos required mastering new lobbying skills. At the time, the Colombian diplomatic corps was undergoing a painful process of professionalization, transitioning from jobs distributed as political rewards—extended vacations abroad offered in return for political support—to a career path requiring intense work and a sophisticated understanding of international relations. Part of this process involved learning the lobbying system, including "the ask." Colombia officials needed to know "how DC works, all the linkages between the media, the NGOs, the contractors, the agencies, all the relationships and the constituencies, how they all come together to make policy," according to then-Colombian ambassador Alberto Moreno, who was widely touted as a key figure in this professionalization process. As an example, Moreno described his first day in Washington, which coincided with a congressional vote condemning Pastrana's decision to pull troops out of southern Colombia in an effort to facilitate peace talks. When the Colombian press called for comments, no one in the embassy had any idea what they were asking about. Moreno quickly focused on learning the power levers in Washington, to "figure out how things worked," in particular, the power of members of Congress in setting policy. "If I went as the ambassador, or had the foreign minister come [to the State Department], that wouldn't get anything done, but if a member of Congress called, it would." According to a former coworker, Moreno "realized early on that you just have to ask the right people, and tell the right stories at the right time, to get things to move." Moreno worked the congressional system, figuring out who were the key committee position holders. In lobbying, he tied the Colombian funding to representatives' local concerns, generally through the drug issue, including writing editorials for U.S. newspapers in key congressional districts.

Without exception, the U.S. officials I interviewed described Moreno as an extraordinarily skilled Washington power player. Talking points prepared for a senior U.S. official in advance of his meeting with Moreno included reminding him to offer Moreno congratulations "on the key personal role you played in achieving Congressional passage of the Colombia assistance package" and went on to provide a joke recognizing his lobbying skill: " 'I've heard rumors that the Clinton Administration is considering you for the position of Director of Legislative Affairs.' "[24] Moreno was also ideally positioned in the Colombian political scene: his close relationship with the president guaranteed him the autonomy to design policy. After serving as Pastrana's campaign chief, he had turned down the job of minister of the interior—"like prime minister"—for the only job he wanted: Colombia's ambassador to the United States. Moreno rightly anticipated a dramatic shift in U.S.-Colombia relations following the intense U.S. critique of former president Samper. The Colombian Embassy also had professional help for its lobbying efforts. According to the *Wall Street Journal*, the embassy was paying approximately $100,000 a month to public relations firms to lobby in support of additional assistance to Colombia.[25]

Although Moreno described the Colombia Plan as "an alignment of interests," Colombian officials were well aware that their proposals had to fit within U.S. policy priorities, despite their disagreement with some of the central elements of U.S. counternarcotics policies. Ruiz described, for example, his frustrated efforts to modify the assessment metrics imposed by the gringos. U.S. officials returned the final draft with a note that he had failed to include an important number: the percentage of the decline in coca production that would be the objective of the plan. Without such a number, he was told, the package would never be passed by the U.S. Congress. He countered by arguing that he was an economist, living by the rules of supply and demand, who rejected the premise of U.S. source-country drug strategies and viewed them as doomed to failure. "I will put in zero coca [as a goal]," he claims to have told his U.S. official counterparts, "but only if you put in the same plan that within six years there will be zero demand." The eventual compromise was to list 50 percent reduction as the goal—"a bit pulled out of a hat," Ruiz told me, "because they told me that if you don't put down a big number, you could be right, but the US Congress won't approve the funding." Yet, in the final document "even then, the U.S. Congress didn't accept the 80,000 [from 160,000 hectares], they didn't accept 50%. They put in parentheses that it should be zero."

Moreno and the Colombian diplomatic corps were well positioned to take advantage of U.S. assistance for their political agendas because the expansion of existing security forces mapped onto the policy priorities that dominated Washington debates. At the same time, they professionalized their advocacy in order to better navigate the possibilities of U.S. policymaking. These efforts, however, were profoundly exclusionary, ignoring the political plans and claims of local officials in southern Colombia who rejected the U.S. strategy of militarized counternarcotics programs. These dynamics replicated patterns of exclusion and erasure deeply rooted in the history of center–periphery relations in Colombia. The policymaking aspirations and alternatives of Putumayans are explored in Chapter 7.

Origin Story VI—Dissent: Development and Nation-Building vs. Counternarcotics

Some lower ranking U.S. officials disputed the description of Plan Colombia as a plan born of consensus; they were the losers in the bureaucratic battles dominated by militarization. Rather than the plan being based on universal agreement among the agencies, these officials described the package as shifting dramatically in focus and content as it was put together, and as generating interagency conflict. One senior USAID official told me,

Originally Plan Colombia was about how to strengthen democratic institutions. In the process of being put together, it became focused on the threat from the FARC and drug trafficking. The drug thing was how to get Congress to approve resources for Colombia. The objective was to expand governance and the presence of the state in Colombia, as part of the requirements for a negotiated settlement with the guerrillas. But of course the only way to get money from Congress is to talk about drugs.

In these stories, the consensus produced through the interagency task force process masked real disputes within U.S. government agencies and obscured alternative policy visions. One such conflict was over the appropriate focus of rule of law programs, such as whether to prioritize addressing neighborhood conflicts or targeting high-profile drug traffickers. The use of NGO partners, common practice among USAID and other agencies, was opposed by some within the Defense

Department because, as one USAID official recalled being told, "They work with the FARC and they criticize us [the DOD]". In this section, I focus on some of the most intense disagreements between officials from the Bureau of International Narcotics and Law Enforcement (INL) and USAID over how to address and manage counternarcotics programs that targeted coca farmers in southern Colombia.

The disputes between USAID and INL reflected their different institutional histories and positioning within the State Department's bureaucratic hierarchy. USAID was widely seen as an agency in decline, with its mandate for "soft" programs—development—seen in a context of extensive institutional militarization, which privileged technical and punitive approaches. It was founded in 1961 to provide money for long-term development; the focus of such programs shifted, depending on the fashion of the times, from "basic human needs" to "free markets" to "sustainability" to "nation-building," according to USAID promotional materials. Reaching its height of influence in the late 1970s, the agency then steadily contracted, with declining funding and staff, and was frequently targeted by members of Congress as a site of wasteful and ineffective spending. The agency attracted stringent congressional oversight and intervention, even to the point of having some of its individual programs managed through line items in the congressional appropriations process. In other words, individual congressional staff members could insert program budgets and mandates—or delete them—from legislation independently of USAID's own planning processes. As one long-term AID staffer put it, the agency got "lots of dogs and cats thrown in because of people on the Hill, that is where AID loses respect. People think that they can't keep their eye on the ball," he continued, "but between the Interagency process and the Hill it is a tough place to be in. AID is not a valuable player for that reason." As the bureaucracy with the smallest budget, most congressional intervention, and least independence, USAID was the weakest player in the room. The former AID staffer concluded, "AID is just told what to do, not to think too much. The job is to implement other people's ideas."

In the case of Colombia, USAID officials were pitted against those of INL. In contrast to USAID, INL has consistently expanded since its creation in 1978 as the Bureau of International Narcotics Matters within the office of the undersecretary of political affairs during the Carter administration.[26] As both a "policy shop and as an assistance agency," INL develops programs at the policy level and provides technical support and training for foreign governments efforts in interdiction and law enforcement.[27] Presidential Decision Directive 14 of November 1993 broadened its mandate to other forms of transnational crime, including money laundering and human and weapons trafficking, and to allow for the provision of military, economic, and security assistance for counternarcotics operations, including rural development programs. These changes were reflected in its name change to the INL in 1995. As part of their policy work, INL officials prepare the annual International Narcotics Control Strategy Report, as well as manage the yearly certification process in which they assess other countries' cooperation with U.S. counternarcotics efforts. The INL has the State Department's only Aviation Unit, made up of almost two hundred helicopters and fixed-wing aircraft units used in fumigation efforts in Colombia, Peru, and Bolivia. The military contractor DynCorp in Florida operates this unit out of Patrick Air Force Base; their contractors pilot and service the aircraft in-country.

The INL/AID debates during the drafting of the Plan Colombia programs stemmed from their widely divergent views of what should be the appropriate focus of counternarcotics programs in Putumayo. Should the United States be targeting coca plants? Such an approach would focus on a criminalized object that could be accessed relatively easily with an array of specialized technology, including chemicals and airplanes equipped with GPS systems and long-distance nozzles. Or should the U.S. programs be oriented toward peasant farmers seeking a sustainable alternative livelihood? If so, they would have to address myriad complex factors, including the environment (weather, climate, soils, and water sources), existing agricultural practices, land tenure, markets (including access to them and becoming competitive in the context of international pricing and agricultural subsidies), as well as the long temporal cycle of planting, growing, and harvesting. An additional factor was the legal status of local producers: should they be treated as farmers or as criminals? AID officials argued that it was critical to differentiate between small farmers, who should be treated as peasants, and large-scale plantation producers, who should be treated as drug traffickers. Yet the Narcotics Affairs Section (NAS) within the U.S. Embassy (which reported within the State Department hierarchy to the INL) doubted this distinction. In a 1998 embassy cable, the NAS was reported as arguing, "Even a 1-2 hectare 'peasant-run' coca plot requires some $10,000 in start-up capital–available only from your local traffickers." The cable concluded, "Whether the coca is planted plantation style or in multiple, dispersed plots to foil eradication . . . the result is identical."[28]

AID officials argued forcefully that the needs of local people should be taken into account. They claimed that Putumayo residents "deserved alternative development programs" rather than being viewed as settlers who should be forced to return to their home communities (the issue of ongoing political violence in those communities was never discussed). According to one former senior AID official,

It was hard fought. The INL were spraying people, they just wanted to spray the bejesus out of it . . . There was a big fight. I said, what you want to do is to spray the bejesus out of people, and then have me sit with a burlap sack on the border to catch the cockroaches as they cross over the border? And Brownfield said, well that is an ugly metaphor but yes.

Numerous AID officials told me of the pressure they felt as a small and underfunded agency, with one summing up AID's situation as follows: "AID more than anyone is caught up in money politics." Another AID official gave me an example of such a funding squeeze. As he prepared to implement the Colombia programs, he reported the tremendous pressure "to get stuff moving; Congress says, here is the money today, we want results tomorrow." When the budget for the Colombia AID mission was the same in the House and Senate bill, he told the in-country mission to go ahead and start drawing up contracts for the programs. However, the bill was changed during the reconciliation process, the private meetings in which the different versions produced by the Senate and House are rewritten as a single final document—frequently the occasion of last-minute negotiations and insertion of new language (including the Leahy Law, for example). A dispute over the kinds of helicopters to be used was resolved with a compromise that required additional funding. The money was taken from the AID budget. In the final bill, funding for the rule of law and conflict-resolution programs (*casas de justicia*) budgets was reduced from a total of $10 million to $1 million each, because more money was needed for the more expensive Black Hawk helicopters. "This was a lesson on the political mathematics of aid debates."[29]

"The big battle was at the end, when the drug thing came to be more central to what was going to be presented," one former senior AID official told me from his new office as the head of Latin American research for a think tank. "It was a big battle, and we lost." The original plan was a 50–50 split between nonmilitary and military aid, with some programs having a larger proportion of nonmilitary aid. "Then it went to Congress, and that was when it changed, because of the negotiations with the Republican Congress. They wanted the helicopters for the spraying, and helicopters are expensive. The OMB [Office of Management and Budgets] only has so much money, so they have to squeeze the other side."

Origin Story VII—Militarized Consensus

Congressional debates over the proposed package reflected the militarization of the policy process. After only a few hours of debate on the substance of the policy, Democratic Representative Nancy Pelosi (CA) proposed moving some of the money from military aid to domestic drug treatment programs. However, most of the debate over Plan Colombia focused not on the efficacy of military assistance or the substance of the policy but on which kind of helicopter to provide. Passionate speeches were focused on the differences in capabilities for personnel carrying, altitude flying ability, and expense. Hours were devoted to the superiority of the Blackhawk helicopter compared to the Huey II, because of its ability to carry twenty-four people rather than only eleven and to fly to an altitude of 20,000 rather than 16,000 feet (important for eradication in mountainous areas and to keep the helicopters out of the reach of guerrilla fire). The additional expense was the sticking point: $13 million for a Blackhawk versus $1.8 million to upgrade a recycled Huey to a Huey II.

The emphasis on specialized military vocabulary and knowledge was both profoundly gendered and established the forms of authorized expertise acceptable in the debates.[30] Assistant Secretary of State for International Narcotics and Law Enforcement Rand Beers was involved in the extended dispute with Congress over whether to provide Blackhawk or Huey helicopters. He recalled a senior female State Department official involved in the congressional debates telling him, "You have to stoke those boys with toys." A former infantry officer, Beers concluded that his military expertise effectively silenced the congressional opposition. For many staffers who were former military officers, policemen, or FBI agents—or who identified with such professions—the focus on weapons technology allowed them to further position themselves as experts in the specialized, hypermasculine domain of military knowledge. Now a lobbyist with a high-profile Republican firm in Washington, one former aide located his authority in policy debates in his superior knowledge of weaponry and military training gained during his six months as a Marine officer. He launched into an extended discussion of the forms and functions of different makes and models of miniguns, their helicopter placement, and their impact on targets, asserting that this knowledge distinguished him from civilians familiar with such weapons only from movies and other popular culture representations. In his accounting, his military experience and travel to remote Colombian military bases, where he was able to witness training exercises and weapons displays, provided him superior expertise. He went on to describe a confrontation with the senior Republican leadership, where he was able to convince them to support the kind of helicopters he advocated.

SouthCom officers actively lobbied Congress, long skeptical of the Colombian military, on behalf of their new allies, connecting the dots between military aid and the drug consumption in their districts. "They would say, Colombia has a problem; we tried to show them that it was their problem [in their districts]," one officer told me. Their lobbying efforts included getting "emergency room statistics for youth drug overdoses in their districts, trying to get them to see that drug issues were their problem," and that SouthCom and Latin American militaries were the solution. "It is wise marketing, to know your customer, know their interests. We did this with other members [of Congress]; we would go in by district. It was always a shock to them." In this recounting, the customer became the U.S. Congress, with the U.S. military attempting to sell a product. For SouthCom, counternarcotics operations provided new avenues for expanded military relationships in their theater of operations, and the Colombian military was the perfect new ally in this fight. Other lobbyists in support of the military components of the package included the U.S.-Colombia Business Partnership, which included representatives of corporations with interests in Colombia and officials from the Colombian government. Founded in 1997 and initially convened by the Colombian Embassy during the certification crisis of the Samper administration to bring the perspective of business community to the debates, the Partnership actively supported the aid package for Colombia.

These debates were also the product of the material politics of foreign aid. Military contractors played a direct role in generating support for the military assistance to Colombia; helicopter manufacturers spent $1.25 million on campaign contributions between 1997 and 1999.[31] The site of manufacturing facilities determined which congressional members championed which product. Connecticut-based Sikorsky Aircraft Corporation stood to gain $360 million by selling thirty Blackhawk helicopters, whereas Texas-based Bell Helicopter Textron Inc. would earn $66 million for selling thirty-three Hueys. The final package reduced the number of the more expensive helicopters, with sixteen Black Hawks ($234 million) and thirty Huey IIs ($81 million) for the Colombian military and two Black Hawks and twelve Huey IIs for the Colombian National Police. In a February 2000 hearing, then-drug czar Barry McCaffrey called Black Hawks "the best helicopter on the face of the Earth; the next time you see me, I'll probably be peddling them, I hope." He went on to serve on the board of Dyn-Corp and to earn hundreds of thousands of dollars a year for consulting and public speaking in what the *New York Times* labeled "One Man's Military–Industrial–Media complex."[32] Other officials supporting the aid package also went on to work for defense contractors, such as Assistant Secretary of State for Special Operations and Low Intensity Conflict Brian Sheridan who at the time of this writing is working at Betchel. Others became lobbyists. Textron retained Charles "Tony" Gillespie, a former ambassador to Colombia; former official Michael Skol founded his own consulting group and was a spokesman for the U.S.-Colombia Business Partnership.

After a delay of almost a year because of partisan wrangling over the appropriations bill, Plan Colombia was officially signed into law on July 13, 2000. The bill authorized $1.3 billion dollars in additional spending for Colombia, almost 80 percent of it military aid.

Conclusion

Through the excavation of origin stories, anthropologists' broader field of vision can trace the multiple institutional agendas at play and help bring excluded accounts into view. The dominant participants in the Plan Colombia Interagency Task Force were able to produce a policy narrative that highlighted consensus because of the multiple institutional interests that coalesced around increasing military aid to Colombia. The dominant origin story of Plan Colombia described the package as the result of a painless agreement leading to an inevitable policy outcome. In numerous interviews, State Department officials recalled the policy formation as a consensus process without significant dissent or debate. As one former official told me,

One thing about Plan Colombia, on the U.S. government side, within the U.S. government there was no interagency debate about what we should be doing. This was because of two facts, because we had all the money we needed, so there was no arguments about my program is more important than yours. But also because of the general conviction that Colombia was in crisis, and the conviction that the U.S. should do something. . . . We had money. We had seventh floor direction. There were no real battles about what we should do.

The multiple origin stories, however, revealed that this consensus was actually the product of strategic ambiguity. This predominantly military aid package was designed not in the absence of multiple institutional agendas, but through the claims that the same package addressed these multiple spheres of concern.

Policy origin stories also function as a particular form of policy knowledge. Within Washington, such narratives are produced by and circulate among journalists, activists, and other policy actors, all with distinct agendas and perspectives. Thus, anthropologists must read these accounts as part of a political economy of knowledge production in policymaking spaces. Material rewards flowed to those policy actors who were able to position themselves successfully within existing power hierarchies. In the case of Plan Colombia, because the policy produced was deemed a success according to the metrics of Washington policymakers, multiple policy actors claimed to be its originators (explored further in the Conclusion). In one example, Rand Beers, who had been the assistant secretary for international narcotics and law enforcement at the State Department when Plan Colombia was created, but at the time of this interview was working as a security consultant and campaign advisor to Barack Obama, told me the same origin stories he shared with a reporter at *Rolling Stone*. Although the article's editorial line was critical of the drug war, it portrayed him as a powerful policy actor capable of maneuvering within distinct institutional power structures, almost singlehandedly producing the aid package that President Clinton claimed as a major foreign policy success.[33]

Strategic ambiguity—described as consensus—achieved multiple political ends, building coalitions as well as silencing dissent. "Now, looking back on it, the consensus was forced," one USAID official concluded with a sigh, at the end of a long interview in a Washington coffeehouse chain. "The hard questions weren't asked, and we stopped thinking about them after a while. It is all compartmentalized so there aren't any questions to ask." However, the multiplicity of policy agendas encompassed in strategic ambiguity was neither infinite nor completely open to interpretation and assignment. What was made "unthinkable," erased, or silenced was equally important for how policy unfolded. The absence of specific social actors in policy debates and the failure to consider some phenomena as social problems worthy of policy solutions were the result of material and cultural processes—not the natural or inevitable result of the inherent qualities of social issues. The consensus narrative effaced the policy stories of weaker institutions advocating nonmilitary development strategies. It also excluded Colombian local officials and Putumayo farmers. I turn to their policy claims in Chapter 7, examining the ways in which they attempted to present policy alternatives.

Part IV
Advocacy and Inevitability

Figure 6   Farmer displaying photos of his fumigated crops and pasture land at a public forum in Putumayo, 1999.

Photograph by Winifred Tate.

Chapter 6

Competing Solidarities

IN THE DEBATES over Plan Colombia, supporters and critics imagined themselves as acting in solidarity with distinct categories of Colombians, from counternarcotics soldiers to human rights activists. Solidarity—a community of feeling and a sense of relationship generated through issue and identity resonance—has come to circulate untethered from its ideological and political origins and is now deployed by actors across the political spectrum.[1] Rather than dispassionate, distant analysis, sentiment structures the ways in which global action is imagined, relying on solidarity as a political and emotional stance emanating from institutional actors across the political spectrum. Ann Stoler has identified the ways in which sentiment structures and informs systems of governance, analyzing how colonial projects extend into the domestic realms of desire, affinity, and respectability.[2] At their core, foreign policy narratives are about the imagined affective attachments we create as we order the world and those to whom we connect and strive to protect. The obligation to connect and protect is implicitly contained within discourses and practices of solidarity as both a burden and a noble birthright; it reproduces global, racial, and class hierarchies through the calculus of who is to be helped, who is to do the helping, and how that help is constituted.

The utopian visions and emotional entanglements of policymakers play a central role in their efforts to orchestrate and impose social transformation abroad. Solidarity is never transparent or self-evident, but involves ambivalence, issues of scale and geographies of blame in transnational social movements, as well as profound limits in the new global regimes of labor and consumption.[3] Just as political scientist Clifford Bob extends the consideration of transnational activist networks to right-wing political projects, and as Danilyn Rutherford describes colonial sympathy, here I extend an analysis of solidarity to policymakers' imagined role in transnational policymaking.[4] Rather than being understood as a particular form of oppositional political expression, solidarity is a fundamental structuring logic of U.S. political culture and a central way in which Americans believe themselves to be acting in concert with transnational political projects in other countries. In other words, solidarity can be a justifying logic of intervention, explored here in the case of neocolonial U.S.-Latin America relations.

Solidarity does not emerge from concern over what constitutes the most violent place or beleaguered people, but from the resonance that a particular issue or population has with a set of could-be advocates. In cases of activism targeting foreign countries with their distant wrongs, solidarity requires generating an affective resonance among the Western activists expected to act. Victims and their situation must resonate with them, thereby generating feelings of identification and connection that motivate activist identities and practices. Resonance and affinity are produced through specific subjectivities and practices, deeply embedded within U.S. political culture; this imagined connection between victim and activist requires a reciprocal relationship between deserving victim and heroic savior. For activism to be mobilized both factors of this binary are required to be in play: a deserving (innocent) victim connected to a savior capable of heroic action. Such resonance can originate from a focus on similar identities, such as maternal responsibility (as mothers), on professional role (as journalists, doctors, teachers), or through political identification (reformists, radicals, revolutionaries, unions).

These emotional identities and relationships are not simply conjured from existing ideologies, however, but must be materially fashioned through institutional and organizational channels. In examining the production of solidarity in the Plan Colombia debates, I focus on travel as a technique of emotional management, which produced new forms of political subjectivities accompanied by expectations of political action.[5] Travel is one of what Susan Greenhalgh calls the "hidden sites" of policymaking, occurring largely out of the public eye but profoundly shaping policymaking debates and practices.[6] Scholars are beginning to turn their attention to how tourism encounters engender particular histories[7] and to its role in diplomacy,[8] as well as how tourism to sites of tragedy, conflict, and pollution produces political practices and identities.[9] Anthropologists have been particularly attuned to the performances of suffering generated by such travel,[10] whereas scholars of the Central American peace movement have examined the ways in which travel played a central role in developing solidarity networks and new activist identities.[11]

Inspired in part by those histories, opposition activists attempted to employ travel to mobilize opposition to Plan Colombia, even as architects of the policy used travel to engender authorizing expertise for supporters of the policy and to create affective relationships and solidarity between U.S. and Colombian officials in official delegations authorized by Congress known as "codels." Like delegations led by NGOs, codels are part of a broad category of political travel intended to educate and transform political subjectivities and motivate particular forms of political action. Both are examples of the growing number of forms of political tourism that have emerged as a central vehicle of transnational political encounter.

In considering NGO solidarity, I am drawing on comparisons between U.S. activism and advocacy focused on Colombia in the late 1990s and early 2000s and the movements that emerged in opposition to U.S. policy in Central America during the late 1980s and early 1990s. The comparison with the Central America movement is very fruitful, in part because of the multiple connections between these two historical moments. Most of the institutions that became involved in Colombia advocacy originated in the Central America movement. Activist identities that had been largely dormant since the dissolution of the Central America solidarity movement in the early 1990s were galvanized and reenergized by the emergence of Plan Colombia. I explore how activists made this transition, examining the efforts to revive institutional and activist practices, including the use of testimony in speaking tours for public education, travel in consciousness-raising delegations, development of congressional allies and targeting of specific legislation, and efforts to form coalitions and allies in other movements. This comparison also highlights the many ways in which the profound differences between the two moments contributed to minimal mobilization and fewer new activists in the case of Colombia.

"If You Liked El Salvador, You'll Love Colombia": Emblematic Memories and Resurgent Activism

For many of the NGO activists and advocates who focused on Colombia during this period, their work was sparked not by their connections to that country but by the ways in which U.S. policy toward Colombia resonated with their experiences with Central America during the 1980s. Spurred by another military aid package being delivered to abusive Latin American forces in the context of a counterinsurgency war, emblematic memories of their political identities, commitments, and responsibilities generated during their previous Central American activism reanimated their activism.[12] This dynamic was encapsulated in the ironic bumper sticker that I first saw in the office of an Amnesty International staffer, which read, "If you liked El Salvador, You'll Love Colombia." The complex terrain of emotions awakened by the Colombia debates included anger that the United States continued to play a destructive role in Latin America and a continuing sense of responsibility to the victims of these policies. Most felt that they had an opportunity to play a unique and important role in the public policy debates because of their earlier experience working on Central America issues. Their language skills, ongoing ties to Latin America activists, relationships with sympathetic policymaker allies, knowledge of critical analytic frameworks, and experience with particular repertoires of activist practices and networks contributed to the sense that their history as activists and their understanding of U.S. Latin American policy privileged them for Colombia activism.

One policy activist who began doing Central America solidarity work as an undergraduate in college recalled springing into action when he heard on the radio that a congressional hearing was planned on Colombia. The intensity of the moment was reflected in the specificity of the details he recalled almost ten years later, including the date of the radio broadcast and the details of the hearing: "It was on August 5, 1999; the next day [there was going to be a hearing with Drug Czar General] McCaffrey proposing a billion dollar counterdrug program for Colombia. I remember thinking, holy fucking shit, this is Central America all over again, the U.S. is getting involved in counterinsurgency, I have to nip this in the bud." Drawing on his activist experience and connections, he was able to immediately produce questions to be posed by congressional representatives in the Progressive Caucus during the hearing, and he soon made lobbying and advocacy on Colombia a major part of his work.

Other activists were "looking for new projects" as the wars in Central America were "winding down," recalled one staff member with the Fellowship of Reconciliation, an interfaith pacifist organization. They prioritized focusing on the worst violence; in trying to decide where to channel their energy, the Fellowship of Reconciliation's director bluntly asked, "Where are the most killings in Latin America?" Colombia was the answer.

Lisa Haugaard's emerging interest in Colombia was typical in many ways. Her life as an activist began with protests against the U.S. role in Central America and the Contra War. Artifacts in her home and office embody her ongoing felt connections to Central American political causes. Hanging on the wall in her entrance hallway, alongside her wedding photos and her daughter's birth announcement, is a framed mimeographed notice of a demonstration being held to protest a vote on aid to the Contras; she met her husband at that protest. Anger was her first motivating emotion as she learned about the growing role of the United States in supporting Central American military forces. She was active with several grassroots groups in New York and eventually moved to Nicaragua, where she lived for three years, researching peasant organizations and working at a Jesuit university. At the time of this writing she is a professional advocate who, as director of the Latin America Working Group, makes Colombia her primary focus.

As she recalled her years of protest and work in Central America, she focused on two elements: the credibility of her analysis and the emotional power of witnessing abuses and knowing that they were the result of U.S. policy. She took pains to explain that her position was not itself based on emotion or blind partisanship. Although emotion motivated her, she emphasized that she was not a "starry-eyed person. I entered into the debate to understand what was going on, and I confirmed that the U.S. willingly helped people commit the most terrible human rights abuses; the Contras, they mainly targeted civilians." This strategy, she argued, was repeated in Colombia. Recalling incidents she witnessed of families killed in buses bombed by the Contras, she drew parallels with the violence enacted by Colombian paramilitary groups:

That was the U.S. strategy, it was not accidental. That was the strategy, *the* strategy. I visited co-ops [in Nicaragua] that had been targeted 4, 5 times. They had been overrun by the Contras, burned to the ground, their children killed. I went to one funeral in Estelí of two men who had run outside the perimeter of the coop to chase a pig and the Contras captured them, slit them from end to end and filled them with stones, cut off—well, you know, they did everything that the [Colombian] paramilitaries did. And they were trained and equipped by the U.S.

Bearing the emotional weight of viscerally knowing the cost of U.S. policies was profoundly inspiring to her during meetings with policymakers discussing Colombia:

When I think about those days I keep flashing on [Assistant Secretary of State for Human Rights Harold] Koh, begging Koh not to do it, and we were right. [Pointing to a chart of paramilitary violence] this is when we were meeting with Koh, look at how the numbers of people going up, how many people died. It was Central America all over again, but with a Democratic administration. I was really motivated by that, that history was repeating itself. It was very disturbing.

Even younger activists born too late to participate in or have firsthand knowledge of the Central American movement were inspired by it. Many spoke of their anger—in the words of one young volunteer, "becoming infuriated"—in learning of U.S. policy in Latin America. Many had spent time in study-abroad programs, learning alternative histories of U.S. policy from Latin American students and activists. These histories naturalized the connections of Colombia activism to the movement that had come before. "It was natural, given my political orientation from the solidarity movement, the notion of 'we're responsibility for all the shit that our government does,'" one younger activist told me. "It was natural coming off of the Central American solidarity movement." Colombia was described by many as the new "hot spot" for young, committed activists searching for the chance to play a political role similar to those played in movements in the 1980s. One described his choice to travel to Colombia with one of a growing number of accompaniment projects, organizations that use the physical presence of international volunteers alongside threatened human rights workers as a means of deterring violence. The organization had played an important role in Guatemala "back in the day," he told me, but now the situation there had improved with the negotiated settlement of the civil war. "If you want to make a life-or-death difference, go to Colombia," he recalled being told. "And at that moment I knew I was going to Colombia."

These activists' policy work also drew on repertoires of political activism developed during the Central America movement that they reoriented toward influencing specific legislation, primarily amendments offered to reduce or shift military funding for Colombia.[13] During congressional votes on assistance to Colombia, activists working within the Latin America Working Group (LAWG) would identify "swing" members—those who seemed that they might change their votes—and would attempt to mobilize voters in their district. LAWG director Lisa Haugaard was co-chair of the Colombia Steering Committee, constituted in 1998 as a loose coalition of more than fifty politically progressive human rights, humanitarian, and religious organizations. The Steering Committee would send policy analysis and guidance to its member organizations, which included religious groups, Amnesty International, labor unions, and other grassroots organizations. Frequently the focus of this information would be on lobbying Congress in support of specific positions, such as yearly amendments to reduce military aid.

Jim McGovern (D-MA) and other congressional critics pursued a strategy of presenting amendments to the aid packages on a yearly basis, thereby providing both an institutional forum for debate and a means to gauge support for alternative policies. These amendments were largely aimed at transferring military aid into humanitarian programs or, in some cases, cutting aid. "When we offered the amendments, people would roll their eyes, seeing our efforts to cut military aid as a waste of time," McGovern told me, describing his frustration with the congressional debates. "But that was the only way to have any debate over billions of dollars. Otherwise, there was no debate, no accountability." Colombia Steering Committee members would distribute "hill drops" (a one-page policy brief or list of talking points distributed to every member of Congress). They also organized public education events in Washington and in swing districts, attempting to mobilize constituents to lobby members identified as possibly willing to switch their vote to support these amendments.

Colombian activists played a central role in these efforts through a process of proxy citizenship, in which certain rights of citizenship—in this case, the ability to make claims for redress to a state—are conferred on activists through their relationships with NGOs. According to LAWG executive director Haugaard, the organization hoped to create mechanisms for Colombian human rights groups to participate directly in policymaking, rather than simply using Colombian activists to educate the U.S. public. Washington activists helped create a new NGO specifically with this mandate. The Colombia Human Rights Committee received funding in 1998 from the Ford Foundation to create a small (two-person staff) NGO—the U.S. Office on Colombia (USOC)—to work with broadly defined sectors of Colombian civil society. The USOC was only one of the many U.S.-based organizations that incorporated speaking tours, presentations, and lobbying by Colombian activists as central strategies in their work to promote policy changes in Washington. It was originally a counterpart organization of the *Coodinación Colombia-Europa-Estados Unidos*, a coalition of progressive Colombian human rights organizations. Over time, however, the USOC developed an increasingly autonomous profile because of its independent funding base and growing differences with Colombian groups over how to design U.S.-based lobbying strategies. U.S. activists came to articulate their solidarity by facilitating Colombian participation in policy formulation, a process explored in greater detail in the next chapter.

Travel to Mobilize Activism: Witness for Peace

Travel was a central site for consolidating activist commitments, so as Washington-based NGOs began considering becoming involved in Colombia, the first step was to go there. In 1997, WOLA hired me to lead the first NGO delegation to Colombia. Participants included the executive director of WOLA, the deputy director of the Latin America Working Group, and the lead Latin America researcher from the Center for International Policy, as well as several grassroots and faith-based activists. The trip was intended not only to educate but also to inspire emotional commitments.

Some groups made facilitating travel their central project, foremost among them Witness for Peace (WFP). The group was founded in 1983 to bring Americans to directly witness and experience the impact of U.S. policy first in the U.S.-funded Contra War in Nicaragua and then throughout Central America. This methodology privileged both the direct experience of witnessing oppression as a transformative moment and the presence of U.S. citizens as a deterrent to violence in the context of a U.S.-sponsored conflict. WFP's publications focus on the deeply emotional personal and political transformation generated by the experience of accompanying communities threatened by U.S. policy.[14] As one member of the board described the WFP's work,

There is nothing like the personal connection to get people invested. The witness methodology is quite profound. *We are in the business of transformation. I came back changed, I still come back changed.* Through travel, I learn so much about myself, about the others on the trip, about my own country. There is nothing like travel to make you think differently about your own country. [emphasis added]

During the 1980s, WFP maintained a permanent staff presence in Central America, conducting human rights research and providing logistical support for periodic delegations whose trips generally lasted about two weeks. More than 100,000 people traveled to Central America in WFP delegations during the 1980s; hundreds of people spent extensive time in-country as part of the permanent accompaniment teams.

Like many of the groups formed during the 1980s that focused on Central America, after the negotiated settlement of the Contra War and the defeat of the Sandinista government in 1990 elections, WFP began an internal debate on whether and how to continue its work. It considered expanding into other regions and sent exploratory delegations to South Africa, the Middle East (Israel and the West Bank), Colombia, and Panama. According to former WFP staff, the decision to remain focused on Latin America reflected a recognition of the group's existing strengths and limitations, including language capabilities, the need for a "culturally sensitive" footprint in order to get reliable information from partner organizations, and the challenges of recruiting people for more distant travel. While maintaining its regional focus, the group decided to expand its mission from addressing the political violence that characterized Central America during the 1980s to the poverty and inequality exacerbated by globalization. Maintaining its headquarters in Nicaragua, WFP created programs in Mexico and organized delegations to educate Americans about their role in the global economy. During this period WFP suffered a steep decline in membership and revenues, in part due to what some saw as a rejection of its fundamental role as a peace organization focusing on the role of the U.S. government in political violence. From 1990 to 1996, the budget shrank 40 percent, from $1.2 million to $480,000.

For many within the group, the focus on Colombia was a return to their activist roots and the focus on political violence connected to U.S. policy in the region. Other factors contributed to WFP's expansion in the late 1990s, including the opportunity to organize popular and lucrative trips to Cuba after the Clinton administration reduced restrictions on travel to the island. There was also a growing interest, particularly among a new generation of activists, in economic justice issues and globalization, for which WFP was well positioned to capture activist commitment because of its relatively early attention to these issues.

In 1999 the board agreed to send an exploratory mission to assess the possibilities of WFP work in Colombia, after rejecting earlier requests from Colombian religious organizations for a WFP presence, arguing that, although the country was clearly experiencing a human rights crisis, that crisis lacked a clear connection to U.S. policy. With the massive new U.S.-funded initiative, Plan Colombia, the U.S. connection and role in the Colombia became clear, and the WFP undertook a six-month feasibility study, and staff members recalled the emotional appeals made by Colombian activists, who drew on the deep organizational roots of WFP as a faith-inspired response to suffering and persecution. The board was deeply moved by the "emotional testimony" provided by Colombian economist and indigenous-rights activist Hector Mondragon. According to one of the first WFP staff members in Colombia who was active in this debate, Mondragon was a "deep Mennonite" and Sunday School teacher who described the many death threats he received: "how he couldn't sleep in the same bed each night, had to keep moving around, how he couldn't teach Sunday school. That had a big impact on the team."

WFP founder Gail Phares was one of the most passionate advocates for becoming involved in Colombia. As a Maryknoll nun, she had worked in Guatemala and Nicaragua in the 1960s; one of the four American churchwomen murdered in 1980 by Salvadoran soldiers had been a close friend and colleague. She has remained a devoted activist, as founder and director of the Carolina Interfaith Task Force on Central America, as well as with School of the America's Watch, and spent ninety days in federal prison after committing acts of civil disobedience during protests. Phares traveled on the first public WFP delegation to Colombia in March 2001 and described being profoundly moved during meetings with Colombian activists and while witnessing the poverty and suffering in the small towns and cities where the WFP delegation traveled. The 100-member trip was described by one of the organizers as a "shot in the arm for the movement;" he went on to say that the delegation had a "huge impact, within WFP and within Colombia." After visiting different regions of the country, members of the delegation carried out a protest vigil at the U.S. Embassy. Phares recalled the emotional impact of the scene:

All wearing our blue shirts [with the WFP logo as required during all delegations], we had doves and did symbolic acts. We had a cardboard helicopter that we covered with the doves. We brought gifts of flowers, fruit and bread, to show as American citizens the kinds of gifts we thought we should be bringing to Colombia. The BBC, NPR, all the main Colombian newspapers covered it. It was touching to see, the cameramen, they had tears in their eyes to see U.S. citizens willing to go in dangerous places.

Another organizer of the delegation recalled the power of affective appeals made by delegates to the Colombian people. "One of the sound bites was that we as people from the U.S. ask for forgiveness from the people of Colombia for the policies of our government. And there hadn't been that kind of thing here before, it made a big impact on people."

A range of groups, including small human rights committees and religious organizations, used travel to generate political commitments to Colombia. For example, Barbara Gerlach, a United Church of Christ (UCC) minister who had adopted two children from Colombia in 1979, got involved in solidarity work after participating in a 1997 human rights delegation to Colombia organized by Cecilia Zárate-Laun, a Colombian immigrant who established the Colombia Human Rights Network based in Madison, Wisconsin. On the trip, Gerlach met the head of the Colombian Catholic Church's Social Ministries; their work with displaced communities made a dramatic impression. In recalling a visit to a convent that was involved in smuggling out families pursued by armed actors, she described their work as "a real underground railroad." On her return, she sent letters urging action on Colombia to Church World Service, an organization of thirty-seven Christian denominations focused on humanitarian aid, and to the UCC Global Ministry department, but received no response. Gerlach prioritized mobilizing U.S.-based churches, particularly around the issue of internal displacement in Colombia.

Thanks in part to Gerlach's ongoing lobbying and network of religious connections, faith-based activism on Colombia began to increase slowly. A delegation of Presbyterian ministers traveled to Colombia and representatives from the Lutheran church began to get involved in 1998; the UCC passed a resolution on Colombia as well. Gerlach said her work was "ecumenical," trying to link existing small-scale projects such as sister congregations and humanitarian and development projects with broader advocacy efforts. Over the next few years, Gerlach led three delegations focused on the issue of internal displacement to Colombia, and others led denomination-specific trips. After they returned to the United States, Gerlach told me that delegation participants "worked on the days of prayer and action, to get churches to lift up Colombia on a Sunday, and then go lobby Congress during the foreign ops process." Activists were expected to write about their experiences for local publications and to get involved in education and advocacy efforts within their community or congregation. In the case of religious groups, they were also to present resolutions for their denomination. Travel in these delegations was designed be a tactic of personal transformation leading to specific forms of political intervention and advocacy.

These delegations were successful in mobilizing a few activists, but on a much smaller scale than during the Central America movement. For example, in contrast to the thousands of participants sent by WFP to Central America, only a few hundred people traveled to Colombia under its auspices. A handful of staff managed the WFP program in a country of 42 million, as compared to hundreds of permanent staff in Nicaragua, a country of 6 million approximately the size of the state of Alabama. Other religious, academic, and humanitarian networks that had historically brought people to Latin America were also much less present in Colombia. Whereas Catholic and mainline Protestant denominations and missionaries had played a central role in previous solidarity work in Central America, Colombia was a net exporter of priests and religious workers, sending many to other parts of Latin America and Africa. As a relatively well-developed middle-income country, the nation was host to few humanitarian workers. The Peace Corps program in Colombia lasted from 1961 to 1981, with larger number of total volunteers than in Central America, but without the annual flow of new volunteers returning to form a critical base of interest in the country. On U.S. campuses, there was little academic focus on Colombia and relatively few scholars of the country, the result of the real and perceived dangers of fieldwork there and the general view that Colombia remained an exception to the academic models and theories of the region.

There were also relatively few Colombians traveling to the United States.[15] Colombia has historically maintained relatively few academic connections with U.S. universities, preferring to send students to Europe, particularly France and England. Most importantly for the creation of solidarity networks, there was no mass presence of Colombians within the United States. The presence of millions of Central American refugees in the United States brought compelling stories of persecution by U.S.-funded military forces directly to American audiences. These refugees played an active role in recruiting U.S. activists and in particular galvanized the Sanctuary movement.[16]

However, rather than fleeing the country, most Colombians seeking to escape violence left their homes as individual family units, resettling informally in shantytowns within Colombia, thereby creating one of the world's largest—but largely invisible—internally displaced populations.[17] In part, this resettlement pattern was a function of geography. Getting to the United States from Colombia is much more difficult than from Central America. The trip required a plane ticket, because there is no land route from Colombia to the United States: the

Darien Gap, the jungle separating Panama from Colombia, is the only remaining break in the Pan American highway. The number of Colombians emigrating to other countries did increase (including those to Spain and Ecuador), but they were largely educated and middle class, often supportive of government expansion and not natural allies of U.S.-based activists protesting U.S. assistance to the Colombian military. Within the United States, Colombian refugees' primary political agenda was the provision of favorable immigration status, such as Temporary Protected Status, for Colombians.

The Limits of Resonance

As one congressional aide who actively opposed Plan Colombia observed, compared to Central America, "Colombia feels a lot more far, geographically and psychologically." This distance was produced in part through the lack of resonance between U.S. activists and the Colombian conflict. The coexistence of criminal networks with insurgent politics generated confusion and suspicion. Colombia's complicated political panorama made it more difficult to recruit American activists (who, like policymakers) often desired black-and-white scenarios with clear "good guys" and simplistic solutions.

Innocence remains a critical ontological category that victims of human rights abuses must fit into to gain political and social recognition.[18] The presumed and real criminality of Colombian communities made the human rights issues less salient and these communities less sympathetic. Putumayo, the initial focus of the Plan Colombia's "Push into Southern Colombia," was a center of drug production and trafficking. For U.S.-based groups attempting to establish institutional relationships with Colombian communities affected by U.S. policies, the extensive criminal activity in the region was extremely difficult to navigate, and the official dismissal of the entire population as criminals was hard to contradict. In recruiting new activists to participate in Colombia campaigns, there was often concern that such activism would be in some way tolerant of illegal drug trafficking. U.S. and Colombian officials also frequently accused critics of militarized drug policy of sympathizing with drug traffickers and guerrillas.

During the past thirty years, within the United States the primary narratives of Colombian violence presented by the mainstream media and popular culture have focused on the illegal economy and on violence among and by drug traffickers. U.S. and Colombian government officials consistently labeled insurgents as "narcoguerrillas," arguing that these forces were simply another form of

organized crime, as explored in Chapter 1. Tracing the evolving and complex relationships between guerrilla forces and the illicit drug trade is extremely difficult. Although scholars have documented how guerrilla forces became more
deeply enmeshed in illegal economies, including becoming involved in multiple forms of criminality,[19] the details of this history remain hidden, contested,
and ill suited for the linear, black-and-white stories mobilized by activists. For
activists, the drug issue made the narrative of the United States siding with
oppressive military forces against liberation movements impossible.

In contrast, for many activists in the 1980s, the Salvadoran and Guatemalan
guerrillas and the Nicaraguan Sandinista government were the good guys. Even
groups that rejected the revolutionary violence of Salvadoran insurgent groups
advocated a negotiated settlement to the conflict, believing that the leadership
could be trusted as good-faith negotiators. In the Colombian context, such sympathy for the insurgents has been impossible, given the escalating brutality of
the conflict, declining popular support for guerrilla groups, and widespread criminality within their ranks. Colombian insurgent groups have never been the recipients of transnational political solidarity (with some exceptions in parts of
Europe). Colombian guerrillas have consistently rejected human rights standards
and international humanitarian law and have been largely unresponsive to international pressure. The FARC has held a number of Americans hostage over
the years, including several who are presumed to have died in captivity and three
who remained in their power for more than eight years. They killed three American indigenous rights activists in 1999. Many Central American activists with
direct links to insurgent movements played a critical role in mobilizing U.S. activists in the 1980s.[20] The FARC's limited efforts to galvanize similar support in
the United States were unsuccessful.

Connecting human rights atrocities to U.S. military aid was more complicated
in Colombia than in Central America as well. In the case of the Salvadoran military and the Contra forces, U.S. military aid clearly enabled them to continue
their military operations; many U.S.-supported battalions were directly implicated in human rights atrocities. In the case of Colombia, tracing a direct line
between U.S. military aid and such abuses was more difficult. Paramilitary forces
had to be first linked to the recipients of U.S. military aid. Their independent financing from the narcotic trade also complicated the panorama. Untangling
these causal factors led to questions, such as whether the violence was the re-

sult of U.S. military aid, or perhaps the conflict was simply the result of drug money and infighting.

Providing a clear narrative of Colombia's alternative future transformation was also impossible. Many activists in the Central American peace movement were motivated by their belief that real political transformation was possible in the region either through revolutionary triumph or a negotiated settlement that would result in significant social and economic restructuring. In the case of Colombia, such a future seemed out of reach. Given the multiple forms of violence and criminalization, activists were unable to convincingly articulate how the region could be transformed through alternative forms of U.S. intervention, such as money for development projects rather than military expansion. One activist summarized this conundrum, telling me, "A lot of what we did was to try to explain how bad things in Colombia really were, how bad and fucked up and sad, how violent." But, he continued, when people wanted to do something in response, "We didn't have really attractive alternatives; we couldn't say, do not do x and do y, the alternatives were pretty weak . . . We didn't even believe in the alternatives we were trying to present ourselves. [For example], the alternative development programs, no one thought that would work."

Several relatively large events were organized in the United States to mobilize interest in Colombia in 2000 and early 2001. One Amnesty International activist recalled hundreds of people attending events organized on the West Coast and at Midwest teach-ins. After its first 100-person delegation to Colombia, instead of its usual action planning workshop (including media and local organizing training), WFP held a "movement building session." One of the organizers told me, "The Colombia mobilization was born in 2002 in DC. In April we had 3,000 person march on the capital, we had teach-ins and workshops, that was the high point of the movement." Yet these events were the zenith of organizing around Colombia; a broad social movement in opposition to Plan Colombia never coalesced, and activists soon realized that mass mobilization around Colombia was not going to happen. Peter Clark—who worked for WOLA, spent a year in Colombia as a volunteer with the Peace Brigades, and then returned to Washington to work with the U.S. Office on Colombia—described "putting a lot of effort" into connecting with grassroots activists throughout the country, attempting to get them interested in Colombian issues and providing them analytical tools and educational resources. Despite this work, "I don't think we had a significant impact," he concluded. "We could generate a handful of calls, letters and visits, but not a lot."

Some activists claimed that it was the activists' focus on advocacy and policymaking that kept a larger interest in the issue from igniting. I argue instead that broader political and material constraints—including the lack of issue resonance in the post–Cold War context, the particularities of the Colombian conflict, and the absence of specific institutional channels to facilitate such mobilization—hobbled the development of a stronger political movement.

In post–9/11 America, competing demands for activist attention also diluted activists' concerns with Colombia. Many viewed the dramatic escalation of U.S. wars in the Middle East as a much more urgent priority because they involved U.S. military combat operations, billions of dollars, and high civilian casualties. Groups that attempted to organize Colombia-focused events found that they were drawing on a limited universe of activists who were now devoted to organizing against the U.S. invasion and occupation of Iraq. "We measure the amount of interest via the number of delegations," one WFP staff member told me. "They were still strong in 2003; in 2004, we were hit hard, by the Iraq war more than by 9/11." Moreover, public support for the Bush administration's use of the 9/11 attacks to justify a complete withdrawal of support for human rights issues when measured against U.S. military objectives greatly reduced the political terrain for human rights advocacy in the United States. The earlier public human rights consensus dissolved as officials publicly sanctioned the use of torture and secret and indefinite detention. Although a small cohort of dedicated advocates continued to work to transform U.S. policy, they no longer imagined that a broad-based social movement would accompany them.

Congressional Travel, Affective Ties, and Militarized Solidarity

Solidarity and resonance also played a major role in galvanizing proponents of Plan Colombia. Supporters of military aid imagined themselves as acting in solidarity with Colombians, but with counternarcotics soldiers, not threatened human rights defenders. Increased weapons transfers, military training, and intelligence assistance was not simply justified by the logics of cold political calculations. Supporters' claims were couched in the emotional language of affective relationships and the responsibility of U.S. officials toward their Colombian military counterparts, a form of policymaker solidarity. The weight of these emotional foundations for policymaking became visible to me as I realized which tales of suffering and injury resonated with U.S. officials. In the course of my advocacy work, U.S. and Colombian officials frequently instructed me that, rather than the human rights defenders and peasant communities under attack by right-wing paramilitary groups allied with the Colombia security forces, the true victims were others: I should be devoting my political resources to kidnapping victims and the police and soldiers killed in the line of duty. Representative Dan Burton (R-IN) issued one such public rebuke in a statement during a 1997 congressional hearing about Colombia, "We never hear debate by the human rights groups in Colombia about the human rights of these Americans who have been dragged through the jungles of Colombia for years now, nor do we hear anything from these human rights groups about the thousands of CNP and Colombian military who have been murdered by guerilla groups who long ago abandoned their Marxist ideology for the enormous profits of the drug trade."

Architects of Plan Colombia used travel to engender authorizing expertise for supporters of the policy and to create affective relationships and solidarity between U.S. and Colombia officials. Numerous members of Congress and their staff traveled to Colombia on official congressional delegations, the codels.[21] However, Colombia codels were colloquially known as "drugs and thugs tours." The typical tour consisted of a two- or three-day trip to Colombia filled with meetings with Colombian civilian and military officials and a tour, often by helicopter, of U.S.-sponsored operations, frequently in the southern jungle regions. The Republican majority in the House of Representatives and their resulting control of key committee positions made such travel possible. According to congressional rules, the majority party had to approve all official travel, with a member of the majority party leading each congressional delegation and the chair of the authorizing committee (controlled by the majority party) signing off on each trip.

Codels are part of a broad category of political travel intended to educate and transform political subjectivities and motivate particular forms of political action. Congressional representatives and staff who traveled to Colombia did so as a form of political witnessing and activism for the purpose of constructing particular relationships and genres of policy expertise as part of a clearly articulated strategy. In one example, a staffer told me of his office "targeting" William Delahunt (D-MA), who opposed military aid, by inviting him on a codel intended to change his political priorities. In describing the transformative power of travel, the staffer told me with pride, "He [Delahunt] voted one way [against military aid] before he left, and voted another [in favor] after he came back."

Codels produced an affective geography of relationships and networks of reciprocity.[22] Codel encounters were designed to inspire forms of solidarity and affective political commitment between Colombian officials and U.S. policy-makers. During interviews, participants repeatedly stressed that the highlight of these trips were the personal relationships developed with Colombian "front-line" officials; former congressman Cass Ballenger (R-GA) told me that, on his trips, "the most important thing was the people themselves." Some staffers boasted of weekly contact with celebrated Colombian Police General Rosso José Serrano. One aide critical of U.S. policy toward Colombia reflected on the importance of personal relationships created through travel and their impact during policy debates:

When you go down to Colombia, you start to believe. You spend time with [president] Uribe and [vice president] Santos, [defense minister] Santos. They are articulate, they speak English, they are interested in your views and concerns . . . You come back really liking these people. Then you are placed in the position of defending them, not analyz-ing the effect of the policy on people, the different streams of aid, how it could be modi-fied, the impact of the policies, the consequences on the ground.

Congressional travel cemented a system of reciprocity, in which Colombian military and police personnel risked injury and death in counternarcotics op-erations, offering their bodies as a sacrifice in the frontlines of the war on drugs, while the United States provided military hardware and training in return. These relationships drew on a long history of proxy conflicts in Latin America in which the United States channeled military aid to military forces. In the immediate post–Cold War period, militarized counternarcotics operations came to occupy a privileged place in U.S. foreign policy.

Masculine calculations of responsibility, courage, and military honor were central to these relationships, in which both Colombian officers and U.S. politi-cians positioned themselves as defenders of American children. During inter-views, the emotional intensity of these commitments and encounters—and the role of classic American male-bonding behaviors such as leisurely beer drink-ing after dangerous operations—was communicated nonverbally, with pauses and extended eye contact. One former staffer described getting to see the CNP "in action" after hearing guerrilla gunfire as the codel arrived at a remote airport. After the police "went out and took care of the situation," they returned to the pool in the multinational complex where the staffers were drinking beer.

Of course we bought them [the counternarcotics cops] the beverage of their choice. The police told us they ran them [the guerrillas] off. Of course if they dispatched [killed] anyone, they would never say [pause]. Those guys don't say. I asked one guy, "Why do you keep doing this?" He said, [looks very seriously at me], "I love my country, and you guys are helping us. Without you, we couldn't do the things we do." He was a counternarcotics cop, and I asked him if they did stuff against the guerrillas, and I was surprised when he said, "Yes, I do a lot of fighting the guerrillas. Every time I catch guerrillas, kill guerrillas, that means less drugs on your streets killing your children," he said. "Maybe someday, they will stop killing mine." [Pauses while looking at me] So he was a pretty serious guy.

In staffer accounts, the wounded bodies of the CNP embodied their commitment and sacrifice, whereas the wounded bodies of addicts were invoked not for the feminized world of physical care and treatment, but as justifying a military logic of weapons technology and combat. One senior Republican foreign policy aide in the House, a former FBI agent who boasted of his close relationship with the police in both his home district and in Colombia, told me in a phone interview of his frequent visits with wounded counternarcotics police in military hospitals during trips to Colombia: "It would eat my heart out to see these young kids who had lost their legs, had no feet, because of land mines. I would go on every trip." At the conclusion of the interview, he returned to the bodies of the Colombian police. When I asked what his strongest memories of Colombia were, he responded,

Of the physical recovery room of the CNP hospital, all the crippled, maimed, distorted bodies of young men and women who had been in the counternarcotics fight. Those young bodies, and the young kids lying on the stairs [overdosing heroin] in Harlem.

Other staffers described the pilgrimages to the hospital to see wounded police as a constant feature of their trips to Colombia, one of a number of commemorative practices intended to enshrine the CNP as war heroes fighting for the U.S. cause. Many anthropologists have analyzed the ways in which public mourning and memorialization of war dead contribute to particular political, national, and ethnic identities; these practices include public naming, monuments, and shrines.[23] In the case of the CNP, their sacrifice was honored through these personal visits, as well as the public reading of lists of names of officers killed in action during congressional hearings and subsequent publication of their names in the *Congressional Record*. Their role as frontline fighters was frequently referenced, as speakers lauded the CNP as the "bravest men and women in the world," "honest," and "heroic." In passionate and contentious congressional hearings, Republicans contrasted these heroes with the presumed corrupt and cowardly Colombian drug producers and the inept and career-minded State Department officials (see Chapter 1). These affective connections were also demonstrated through physical talismans, including inscribed hats and clothing and other emblematic souvenirs such as shell-casing paperweights.

Photos from these travels were also displayed as evidence of the technological prowess, affective relationships, and political commitments embodied in codel travel. During phone interviews, staff frequently described photographs of themselves in remote jungle locations, standing alongside military hardware. Former member of Congress Ballenger recalled with pride the "ton of pictures" of himself with then Colombian president Andrés Pastrana and with Huey helicopters that commemorated his important role in promoting military assistance. One former aide concluded our interview by rifling through a stack of photographs of his travels to Colombian military bases with Colombian military officers; he also proudly showed me the multiple visa stamps on his passport. In addition to being a means of constituting private political subjectivities—used for display in offices, homes, and among colleagues—photographs of members of Congress in the field were sometimes circulated as campaign materials. For example, one aide described codel photos of members of Congress participating in counternarcotics operations as "a great shot for the constituents."

Travel made politicians effective advocates for the policy in part because it transformed them into experts through their ontological status of having experienced conditions "on the ground." They gained authoritative knowledge not through extensive study or analysis, but through direct witnesses and experience. As one former Republican staffer who traveled frequently to Colombia said, "I had the chance to see stuff I had only read about, or seen in the documents." One member of Congress, who led three congressional delegations to Colombia in one year, spoke frequently about the importance of being able say "firsthand" what they learned. He went on to critique U.S. and European human rights organizations that claimed that violations had occurred: "the view from Bogotá looks very different."[24] In a 2001 *Washington Times* editorial titled "A Wound that Still Bleeds," Oliver North wrote an editorial that began, "Rep. Cass Ballenger . . . says that 'the best way to find out what's going on is to go see for yourself.' " One Republican staffer, who had been on six delegations to Colombia in four years, described the tours this way: "We [use travel] to build bridges, educate members in the complexity of the challenges that the Colombian government is facing, so that members can feel at the table [in the debates over policy]." In this case, "at the table" meant being empowered by expertise to participate authoritatively in policy design, contributing insights that would be accepted as appropriate and important by other members. The staffer went to explain how travel was essential for constituting such qualities: "There is no way that briefing materials can match what the members see and experience on a trip."

Although orchestrated and limited in time and scope, codels provided access to conflictive regions, restricted knowledge, and embodied experiences that were unavailable to others. Congressional delegations allowed members of Congress, their aides, and their allies access to forbidden landscapes within Colombia through travel in military vehicles to remote jungle bases and outposts, with armed guards and military escorts. "In-country," codel members participated in classified briefings with U.S. and Colombian officials that revealed secret information. Summerson Carr notes the importance of intimate knowledge of "inaccessible or illegible" things in the construction of expertise.[25] The value of this knowledge was further increased by the association with risk and the willingness to travel in "dangerous" areas that were outside the perimeter of permitted places—to be, as one staffer put it, "to be in a place where no gringos had ever been."

Catherine Lutz has written about how the love of technology, what she calls "technophilia," has influenced the evolution of the U.S. military and the growing militarization of American industry. Such technophilia is a central element in policymakers' enthusiastic support of funding for military hardware. A central feature of the "drugs and thugs" tours was the use of military hardware to impress U.S. officials. Such displays drew on the high value of militarized masculinity.[26] In interviews about their travel to Colombia, staffers frequently mentioned the impressive displays of technology, recalling military training exercises, exotic forms of military travel, and mortar exercises. The aesthetic experience of weaponry, although often overlooked in conventional political science accounts of such policies, is profoundly motivating for officials.[27] One staffer who traveled on six codels to Colombia emphasized the importance of such issues when considering which minigun model to supply to the Colombian police for "softening the enemy." In addition to the material requirements of having sufficient force to break through lush jungle, he explained to me how the minigun

has a psychological effect; the barrel is this big [holds his hands in a circle as wide as his face], with individual barrels around it; it can fire 3,000 rounds a minute. That is a lot of ammunition going down range at once, it tears through the canopy and can reach the ground. People don't think of that, a lot of things can stop bullets, but this one can reach the ground. The psychological effect in part is because of the sound, a very distinctive sound [vvvvooot]; you know that there are 600 rounds coming at you. That is very productive from a military perspective.

Through travel, participants experienced the pleasure enabled by military machinery—the physical sensations of helicopter and "go fast" boat travel, the sound and smell of munitions exercises, the dramatic explosive destruction of captured cocaine. Congressional aides and members of Congress described the rush of peering out helicopters flying over "triple canopy" jungle. Codel participants had the opportunity for embodied participation in counternarcotics operations, including "doing manual eradication": physically pulling up coca plants and assisting with their destruction. Travel produced a sensory geography linking their visceral experiences of technological displays and vulnerable bodies to political action supporting military aid.

In a 2008 interview, I asked Jim McGovern (D-MA) to reflect on congressional travel. One of the most liberal members of Congress, McGovern and his staff went to Colombia six times on trips organized and paid for by NGOs. On these trips and other nonofficial delegations, NGOs created their own restricted geographies, privileging encounters with civilians and opposition activists—among them human rights, peace, labor, and religious leaders who had for several generations criticized and opposed existing counternarcotics and counterinsurgency programs. He began by recalling his congressional-sponsored travel in the 1980s. As a congressional aide, McGovern had worked for the Speaker's Task Force investigating the killing of four Jesuit priests, their housekeeper, and her daughter by an elite U.S.-trained Salvadoran military squad in November 1989. As a result of this experience, he told me, "I don't trust what my government says on human rights. Not anyplace. I want to see for myself. That is why I don't ask the embassy to put together my trips." He described how official codels reinforced support for existing policies through their carefully orchestrated encounters:

The US embassy says there is no problem. The English-speaking president says there is no problem . . . They can count on members of Congress to go to Colombia on codels, to spend between 24 and 48 hours in Bogota. At most they go to one area that is fully prepared to look like a raging success.

Conclusion

For Plan Colombia critics, the resonance with previous policy struggles over the U.S. role in Central America in the 1980s proved to be a galvanizing force. At the same time, real and perceived criminality among Colombia insurgent movements and victim populations resulted in the absence of political solidarity and limited affective affinities. The concrete material connections of embodied flows—of refugees, Christian churches, and educational exchanges—established the routes channeling these affective attachments; the minimal presence of these connections hindered the mobilization of a wider solidarity movement. Those who did participate traced their activism to resurgent activist identities linked to their earlier involvement in the Central America movement that was channeled through their professional activity. Now engaged as salaried employees of NGOs that grew out of previous volunteer social movements, they were largely sustained by foundation grants and engaged in policy advocacy as experts. However, their activist identities, forged during their previous participation in social movement mobilization, remained a powerful motivating force for many participants.

Policymaker solidarity, an articulation of political identification resulting in material commitments in transnational politics, is critical in mobilizing support for policy, and supporters of military aid to Colombia were extremely successful in this endeavor. Travel in official delegations organized and paid for by Congress was central to this process and in the production of sensory and affective geographies linking U.S. and Colombian officials in affective relationships and calculated reciprocity. Codels were orchestrated to present participants with particular geographies and spectacles of technological performance and personal suffering—and to spur them to political action. The masculine realm of military sacrifice was witnessed, commemorated, and rewarded. Policy expertise was produced through the sensory pleasures of travel to restricted military bases, the embodied awareness possessed by former military officers of distinct weapons systems, and the conviction of technological superiority. By claiming such knowledge as superior to other forms of expertise, congressional support-ers of militarized counternarcotics operations erased alternative policy argu-ments, creating the boundaries of what was politically possible to discuss. In the case of nuclear weapons testing, Joseph Masco has argued that the chang-ing "technoaesthetics" bounded the scientists' political analysis of the stakes of these operations.[28] Similarly, in congressional disputes over miniguns, Huey IIs, and Blackhawks, there was no opportunity to debate alternative visions of what if any social issues were posed by the consumption of drugs and the appropriate collective response.[29] The ongoing failure of source-country drug policies to af-fect the availability of illegal drugs was positioned not as a substantive critique but as the failure of technology. The robust, extensive, and long-standing cri-tiques produced by both academics and think tanks of U.S. counternarcotics poli-cies were excluded, as were alternative policy formulations produced through the "harm reduction" paradigm and programs implemented in Europe.[30]

These debates also charted a moral discursive and political terrain in which policymakers passionately claimed to speak for victims of violence enmeshed in a transnational chain of material and symbolic relationships. Congressional members of the drug warriors and their staff and supporters articulated a moral geography positioning themselves as acting in solidarity with some suffering Colombians—that country's national police and later, military forces—while ar-guing that those policymakers acting on behalf of other suffering Colombians by attempting to enforce human rights legislation were in fact characterized by moral failings: they were inept, driven by bureaucracy and careerism rather than legitimate moral concerns. Although such analysis is often applied to human rights and humanitarian NGOs, this case revealed that sensory geogra-phies, affective relationships, and moral commitments play a critical role in policymaking across political fields.

Chapter 7

Putumayan Policy Claims

"WE CALL ON STATE AGENCIES, the human rights NGOs of the world, the human rights NGOs of the country, the departmental and municipal institutions, the countries that intervene," a tall man began over the hum of the rain. During this public forum, ambitiously titled "The South Evaluates Plan Colombia," NGO representatives, state officials, and local residents came together in the final month of 2001 to respond to the projects being unveiled in the region. A quiet group of solemn-faced farmers sat on green plastic lawn chairs in the largest assembly hall of the Puerto Asís regional high school while clusters of small town officials enthusiastically greeted old friends and political rivals. More a pavilion than a room, the space was open on four sides to the damp air, with green-painted cement columns holding up the tin roof. Over that afternoon and the next, in classroom breakout sessions and private conversations over small plastic cups of sweetened black coffee, the participants discussed political violence, coca, and alternative development. They decried fumigation as an example of the ongoing betrayal of peasant trust and of the expectations raised by state promises. They expounded on fears that planned development projects would share the same fate. Some ventured to make hushed and coded comments about the dramatic rise in killings and the armed gunmen occupying many small towns.

In their welcoming remarks organizers referenced the history of local demands on the state, reminding listeners that "this is not the first time that Putumayan peasants tried to provide a means to end coca cultivation with social support," and listing in numbing detail the multiple avenues pursued by local coca farmers. They characterized the state as an unresponsive traitor and the coca-farming local residents as aspiring citizens. Organized by Colombian NGOs based in Bogotá, this gathering was only one example of the political alliances between residents, local state officials, and NGOs as Putumayans attempted to speak back to policy in this and other public forums, during encounters with official policymakers, and through testimonial accounts of their suffering. They also offered policy alternatives. Even though most of these efforts were invisible or discounted in official Washington policymaking arenas, the policy imaginaries and practices of the targets of intervention are a critical site for apprehending the full process of policymaking.

The residents of Putumayo faced many barriers to participation in policy-making. Remote rural areas during this period were largely inaccessible much of the year because of flooding, with travel to municipal centers costly and time consuming. Many residents lacked the formal education that is required to navigate governmental bureaucratic processes. Most significantly, residents were not considered legitimate political actors, but were stigmatized as criminals whose views could be appropriately excluded from policy debates in Colombia and the United States. Thus a central goal of Putumayan policymaking was recasting residents as legitimate citizens with credible proposals that were worthy of respect from national and international state actors.

During this period in Putumayo, humanitarian, counterinsurgency, human rights, and nation-building projects all converged in the same theater of operations, to use the military phrasing. Anthropologists María Clemencia Ramírez and Oscar Jansson have explored the implementation of these programs in Putumayo, illuminating the complex entanglements of security and development and their coercive effects.[1] In the United States, Putumayo was rarely in the public eye except in news footage of fumigation planes: it was both literally and politically a marginal place. Yet as Anna Tsing reminds us, marginality is foremost "an ongoing relationship with power."[2] Here, my focus is not on the process of implementation, but on how Putumayo residents and officials attempted to engage these distant powers and mobilized to shape the policies affecting their region.

As the United States began funding fumigation efforts, counternarcotics army battalions, and finally alternative development in the region, the conflict was reaching its zenith as paramilitaries and the guerrillas struggled to control the region. Intense militarization profoundly affected daily life as encounters with armed actors involved checkpoints, detention, surveillance, coercion, and incidents of harassment, rape, and torture. Negotiated systems of arbitration broke down, and power was expressed through the point of a gun.[3] As this violence consumed local residents, they turned to the possibilities of policy advocacy in venues outside the region. Here, I examine how people made political claims in this complex and contested terrain, to whom, and on what grounds. Despite their inability to shape the policies in question, through this process, local residents and officials generated new subjectivities and practices and laid the groundwork for future claims and emergent forms of political action.

Proxy Citizenship and Putumayans in Transnational Networks

Local state officials in the Putumayo government built transnational partnerships with NGOs to facilitate travel and advocacy in Washington, upending the traditional model of alliances among activists intended to influence Latin American central governments. At the same time, local residents mobilized existing institutional channels to present proposals for an alternative model of crop substitution based on a logic of agricultural development, rather than on the counternarcotics assessment metrics of coca eradication. Such efforts were limited by the contradictory imperatives of development and counterdrug programs, as well as by the demands of scientific assessment, which dismissed testimony of lived experience as anecdotal and hence unacceptable policy knowledge. Thus, although Putumayans attempted to produce forms of legitimate policy knowledge to justify their opposition to Plan Colombia and bolster their alternative policy claims, their efforts were largely unsuccessful.

The fundamental policy decisions involved in Plan Colombia, including program design, implementation strategies, and funding levels, were made in Washington without the participation of Colombian local state officials, much less the region's residents. In their attempts to gain access to these policymaking spaces, Putumayans relied on proxy citizenship, in which some of the rights of citizenship—the ability to make claims for redress to the state based on the experience of governance—were conferred and enacted through their relationships and affiliations with networks of human rights NGOs.[4] This policy advocacy was made possible through transnational linkages mediated by nongovernmental policy advocates in Colombia and the United States. U.S. NGOs allowed Colombian activists to function as their proxies, delegating to them authority, political legitimacy, and political rights of access to these spaces of confrontation with the state. The Colombians' claims to partial citizenship emerged from the experience of governance, articulated through testimony as a particular kind of expert policy knowledge. Colombian activists spoke as victims of U.S. policies—experiencing governance via U.S. programs, requesting political changes in Washington, and offering guidance on how these policies should be redirected.[5]

Proxy citizenship expands the concept of partible personhood[6] to explore the ways in which partible packages of rights and obligations are mobilized through transnational processes of governance and activism. These Colombian activists did not carry a U.S. passport, vote, pay taxes, or claim any of the other multiple duties and rights of U.S. citizenship. Yet they claimed political rights to redress before the state as subjects of governance, rather than a legal relationship with the state, in a process legitimated by their relationships with citizen-advocates. Proxy citizenship is a form of citizenship rescaled to the "Americas" to encompass proxy governance exercised by U.S. agencies throughout the continent and how this individual lived experience changed people's self-identity as subjects of governance.[7] At the same time, access to the state required a process of legitimization from strategically placed U.S. allies, involving "encounters between actors from vastly different, yet connected, social and political spaces."[8] This process not only generated political opportunities and created new citizenship subjectivities but also involved political costs as activists were forced to transform their claims.

Opposing Plan Colombia: Articulating Alternatives

Having been excluded from the design of Plan Colombia, Putumayans were confronted with how to influence the aid package once it was announced. Their strategies reveal the multiple ways in which they attempted to become legible as legitimate political subjects and as credible experts about the situation in the region able to assert claims to alternative policies. These policy claims focused on three arenas: the need for sustainable development, opposition to fumigation, and demanding an end to military-paramilitary violence. Their primary strategies involved building alliances with local state officials and with international NGOs, particularly those based in Washington, to facilitate access to policymaking spaces. Claims to legitimacy centered on their particular identities as peasant farmers, on scientific claims about the impact of fumigation in the region, and on eyewitness testimony as witnesses to the harm done by Plan Colombia.

Then-governor Jorge Devia described the Plan Colombia programs announced in the region as "crumbs," rather than the sustainable infrastructure projects required to generate real alternatives to the coca economy. Devia traveled to Washington in early 2000 as part of an NGO delegation organized by a Washington-based human rights organization, the R.F. Kennedy Center for Justice and Human Rights. There he met with U.S. policymakers, including State Department officials and members of Congress, and learned firsthand about the contents of Plan Colombia. On his return, Devia joined with the governors of five other neighboring states to form the Southern Alliance in opposition to the U.S. programs. The governors explicitly rejected Plan Colombia in part because it was developed without the participation of local authorities and communities. After President Pastrana refused to meet with them, the governors built on connections with national and international NGOs to travel to Washington to lobby U.S. policymakers.[9] This visit was organized and funded by Washington-based NGOs, which arranged press briefings and set up lobbying meetings. In February 2001, the Southern Alliance presented its "Southern Project," proposing increased social investment and an end to fumigation, and offering a model of participatory, sustainable alternative development as the basis for peace-building in the region.

Coca farmers saw their connections with the state as the key to legitimizing their organizations, and they realized that through their work with legally constituted municipal committees they could open political space for developing proposals against fumigation. Mobilizing the networks and practices deployed during previous protests, most recently during the 1996 cocalero marches, an alliance between state agents and peasant leaders attempted to use County Rural Development Councils (CMDRs) to propose policy alternatives, postpone fumigation efforts, and reconceive counternarcotics operations in the region. The CMDRs were one of a number of mechanisms for local political participation that were developed as part of the decentralization and democratization efforts of the early 1990s. In many rural areas, mayors and peasant groups worked together on these councils to design rural development plans. ANUC, the national state-established peasant association, and other peasant organizations made the CMDRs a central part of their advocacy strategy to influence national agricultural policy. As a result, the General Law for the Development of Agriculture and Fishing required establishing a CMDR in every municipality.[10] The ANUC leadership promoted CMDRs throughout the country, including Puerto Asís, in an effort to expand their political voice. Within Putumayo, the ANUC had not participated in the earlier cocalero movement; the Civic Movement leaders that led the negotiations ending the protests did not allow the departmental ANUC representative a seat at the table. After the intense persecution of the cocalero leaders in 1997 and 1998, however, the ANUC and the CMDR came to fill a leadership vacuum. By 1999, local officials were promoting CMDRs to coordinate their activities and provide security when traveling to rural communities.

Local officials and peasant coca farmers working together in the Puerto Asís CMDR developed what would become known as the "social pacts" proposal as an explicit counter policy to Plan Colombia. The social pacts were agreements between local coca farming communities and the Colombian government, stipulating the suspension of fumigation campaigns and the provision of food aid and technical agricultural assistance in exchange for the farmers' collective gradual, voluntary manual eradication of coca plants. According to then Puerto Asís mayor Manuel Alzate, who took office in 2000 and worked with the regional environmental agency and the CMDR, "We thought it would be possible to submit a project proposal to the national government and to the embassies, particularly the United States embassy, demonstrating that manual eradication was another approach, that fumigation was not the only strategy possible." When Plan Colombia national coordinator Gonzalo de Francisco arrived to present Plan Colombia, the CMDR representatives and the mayor offered the "social pacts" as an alternative to Plan Colombia's centralized development strategy and fumigation. Between December 2000 and July 2001, the Colombian government and 37,775 families in nine municipalities signed such pacts.[11]

As the conflict escalated, armed groups targeted travelers between rural *veredas* and municipal centers, accusing them of being informants. The FARC condemned the CMDR as being co-opted by the state; FARC gunmen killed at least one CMDR leader. In early 2000, paramilitaries first killed one peasant leader active in the CMDR process and then two community association presidents. On September 24, 2000, the FARC declared an armed strike that lasted until December, shutting down all road traffic and much of the river traffic in the region. Extensive delays in the delivery of food aid crippled the social pact process. Fourteen months into the program, only fewer than 5 percent of the farmers who signed the first pact had received their allotted assistance. According to the Latin America Working Group, "[m]ore than two years later, only 21 percent of the aid for food security projects had been delivered, and only 24 percent of those participating in social pacts had received all or a portion of the promised aid."[12] Because so much of the aid was not delivered, many families did not eradicate their coca plants. The Pastrana government and USAID declared the social pacts a failure.

The collapse of the social pacts revealed both the complexities of acting in this contested territory and that the dominant policy logic of U.S. operations was the imposition of the counternarcotics agenda, irrespective of the challenges faced by local communities. U.S. officials and their contractor proxies operated on a fixed timeline, responding to political pressures within the United States, particularly the two-year electoral cycle faced by all members of the House of Representatives. Their assessments employed metrics focused on eliminating coca. For many farmers, the ongoing fumigation demonstrated the state's bad faith. Despite the farmers' insistence that the regions attempting to implement the social pacts be allowed at minimum a year of fumigation-free growing time to ensure the viability of legal crops, pressure from Congress led to the resumption of spraying after only six months.

The alliances between Putumayan residents and local state officials, and between these officials with international NGOs, demonstrated the complexity of state-building efforts in such marginal areas. Akhil Gupta has examined encounters between national bureaucracies and supplicant citizens that challenge "Western notions of the boundary between state and society" and has contrasted them with the more fluid relationships between public servant and private citizen in small rural communities.[13] In Putumayo, local officials, community leaders, and NGO staff worked in shifting and tenuous institutional constellations in their efforts to become legible by the central state as legitimate political actors. In this process, state officials recognized the privileged status of national NGOs, which served as intermediaries between local officials and the central state, and in some cases international NGOs. "We have been able to rely on the accompaniment and guidance of these NGOs," one regional human rights ombudsman told me, adding that they "have a great influence on the national government and even on the international community." These relationships demonstrated the importance of distinguishing among the varying political and spatial instantiations of the state that can be marshaled to support or challenge official state positioning and interests.

Although development projects have been widely critiqued as "anti-politics machines," transforming issues of power inequalities into questions of technocratic administration, it was precisely this depoliticization that offered the possibility of political legitimacy for Putumayan coca farmers.[14] Accused by Colombian and U.S. senior officials of being sympathetic to the insurgent politics of the FARC and being motivated by the profits of the drug trade, Putumayan residents, as settlers in the jungle periphery, had only a tenuous claim to the category of legitimate peasant farmer. In rapidly urbanizing Colombia, the role of peasant itself was a contested category, not only a site of sanctioned nostalgia and regional identity but also scorned as a drag on modernizing progress. Unlike coca farmers in Bolivia and, to a lesser extent in Peru, all coca cultivation in Colombia was illegal. There was no widely visible traditional indigenous use for coca to serve as the basis of cultural acceptance and to justify limited legal cultivation.[15] Working with the repertoire of political claims developed through generations of peasant activism in Colombia, local farmers articulated an alternative policy logic of sustainable development. Even while relying on their depoliticized positioning, their proposals were profoundly political documents, demanding long-term regional investment in markets and infrastructure and an end to fumigation.

Mobilizing Against Fumigation

Beginning in the mid-1990s, massive fumigation operations in Colombia began in the south and extended northward over the next two decades as coca cultivation spread into new areas. These programs were funded and managed by the INL, their aviation wing based in Florida, and the military contractor DynCorp. American pilots, a motley mix of former military and crop-dusters pilots, alternated weeks in-country on assignment and weeks off. The U.S.-based agricultural multinational Monsanto produced the chemicals that were sprayed: a mix of glyphosate and unknown additives. Glyphosate, the main ingredient, was then widely used in Colombia and the United States as a commercially available herbicide, sold under the name Roundup Weed Control™. However, the exact chemical composition of the spray unleashed in Colombia has never been revealed.

In aerial spraying operations, small planes unleashed wide swaths of the chemical mix. Spraying was unpredictable and widespread—covering not only coca fields but also homes, schools, pastures, roads, food crops, and waterways. On the first trip to inspect the damage, one local health workers recalled, "Everything was yellow. I was used to seeing green coca everywhere, I was shocked. This is was what we saw: not a green leaf on a tree. Many jungle animals dead, dead monkeys, dead birds, fish farm tanks with thousands of dead

Figure 7   Farmer inspecting his fumigated fields.
Photograph by Nancy Sánchez, used by permission.

fish floating in them. They were the first ones to die." For the first time in their lives, residents saw the perpetually green jungle canopy withered and brown.

The first complaints against fumigation involved the death of children in Puerto Guzmán and the destruction of crops in remote rural communities deep in the jungle. Nancy Sánchez, who came to the region as a human rights researcher, had stayed on as a government employee in the regional public health department. She described the situation as a "death foretold," because civic leaders were aware that fumigation was being conducted in other regions, but did not anticipate its profound impact. "No one knew what to do; they would drink the water that had been fumigated," she said. "Many kids died from diarrhea, and there were also a lot of skin problems." Farmers complained that their animals died "of sadness" after fumigation, reporting that after eating or drinking in fumigated areas the animals would stagger ("act drunk") and grow listless and quiet. Counternarcotics police dismissed these complaints, arguing that if there were any problems from pesticides in the region, it was the result of peasants' use of glyphosate as a weed killer in coca fields.

As the social pacts were falling apart, local public health workers, allied with U.S. NGOs, turned to science as a way of legitimating their claims against fumigation in the region. Yet as activists worked to present fumigation as an issue of environmental justice, they were soon confronted with the restrictive logics of scientific evidence. Kim Fortun, in her study of activism following the Bhopal disaster in India, and Melissa Checker, in her work on neighborhood organizing against environmental racism in Chicago, demonstrate the ways in which scientific categories of risk and impact emerge from existing power hierarchies.[16] Local residents and the advocates working with them felt deeply how the demands of scientific evidence and accounting worked to delegitimize their claims contesting fumigation. The Colombian central government and U.S. policymakers argued that fumigation was harmless and dismissed any efforts to scientifically prove otherwise. The U.S. ambassador famously claimed that a Marine on staff at the embassy had suffered no ill effects after drinking a glass of Roundup™ on a dare. But although he told this anecdote during meetings with activists lobbying against fumigation, the U.S. government was using science as its primary justification for rejecting claims of fumigation's ill effects. According to U.S. officials, what was required was the ability to compare the before and after in order to establish causality. The lack of baseline studies, ongoing monitoring, and health services in the region made it impossible to definitively prove the negative effects of the fumigation or differentiate peasants' use of Roundup™ from fumigation. Spraying proceeded without any environmental impact studies and without lab testing in violation of Colombian law. In this calculus, the chemical was presumed innocent. At the same time, the population in the region was presumed guilty of coca farming, justifying widespread spraying.

To build a scientific case, regional public health workers embarked on an arduous process of gathering samples. Their primary concern was demonstrating spraying's impact on the health of local residents, but this proved extremely difficult to document. Their first effort was to employ a statistical analysis, using the epidemiological approach to violence and murders as a public health issue pioneered by the University of Cali that had been used in a previous report on homicides in the region. The health workers organized a meeting in Puerto Asís to gather doctors' records from throughout the region, which included more than 6,000 complaints about health effects of the fumigation. Based on a statistical analysis of the complaints, they found a dramatic increase in deaths from diarrhea in the region, which they argued was a health consequence of the fumigation and in particular the high concentrations of chemicals in the water.

Another approach to document the impact of fumigation, which involved the testing of blood samples, proved the difficulty of such scientific inquiry in the remote jungle region. One study, funded by the OAS, required the blood to reach Canada for testing within twenty-four hours of the sample being taken. Despite the heroic efforts to transport the samples from the Putumayan jungles to the Canadian labs within the required time frame, the study found no impact from fumigation. Putumayan health workers argued that the study was invalid because the fumigation had been suspended for four months before the study began because of the rainy season; the study's project directors had done no field-work and so did not know the spray schedule. In a second study, public health workers working with Colombian universities and Ecuadoran environmental lawyers spent weeks gathering blood samples in remote regions. Unfortunately, the samples were destroyed in the final leg of their journey to an Ecuadoran lab when the refrigeration system broke.

The government response to these studies was to dismiss their findings and to limit the possibilities of monitoring by state agencies. The Colombian government reduced the mandate of the public health services in the region, stripping them of the power to investigate the impact of the fumigations, which then became the responsibility of the mayor's office. This meant that people could no longer register their complaints at the hospital while getting treatment, but had to travel to the center of town to do so. The regional environmental agency, Corpoamazonia, which had issued a resolution prohibiting fumigation on environmental grounds, also had its mandate limited.

Advocacy and *Testimonio*

Unable to produce acceptable science, public health advocates and others turned to the stories of the suffering produced by fumigation—to narratives of empty bellies, withered landscapes, and blistered skin. The public health workers switched their focus to alleviating and documenting famine and malnutrition in the region, the result of the destruction of food crops by fumigation. These reports were based on testimony from affected families. Through proxy citizenship, in which certain rights of citizenship—the ability to make claims for redress to a state—are conferred to activists through their relationships with NGOs, Putumayan activists came to make their case in the United States.

Focusing on advocacy from within the policy process, U.S. and Colombian NGOs channeled political legitimacy and rights of access to Colombians, whose claims emerged from the experience of governance as articulated through testimony. They embarked on witnessing tours, attempting to challenge the dominant framing of fumigation as only an issue of concern to criminal drug traffickers.

Testimonio has come to circulate as an important alternative form of expert policy knowledge, albeit with contradictory results. Critics of Plan Colombia produced an emotional recounting of experiences of suffering in this genre, historically used as a central mobilizing practice in Latin America.[17] Over the past four decades, testimonio has been strategically deployed in transnational social movements between the United States and Latin America as part of leverage politics to help mobilize U.S. citizens to act on Latin Americans' behalf. During the 1970s, the "boomerang" model employed testimonio to inspire U.S. activists to pressure their government to push for Argentine reforms, and, in the 1980s, Central American activists used a "signal flare" strategy to inspire U.S. citizens to demand change from their government.[18] In an important shift beginning in 1999, Latin American activists began to speak directly to policymakers in an effort to change U.S. policies. From 1999 to the present, hundreds of Colombians, working with a range of U.S. political allies, including unions, churches, solidarity organizations, and human rights groups, met with U.S. officials in Colombia and in Washington to describe their experience of the consequences of U.S. governance and to demand alternative policy formations.

Testimonio's value as expertise is generated through its ontological status as a report of conditions "on the ground," from hidden, inaccessible, and dangerous sites—authentically representing individual life events and producing a collective history of communal experiences and analysis.[19] Testimonio as policy knowledge, however, contradicts the conventional construction and authorization of expertise through statistics, data and other forms of putatively objective forms of expert analysis.[20] The eruption of these accounts in policy forums has paradoxical effects: accepted as legitimate policy knowledge by some, testimonios are delegitimized by others as anecdotal, nonrepresentative, and lacking analytical rigor. The content of their claims is largely ignored by officials who, empowered through the institutional and discursive power of "state speech," co-opt these accounts and use them for their own purposes in configuring state power and legitimacy.[21] Even while dismissed, the production of testimonio in policy arenas can be employed by state actors as evidence of the state's inclusive, democratic practice.

In Colombia, access to the state required a process of legitimization conferred by strategically placed U.S. allies and involving "encounters between actors from vastly different, yet connected, social and political spaces."[22] Legitimacy, a critical political resource for advocacy, was constituted through relationships with NGOs. This process relied, in part, on institutional shifts in policymaking practices, including the increasing reliance on private policy expertise from think tanks in the late Cold War and post–Cold War period.[23] Not just any Putumayo resident could make proxy citizenship claims. Claimants could not be guerrilla supporters or criminals. Small coca farmers were acceptable but not owners of large coca plantations. Local officials were more credible than community leaders. The vetting processes required for proxy citizenship occurred in a nested hierarchy of organizations. U.S.-based NGOs developed partnerships with specific national groups that established links with particular regional and small-town activists. These U.S. allies provided training workshops, vouched for visa applications, paid for plane tickets, brokered meetings, and served as translators. They also assessed potential participants for acceptability and advised on the production of politically acceptable narratives.

U.S. NGOs provided the significant material and political resources required for proxy citizenship. Access to U.S. officials, even those visiting Colombia, often required travel, frequently from distant hamlets to municipal capitals or to Bogotá. National and international NGO partners paid for transportation costs, hotels, and food. NGO connections also facilitated visa applications, bypassing, among other things, the financial requirements for short-term travel and the wait for the required interview, which at times reached as long as two years.

Through informal training sessions, numerous activists were taught the basics of U.S. constituency-based politics and political advocacy. They were also trained in presenting particular kinds of human rights narratives. Several scholars of the Sanctuary movement in the 1980s and early 1990s have analyzed how the production of "good stories" was fundamental to the ongoing activism of U.S. sanctuary workers.[24] These good stories required a particular framing of Salvadoran history and conflicts, a charismatic speaking style, and authentic victims who could perform suffering without exposing evidence of psychological damage. Their stories had to generate "empathy, to spark a sense of urgency, and obligation or responsibility" as well as "be adapted to dominant US norms, values

and [self-] perceptions."[25] Central American activists played a central role in mobilizing the U.S. Sanctuary movement. Even while discursively denying their
political agency, Central American activists strategically deployed it as part of
their political mobilizing strategy.

Similarly, Colombian activists were instructed to be extremely concise, to present linear narratives focused on specific incidents, and to focus their complicated stories of Colombian violence on a single anecdote that could be understood by, and elicit sympathy from, young congressional staffers who could spare
just fifteen minutes for a meeting. Yet in practice, they maintained their agency
in the production of particular narratives. Colombians exercised considerable
initiative when articulating their stories, often subverting their instructions
to remain brief or focus on more recent cases. Instead, they attempted to provide contextual analysis and frequently presented the cases that had been
most meaningful to them—attacks on family members or events that they
had witnessed—rather than the streamlined narratives and up-to-the minute
analysis they were advised to present.

Much of the debate over the genre of testimonio has focused on the issues
of contested authenticity and collective representationality.[26] Here I explore instead how the testimonial form functioned as political practice and expert knowledge. The policy arguments offered by these activists were produced through
and legitimated by their emotional accounts of lived encounters with the U.S.
state through the military and counternarcotics programs the United States
developed and funded in their region. These political narratives were deeply
gendered accounts of suffering rather than of political agency or resistance.
Women in particular positioned themselves as maternal figures and caregivers
in relationship to their family members as well as the broader community. Assuming this role was particularly important in a region like Putumayo, where
inhabitants were doubly suspect as possible guerrilla sympathizers and drug-
trafficking criminals, both widely viewed as male identities. Although both testimonio and policy knowledge attempt to inspire the listener to action, in this
case the audience was not U.S. citizen activists moved to protest, but government officials acting to shift policy. In the arena of policy expertise, the focus
was not on the suffering and political mobilization of the narrator, but on the
provision of hidden knowledge and the production of information about the
role of the state that could be deployed in policymaking.[27]

The November 2008 meetings in Washington of a delegation of five activists from Putumayo illuminated significant features of this process. The delegation was organized to publicize the work of small, fragile, but significant networks of small-town activists, particularly the Women's Alliance of Putumayo (hereafter, the Alliance). The Alliance was founded in 2003 in response to escalating political violence in the region; its work focused on documenting abuses, offering education workshops, and developing support networks for local women. Four of the five delegation members belonged to the Alliance. Ana, a diminutive, soft-spoken rural schoolteacher in her late fifties, exemplified the important role of public teachers as the primary link between isolated hamlets and the capital. Blanca, a stout woman whose broad hands revealed a lifetime of hard labor, had been a leader of family members of the disappeared who were searching for the remains of their relatives in mass graves in the region. She was an insistent witness of her four daughters' disappearance. Marta, in her late thirties with feathered black hair and an anxious gaze, was a new member of the Alliance as well as of the Women's Path to Peace (*la Ruta Pacífica*), one of the country's largest and oldest pacifist feminist organizations inspired in part by the symbolic protests of transnational groups such as Women in Black.[28] A slim, serious single mother in her late twenties, Emilse spoke for the Peasant Association of Southwest Putumayo (ACSOMAYO), which claimed to represent more than 13,000 peasants and 2,300 indigenous people and is a member organization of the Women's Network. She had assumed leadership of ACSOMAYO after paramilitary groups killed the previous president. Willington was the only male participant in the delegation and was a representative of the Cofán people, one of Putumayo's thirteen indigenous communities. The executive director and a Putumayo-based staff member of MINGA, a Bogotá-based NGO that provided legal, moral, and political support for the group, accompanied them.

Arriving in Washington, the Putumayo activists confronted a narrative of their history that cast them as criminals and guerrilla supporters who were transformed into legitimate citizens through U.S. intervention. This view of both the historical problems in Putumayo and the success of the U.S.-sponsored programs in the region was widely promoted by U.S. officials and contractors in English-language newsletters, press interviews, and official reports. In their Washington meetings, the Putumayo activists directly challenged the conclusions of this narrative. Security had not improved, the activists asserted, and multiple armed groups maintained an ongoing presence in the region. The activists argued that the Colombian military, rather than providing security, was in fact contributing to insecurity, increasing the levels of violence experienced by inhabitants and violating their rights. Their critique of U.S. counternarcotics programs in the region was based not on an assessment of the ineffectiveness of these programs in reducing the flow of drugs or the price and availability of illicit drugs in the United States. Instead, they linked the counternarcotics programs to larger regional social problems, focusing on their personal cost to the population. Finally, they argued that U.S. policy should be reoriented away from the military and to humanitarian and development projects.

The highest profile moment of the trip was the delegation's testimony before the House of Representatives Human Rights Commission, a two-hour event held on a Thursday afternoon. The commission, although officially sanctioned by Congress, does not consider legislation, but is instead voluntarily convened to educate members of Congress and the public about human rights issues. The commission hearing replicated many of the expected elements of a testimonio performance as a public event. The activists faced the public on a raised stage, sitting behind a long desk and speaking into arched, wire-necked microphones to address a sympathetic audience. The two members of Congress on the stage did not cross-examine or question the activists, but allowed them to speak uninterrupted and praised their work and bravery. Held in the Rayburn Office Building, the event was open to the public; anyone could enter after passing through the metal detector at the building entrance. However, the audience, sitting on straight-backed metal chairs arranged in tight rows with an aisle in the middle, was primarily a sympathetic crowd of Washington human rights advocates and largely liberal Democratic staffers.

All of the activists who spoke focused on their individual experiences of violence and suffering during their testimony, with Colombian Bogotá-based advocates offering contextual remarks that described the general situation in Putumayo and their research in the region. Among the Putumayan activists, Blanca offered the most sustained testimonial narrative—an account of the disappearance of four of her daughters and her subsequent search for their bodies. Sitting on the raised dais before commission members, Blanca spoke in a loud, deliberate voice of how the girls—at the time nineteen, eighteen (twins), and twelve years old—were taken from a family barbecue on January 1, 2001, by paramilitary commanders whom she listed by nickname. In each meeting during the Washington mission, she recounted the same details, using the same phrases. She described how she fled to a neighboring state with her surviving family members, returning to search for the bodies of her daughters in the mass graves that had been discovered throughout the region. After another leader of the women searching for their families' remains was killed, she fled again, this time to Bogotá. Her delivery was punctuated by brief pauses while she cried, wiped her eyes with tissues, or breathed deeply in an effort to maintain her composure. At times, she directed her words to a large banner, hung along the wall at the back of the room, that displayed pictures of her disappeared daughters— the youngest in her school uniform, her head cocked, an inquisitive smile on her face—and that located her account within a tradition of political presentations set in a visual landscape of the dead and disappeared. Her presentation ended with tears as she explained her current economic misery and demanded that the government return her house—now occupied by supporters of the paramilitaries that killed her daughters—and provide aid for her surviving family.

An earlier meeting at the State Department provided an alternative example of how testimonial narratives were incorporated into policymaking and was more typical of the delegation's meetings. The setting differed from that of the congressional hearing in several ways. The meeting was closed, and only invited State Department officials and the delegation participated. No one else was admitted to the building, much less the meeting, without individual clearance. Unlike the large, open hearing room, the meeting at State took place in a small conference room. Here, the activists did not face their public. Rather, the long narrow table was presided over by the most senior government official present, an older man in a plain blue suit, flanked by two younger women taking notes. The activists were seated in a long semicircle facing him along the table, with a row of chairs set against the wall for lower ranking staff.

There were, however, similarities to the congressional hearing. During this meeting, the activists made their presentations without interruptions or the give-and-take common to the meeting format. Despite an NGO accompanier who opened the meeting with the statement that questions were welcome, the State Department officials present did not question the delegation members or make any remarks until the conclusion. In contrast to the sustained testimony of the congressional hearing, however, the Bogotá advocates did occasionally interject to provide additional information, cite statistics about additional cases, or mention their broader advocacy campaigns. As in the hearing, the activists offered tales of personal tragedy as representations of communal suffering. Blanca repeated the story of her daughters' disappearances. Marta's personal testimony focused on her search for the body of her sister, a two-term state assembly representative whom paramilitaries had taken from her home, hacked to pieces, and thrown into a river along with seven others. She went on to describe how the most basic aspects of daily life had changed, as people could no longer travel outside of town for fear of being accused of participating in an armed group. Ana described having to continue teaching in school buildings taken over by paramilitary groups, her efforts to assist those widowed and orphaned by military attacks, and her ongoing concern about the well-being of young students forced to travel to school from distant hamlets through combat zones. Willington focused on the forced military recruitment of indigenous youth and the abuses by the "security forces [that] do whatever they want . . . because they think everybody is supporting the guerrillas."

The activists' central policy claim was that the state was complicit in paramilitary violence. State security institutions were participating in the conflict through direct action (such as strafing houses in indigenous communities) or collaboration (between the military and paramilitary groups). Marta, for example, emphasized her status as an eyewitness in speaking of the relationship between the military and paramilitary that could be publicly observed in her town: "I saw with my own eyes, how they drank *trago* (alcohol) together, how they talked together, the *paras* (paramilitaries) and the security forces. And we all had to stay quiet." In her account, Blanca did not locate her family's tragedy within political disputes and claims: she lamented her loss as a mother and insisted on being identified in terms of the universal claims of parents seeking to protect their children. Her story, however, implicated the state in several ways. First, she intentionally named the paramilitaries who were working with local military commanders in the area. Second, she described the repeated inaction of specific government officials as they refused to assist her: during her daughters' abduction, as she yelled for help in the village square; then, as she begged the local police and the mayor's staff to take action; and, later, as she returned to search for the bodies among the multiple mass graves in the region. Here she contested the dominant narrative of the absent state, repeatedly describing state agents as actively colluding in brutal violence or actively refusing to intervene despite their presence and her immediate demands that they do so. She concluded with a reference to the ongoing dispossession generated by paramilitary violence in the region: her house, in a final insult, remained occupied by paramilitary gunmen.

During these state encounters, the Colombian activists presented their testimonio as a form of policy advocacy: "the ask." In her discussion of the humanitarian crisis generated by the destruction of food and coca crops and the killings by state security forces, peasant leader Emilse told the State Department officials, "I know that although you don't have complete responsibility, that some of it is the responsibility of the Colombian state, many of the programs in this region that we are talking about are funded by your government." Schoolteacher Ana told them, "We have to live daily with the armed groups, so we ask, how can you keep giving money to the military, when you know that they are violating the right to life, to housing, to tranquility." The "ask" was embedded in the narratives, in which the United States appeared complicit in the abuses of the Colombian state. The speakers also offered specific policy alternatives. Emilce requested that more responsive, long-term development projects be funded in the area. "The best way to help a country develop is to provide the help directly to the social part of development, for children and education," Ana concluded. These prescriptions for political action upended the assumptions of militarization, arguing for civilian- and people-focused policies rather than military- and technology-driven ones. As policy claims, these admittedly vague exhortations were legitimated by the testimonial form, authenticated as expertise by the lived experience of policy's failures.

Advocacy Encounters Remade by the State

For many of the NGO, congressional, and agency staff who traced their political education to participation in or sympathy with activist movements, the testimonial performance was a legitimate form of actionable policy information. The accounts also gained credibility from the privileging of local information, the notion that "being there" provided particular insights and authentic knowledge unattainable in other ways.[29] These emotional accounts of personal loss served to validate the claims of suffering and abuse; they were fundamental to the legitimacy of the policy critique offered by Colombian activists on the basis of their lived experience in the region. The authenticating power of experience was explicitly stated in some of the meetings. Some of the officials repeatedly told the activists of the worth and importance of their testimony as political knowledge that could help them in the policymaking process. In the words of one official, "We appreciate your visit, because it is one thing to hear directly from people, and not just read about the situation." Officials also spoke of being personally affected and moved by the testimony that they had heard.

However, the activists' testimony, fundamental to their gaining political credibility with their allies as required for the production of proxy citizenship, was also epistemologically risky. Some policymakers dismissed it as inadmissible because of the speakers' reliance on emotional, individual narratives. The activists were urged to "make them cry" through their testimony, as a means of generating political commitments from their listeners. At the same time, public grieving by the speakers as they recounted their most painful personal memories was viewed as signs of weakness and excess emotion that clouded their political analysis. The emotional personal stories that legitimated the claims of political knowledge through lived experience were in some cases interrogated as inadequate and excluded from consideration as the kind of expert knowledge required for policymaking. Some advocates felt that testimonial performance risked dismissal by policymakers unless it was accompanied by broader analysis in the shift from activist inspiration to policy knowledge. This double bind emerged from the ways in which the practices of advocacy within existing political systems set up unresolvable tensions between the requirements of immediate political action, including legibility as legitimate political actors, and broader demands for social transformation.[30]

This dynamic became very clear in one meeting with a congressional staffer, a senior aide who self-identified as a political ally critical of U.S. policy toward Colombia. Sitting around a long table in an empty hearing room, he repeatedly and aggressively questioned the speakers about their larger analysis of the dynamic in the region, rejecting their stories of lived experience. When Willington spoke of his indigenous community as being on the road to extinction, the staffer demanded, "When you say, it was 'exterminio,' do you think it was a policy, or a consequence?" When Willington offered a series of statistics about the indigenous communities in the region, the staffer responded, "That is the kind of information we need: concrete data, demographic data, where you can see the difference from one time to another." Is this a policy, a trend, simply a single event, or a consequence of other factors, the staffer repeatedly asked. In his dismissive body language and comments, the staffer clearly signaled his view of the accounts of suffering as obscuring the required analysis and thereby delegitimizing the speakers. He viewed Blanca's emotion as she tearfully recounted once again the disappearance of her daughters as a distraction from a concise analysis of the larger histories of violence. Several times, he looked to me to cut off the Colombians, so that he could ask questions that he felt were more important. This staffer viewed the encounter not as a space for witnessing the delegation's accounts, but as an opportunity for further political training for the activists, who could use their Washington meetings as an educational encounter. He intended to instruct them about U.S. political culture and how interests are defined and weighed in U.S. policy debates. "Politics is done toward another government, not the people, and you have to balance the interests involved," he told the activists. He was unwilling to serve as the expected witnessing public to their performance of outrage and grief as they pressed their moral demands on the state.

This staffer's behavior violated the activists' expectations of appropriate conduct during these meetings and of the suitable response to their emotional accounts. During the evening following the meeting, the last one at the end of a long and intense day, the delegates were full of anger and outrage at what they perceived as the staffer's disrespectful dismissal of their political claims and personal tragedies. Even worse was his effort to explain the U.S. political system and the complex landscape of political interests involved in shaping U.S. policymaking; they felt it delegitimized their political claims through testimony, invalidating their presence. "Why should we bother coming here if everyone knew everything already and nothing was going to change?" one of the activists asked angrily over breakfast the next morning. The Bogotá-based national NGO advocates admitted to me that they were experienced in providing the kind of quantified analysis viewed as legitimate policy information, but that, for the Putumayo activists offering their testimony as a means of staking claims on the basis of their dramatic lived experience, this demand was profoundly alienating.

The personal testimonies offered by the Colombian activists were also reconfigured in the service of state projects. Through the particular power of "state speech" to create legal and political realities, the presiding official's concluding summation at the State Department meeting described earlier rearticulated the activists' testimony into one that exonerated U.S. and Colombian officials. Because it emanated from institutions, state-sanctioned framing of events and histories circulated as inherently more authoritative and credible, rendering ineffective the activists' attempt to contest these narratives. The activists provided repeated and clear allegations that U.S.-supported military forces colluded with paramilitary groups and that counternarcotics policies produced humanitarian crises. Yet officials rhetorically erased the substance of the Colombians' political claims, refusing to acknowledge their assertions of state complicity with paramilitary violence and the ongoing impunity and threats in the region. Instead, they described the population as "trapped between two forces," naming only the guerrillas and not the paramilitaries and their Colombian military patrons. Rather than acknowledging the ways in which the Colombian state was complicit in political violence, the State Department representative instead described it as absent. "Because they are not in the communities, there is no prosecutor, army, or police forces, there is no presence of the state," the official offered as the final lesson of the meeting. "If the army is there, they are just passing through for a moment, the government is not there." Finally, State Department officials rearticulated these claims as a statement of support for the militarized development projects being formulated by the United States.

In their summation of the meeting, officials erased the activists' fundamental critique of an abusive military and of the model of governance that prioritized violence. "We are concerned about not being heard," a Bogotá-based advocate began before outlining a critique of the U.S. program, including the ways in which social development objectives were militarized and made subordinate to military objectives and how they violated the rights of civilians. While arguing for ongoing U.S. pressure on Colombian military forces to "conduct themselves well," U.S. policymakers rejected the shifting of funding to educational and humanitarian development projects, as advocated by the activists, and endorsed instead the increasing militarization of humanitarian and civilian government programs. The activists' profound critiques of U.S. policy were thus remade into support for U.S. programs. The content of their claims—emotional personal testimony to demonstrate the ongoing impunity, violence, and complicity of the government in abuses in their region—was not addressed. Instead the fact of the meeting itself—that activists were able to meet with U.S. officials, their presence rather than their speech—was used as evidence of U.S. democratic practice. "Participation" in policymaking became simply sitting at the meeting, the encounter itself, rather than the incorporation of people's views and critiques into policy or the practice of governance.

Testimonio, Advocacy, and Political Subjectivities

Participation in policy advocacy transformed activists' sense of political possibilities and participation in Colombia in complex ways. Activists feared their public testimony would lead to violent reprisals in Colombia, even as they widely viewed facing this risk as demonstrating their personal valor and commitment to martyred family members. Testimonial performance itself was a fraught process, exposing activists to the contradictions of their temporary safety in Washington and the ongoing violence in their home region and to the emotional consequences of reliving their traumas. At the same time, for some activists, travel to Washington provided new political resources and alliances, as well as contributed to new citizenship subjectivities within Colombia.

The complex calculus of testimonio as political performance, healing exorcism, and personal therapy was a frequent topic of reflection by the delegation. A large and growing literature critiques testimony's supposed specific psychosocial impact on the speaker as a technology of healing and on larger political structures as legal mechanisms of redress when employed in truth commissions that rely on public testimony[31] and in emerging forms of humanitarianism.[32] During their after-hours dinner and taxicab conversations, activists returned again and again to the emotional work of providing testimony as both a burden and a release.

One of the more experienced Bogotá-based advocates reflected on the emotional stress involved in leaving the crisis-driven daily routine of Colombian human rights activism and spending time in the relative comfort of U.S. and European NGO offices and homes. She described a cycle of resentment, despair, and anger that she had experienced during her first trip abroad and had since witnessed repeatedly while accompanying other activists. "Many things that people have not dealt with emotionally emerge," she told me, admitting that she experienced a breakdown "of intense emotions" during her first trips out of the country. This emotional reaction was also evident in the kinds of relationships that the activists developed with each other. Being a witness had become her life's work and she was frequently featured at numerous NGO events, yet Blanca continued to live without a regular salary in the poor conditions of Bogotá's squatter neighborhoods. Blanca's final words in her tragic narrative were repeated ringing calls for financial support for herself and her surviving family. Her constant angry, scolding harangues of the other activists were widely viewed as the product of the toll of losing her daughters, her subsequent focus on their case, and the family's ongoing poverty. "You have to realize that people are affected by these things in different ways," one told me. "Some people get very grumpy and angry; some people react in different ways. It is a long process."

In part, activists' varying responses were a result of the contradictory assessments of the possible violent retaliation generated by their political participation in public testimony. There was a great deal of discussion among the activists about risk—about what kind of talk generated risk and who among them was the most at risk. At the same time, taking on risk was a signifier of political and personal commitment to their dead and disappeared family members and to the suffering collectives and communities that had experienced similar losses but were unable to speak out. These disputes came to a head before the congressional Human Rights Caucus hearing, when heated discussions of the possible effects of Colombian media coverage led one of the activists to refuse to participate. She explained to me later that she was both fearful of future violence and emotionally exhausted by the expectation that she produce a specific narrative accounting of painful events. Those meetings involved "getting everything out of me, *sacando todo*. Remembering everything," she told me later. "All the bodies I saw, that I had to collect, telling the families and figuring out how to bury them."

The activists also described long-term personal, institutional, and political transformations as a result of their trip. Within the complex political terrain of their visit to Washington, they repeatedly described the transformative experience of speaking. "I don't know how we got so brave," Ana told a congressional staffer as she described her work under constant threat. Some felt that the opportunity to speak in a public hearing and in meetings with powerful officials validated their political claims. This was in sharp contrast to their description of daily life in the combat zones of Putumayo as profoundly silencing and of repeatedly having their claims dismissed and ignored by Colombian government officials.

These activists also gained political capital that was useful during their subsequent encounters with local Colombian politicians, in which they demonstrated their newly acquired transnational political standing and increased status back in Colombia. One activist recalled standing up to the mayor after he admonished her for speaking in the United States without authorization. She also used her passport, with the full-page U.S. visa, when stopped at checkpoints and by officials to demonstrate her transnational connections, as a form of political protection.[33] Despite her intense fear during the trip, when she recalled the experience back in Colombia, she described it as making her feel "protected," giving her both the confidence to speak and allies that she could rhetorically and practically call on in times of stress and confrontation.

Conclusion

The Colombian activists had multiple and distinct ways of evaluating their experiences in Washington. Several attributed changes in U.S. policy to their work. Speaking nine months after the trip, over a small glass of wine on the porch of a friend's house in Putumayo, one told me, "We did a great job; things changed afterward." Referring to the decline in military aid the year following the 2008 delegation, she said, "I like to think we had something to do with it." Although the activists did not get the policy changes they advocated—suspension of military aid and the redirection of assistance to humanitarian programs—they claimed that shifts in aid resulted at least in part from their activism (other explanations could include the decline in the U.S. foreign aid budget, the financial crisis in the United States, and the shift in focus to Mexico with the rise in drug-related violence there). Washington-based NGO advocates argued that they contributed to cumulative changes. Such delegations played a critical role in generating the affective relationships that sustained policymaker allies and activists, explored in the next chapter. Thus, although not singularly or directly responsible for subsequent political acts, NGO advocates saw the cumulative effects: letters of support from members of Congress, public statements of support and political support in specific cases, and, in rare cases, funding though budget line items (usually dedicated to government partners such as the human rights unit of the inspector general's office). Another activist, in describing the congressional hearing, excitedly reported that she had seen a member of Congress tearing up during the testimony of her family's disappearance. She repeated the story more than a year later when describing the achievements of the trip.

Others saw the trip as a waste of time and resources and a distraction from the ongoing demands of work among their communities. Along with activists throughout the country, Putumayan activists debated the value of focusing on advocacy within the U.S. political process.[34]

Although Colombian activists and their allies did not produce the demanded shifts in policy and governance, they were able to profoundly transform the broader political terrain by contributing to new political alliances and relationships and the subjective experience of political identities. This is an emergent form of political belonging produced through networked relationships and centered on the trans-territorial power of the United States to exercise governance projects in Latin America. For the Putumayan activists, their experience of the encounter, including the emotional production of testimony before the state, produced new forms of empirical citizenship that they brought back with them to Colombia. Their experience in Washington transformed how they understand themselves as Colombian citizens and their possibilities for political participation within Colombia.

However, the advocacy campaigns and the institutional channels through which they operated were profoundly exclusionary forms of political participation, in which alliances and affinities in relationship with U.S. advocates, rather than simply the experience of governance itself, were a fundamental requirement for access. NGOs conducted multiple gatekeeping and vetting roles, through which proxy citizenship could be understood as part of a process of professionalization with specific ideological agendas. Through this process, they excluded multiple political views, including insurrectionary political projects as well as the significant segments of the population (in some cases the majority) who might welcome U.S. interventions.

For the Colombian and U.S. activists and policymakers, the friction in these encounters produced unintended consequences rather than the stated policy goals.[35] Much of the impact consisted of the ephemeral and immeasurable accruing of political capital and credibility for activists, such the rural Colombian teacher who displayed her U.S. visa before the local officials who were attempting to intimidate her into silence. Several activists I interviewed, whose visits to Washington were not discussed here, described the new political alliances and commitments created when Colombians from different regions and organizations spent days and weeks together in meetings and hotels. In one memorable case, activists from an organization representing family members kidnapped by the guerrillas and one from a group supporting relatives of those targeted by the state security forces formed an unexpected affinity. This was despite the fact that, within the Colombian political landscape, their political alliances were understood to be oppositional: families of kidnap victims were generally vocal supporters of increased military and security aid, whereas those targeted by state security forces were critical of it. In this case, the vetting process conducted by gatekeeper NGOs ensured that the organization representing kidnap victims focused on lower class police and soldier draftees, held in some cases for more than a decade as political prisoners. Through their encounters in Washington, they found a shared political agenda, and in their meetings, they decided to switch testimonies, each describing the others' cases and tragedies as a means of demonstrating their alliance.

As claims embodied in particular forms of policy expertise and communicated through testimonial life histories and stories, the testimonies entered into a complex political field. This advocacy practice demonstrated an important use of testimony as policymaking knowledge, rather than as humanitarian practice or a mechanism for justice. In this social and political realm, testimony as policy knowledge was contested and debated by activists—as an epistemologically and physically risky strategy—and by some policymakers, who dismissed such efforts as insufficiently objective or analytical for the policy process. Activists debated the calibration of emotion, which had to be strong enough to produce politically useful narratives from the complex landscapes of suffering, but not so excessive as to delegitimize these accounts, and these debates are ongoing: are tears an authenticating expression of the profoundness of a political claim or proof of personal instability? The political conditions required for these advocacy campaigns were profoundly particular: proxy governance programs, operated by the United States in Latin America, mobilized U.S. advocates ready to channel material and political resources, as well as activists on the ground willing to submit to this taxing process. The political terrain of such efforts included the absence of a mass protest movement, shrinking political space for dissent, and expanding government bureaucracies dedicated to encompassing human rights. Yet, as the forms of transnational solidarity between U.S. and Latin American citizens have waned in the past two decades, this has become an important mechanism for attempting to articulate political transformation within policymaking processes. For the Colombian activists and in some cases their allies, the experience of producing testimonial policy knowledge through encounter with U.S. policymakers reconstituted a sense of themselves as victims of political violence, citizens, and political actors. These testimonies were not accepted as revelations of truth, but assimilated and absorbed into existing institutional agendas. State agents could co-opt these testimonies for particular political projects, producing the encounters with activists as evidence of democracy in action without acknowledging the content of the critique. Adopting advocacy strategies was part of a history of shifting expressions of solidarity that produced new forms of political subjectivities but only limited policy transformation.

Figure 8   Farmer's house, Putumayo, 1999.
Photograph by Winifred Tate.

Conclusion

Plan Colombia, Putumayo, and the Policymaking Imagination

ACCORDING TO WASHINGTON POLICYMAKERS, Plan Colombia was a success, a happy exception to the troubled U.S. interventions in other places, such as the Middle East, over the past decades. For years, President Clinton wore a woven bracelet in red, blue, and yellow—the colors of the Colombian flag—as a public sign of his close attachment to the country and his view that the aid package was an important legacy of his administration. "Colombia is a model for the region," Secretary of State John Kerry stated at his 2013 Senate confirmation hearing. "It is an example to the rest of Latin America about what awaits them if we can convince people to make better decisions."

Here, I challenge this triumphal narrative and present alternative visions of assessment. The bulk of this book has examined the forces and imaginaries that created Plan Colombia. These include the convergence of the transnational illegal drug trade with multiple militarization projects in the United States and in Colombia, as well as the collision of the hopes and aspirations of Washington human rights advocates, U.S. congressional staff, and peasant farmers of southern Colombia. I conclude with an interrogation of the policy evaluation process. The framing, indicators, and benchmarks chosen for assessment reveal how particular forms of policy knowledge are authorized and privileged while others are discounted. As in the policy problematization process, evaluation statistics presented as transparent actually require narratives to fix their meaning. Such assessments should also be examined for their absences. In this case, such absences included the fumigated fields, brutal paramilitary attacks, and frustrated efforts to organize collective participation in policymaking. The multiple origin stories also contained multiple endings, as policymakers turned to new proxy wars, conjuring unexpected threats and defending against newly discovered vulnerabilities, even as the once-targeted inhabitants of Putumayo turned to new political struggles and imagined futures.

An anthropological approach necessarily includes the appraisals of policymakers and analysts *and* of the targets of policy, their efforts to shape these programs, and their reflections on the process. Local people are never simply the empty receptacles of such interventions; they actively contest these projects, shape their outcomes, and produce alternatives. The process of policy implementation involves profound entanglements with these imaginaries, hopes, and political projects, and the resulting transformations cannot be understood in isolation from them. The efforts of the objects of intervention to shape policy are central to comprehending contemporary democratic processes. The anthropology of policies in democracies attends to how participation is constituted, delineated, signified, and authorized, as well as considering the rituals and practices that certify democratic processes.[1] Examining democracy promotion and nation-building efforts reveals that such projects are less involved with encouraging widespread involvement in governance than facilitating specific policy outcomes. In the case of Plan Colombia, the object of local interventions conducted under the banner of "democratization" was not, in other words, to incorporate local understandings and experiences of social problems, but to produce and maintain the dominance of particular political actors and agendas.[2]

Policy debates in the contemporary United States are relentlessly oriented toward the present. Being policy relevant means being attached to current policy problematization and knowledge production. Other time scales that could illuminate policy impacts, such as decades-long agricultural, environmental, and reproductive cycles, are invisible and discounted. State interventions involving massive aerial spraying of chemical herbicides, crop substitution programs, and changing military cultures demanded such extended time frames. Yet the production of evaluations of those interventions—in the form of reports, op-eds, and other types of discursive analysis—served as a form of advocacy for particular political formations in the present. At stake in the debates over Plan Colombia were the policy priorities for the late 2000s, including Mexican drug violence, reconstructing Iraq, and nation-building in Afghanistan—places with remarkably different situations that were defined by broadly similar concerns with counterinsurgency and state-building in the contexts of entrenched illegal economies. Even as Plan Colombia became a model for other countries and other aid packages, the ways in which this policy was made, how it facilitated the paramilitary forces' ongoing influence on political life, and its failure to consider how sustainable rural lifeways might be maintained were obscured.

The vision of Plan Colombia as a success was consolidated during the late 2000s by a series of triumphal reports from think tanks and by statements from policymakers and pundits. A 2007 report from the Center for Strategic and International Studies (CSIS), titled *Colombia: Back from the Brink*, credits Plan Colombia with many accomplishments, including expanding state authority, reducing violence, improving human rights, advancing the peace process, enhancing governance, expanding the economy, and providing social services. "Colombia is what Iraq should eventually look like, in our best dreams," according to Robert Kaplan.[3] "This critical ally of America has done all of the right things to try to bring stability, democracy, and prosperity to its own citizens," then Secretary of State Condoleezza Rice said in a 2008 statement supporting further U.S. assistance for Colombia. During my field research in January 2010 at SouthCom headquarters in Miami, the public relations officer forwarded me an article from the *National Standard* titled "The Colombian Miracle."[4] During interviews, I heard similar assessments from those who had been directly involved. "Colombia has been very good to all of us," Lt. General P. K. Ken Keen told me in his office. "It was a great place to work." He recalled how his former boss, General Charles Wilhelm, who had facilitated our interview by calling him and urging him to speak with me, viewed Plan Colombia as a case study for success. One of the reasons these officers agreed to talk to me was the hope that I would write such a case study.

I have witnessed the transformations on which these claims rest. Putumayo has a new airport and, for the first time, paved roads along many of the central arteries connecting the Ecuadoran border to the departmental capital. During a 2008 trip to Putumayo, I sat at a sidewalk bar with the members of the Putumayo Women's Alliance, drinking beer and celebrating the completion of a workshop and the upcoming marriage of one of the board of directors. Women from the small towns of Putumayo could travel once again to rural areas to visit counterparts in small hamlets who had been isolated for years during the intense conflict of the early 2000s. Paramilitary groups no longer openly patrolled the towns. According to many available statistics, the levels of violence in Colombia have declined and the number of homicides and kidnappings decreased. The FARC has been weakened: its troop numbers diminished, leaders killed, and units forced into strategic retreat. FARC roadblocks no longer stopped travel on the main roads. Mobility has increased, with people now able to travel freely without fear of kidnapping. Infrastructure is being built. "The Only Risk Is, You'll Want to Stay," the Colombian government's tourism slogan proclaims.

However, the publicly produced narrative of Plan Colombia as successful nation-building obscures as much as it reveals. In many ways, these efforts at assessment emerge from a priori ethical and political assumptions: either you believe that spraying chemicals over thousands of hectares of land—and all the life they contain—is safe, or you don't. Either you believe that guerrilla violence justified paramilitary attacks, or you don't. Understanding the production of Plan Colombia as a policy success requires examining these assumptions, as well as the ways in which strategic ambiguity is deployed in the assessment process. Finally, this work requires bringing in the complex and contradictory experiences of Putumayo residents, their understandings of the outcomes of these efforts, and their political claims regarding Plan Colombia's as yet unfinished futures. To examine the Plan Colombia success story, I now turn to the stories of three Putumayo residents who have guided my research in the region.

Manuel and the Failures of Counternarcotics Operations

Assessments of Plan Colombia have largely downplayed counternarcotics objectives because these programs have failed according to the metrics contained within the package itself. The 2007 CSIS study reported that the objective of reduction of coca production by 50 percent "has not been met."[5] Rand Corporation analysts acknowledged, "In Colombia, strategic cooperation and large amounts of U.S. aid failed to stem the production of narcotics. Nearly two-thirds of global cocaine continues to be produced in Colombia."[6] By dismissing one of the central goals of Plan Colombia, such assessments prevented a discussion of counternarcotics policy, its goals, practices, and results. The effect was to consign counternarcotics policy to the realm of political fantasy, revealing its utility as an ideological construct for facilitating specific forms of international aid and disallowing any substantive discussions of alternative policy formulations produced through the "harm reduction" paradigm and implemented in Europe,[7] as well as the multiple ways in which users experienced their drug consumption and its effects.[8]

Such analyses also ignored the work that counternarcotics policies actually achieved—moving illegal drug production and its associated violence into new areas or back into old ones—and the devastating effects of counternarcotics programs on the targeted communities. Although the amount of coca grown in

Putumayo has declined, most of Colombia's coca is now being grown in the neighboring state of Nariño. Cultivation in other conflictive areas is also on the rise. Decreases in Colombian cultivation are offset with increases in Peru and Bolivia. At the same time, hundreds of millions of dollars spent on aerial fumigation and ill-fated development schemes have left behind only further accusations of state malfeasance from the farmers these efforts were intended to transform.

Manuel has been trying to stop growing coca for more than fifteen years. After moving to Putumayo in the early 1980s to grow coca with his brother-in-law, he began searching for viable alternative crops, first on his own initiative and then with the help of the Colombian and finally the U.S. government. With twenty-eight friends, he organized a black peppercorn growing collective whose crops were destroyed by fumigation. He then participated in alternative crop programs funded by Plan Colombia; those crops were fumigated and destroyed as well. The USAID contractor Chemonics advised him to register an official complaint in hopes of receiving compensation, but then left the country when its project's funding cycle ended. Manuel and his partners went through the officially mandated channels to appeal for compensation for destroyed legal crops, which entailed an expensive trip to Bogotá and a visit to the counternarcotics police. For his trouble, he received an indirect death threat via a friend whose daughter was the girlfriend of a counternarcotics police officer. The third-hand message: retract your complaint or you'll disappear. So he did.

Manuel was not the only person to have problems with USAID-funded alternative crop programs. Thousands of people attempted to register complaints with local ombudsmen in an effort to claim compensation for destroyed legal crops, to no avail. At the same time, millions of dollars were spent on alternative livelihood projects that were abandoned or left no trace in the local economy except farmer frustration. Such projects included the animal feed plant that cost more than $2 million to build and then was sold off as scrap three years after it opened.[9] Or the infamous chicken project, in which thousands of chickens imported from the United States required expensive chicken feed, were unable to weather Putumayo's climate, and were left to starve or were made into soup. Thousands of heads of cattle were distributed; millions of dollars in seed, credit, and agricultural support spent. Today in Putumayo these programs appear to have simply melted into the landscape with no effect on agricultural production, much less on coca growing. Anthropologist María Clemencia Ramírez's exhaustive study of local development efforts found that USAID programs undermined state legitimacy and eroded public confidence in the state, the exact opposite of their stated goals.[10]

To this day, officials continue to dispute criticism of fumigation. During the early years of implementation of Plan Colombia, State Department officials argued that GPS systems used on the spray planes allowed precise tracking. Yet after the Ecuadoran government brought a lawsuit alleging that herbicide drift was killing crops within Ecuadoran territory, the Colombian government suspended fumigation within five miles of the border. Residents decried the health impact of fumigation, citing unexplained skin rashes and headaches. U.S. officials denied these claims, and frequently, if apocryphally, claimed that young and enthusiastic counternarcotics staff were willing to drink glasses of glyphosate to prove its safety. Health claims were repeatedly dismissed as lacking in scientific evidence and the required baseline studies. Residents lacked access to health care, potable water, and adequate nutrition and were living in remote tropical regions that were inherently unhealthy, so how could any illness be attributed to fumigation? Similarly, claims of negative environmental impact, initially ratified by the Colombian Environmental Ministry, were dismissed, and fumigation was endorsed by the U.S. Environmental Protection Agency. Officials claimed that the environmental damage generated by coca paste production—caused by deforesting remote land for coca farming and dumping gasoline and chemicals into the watershed—was greater than that of fumigation. Yet by the late 2000s, Colombia was increasingly phasing out fumigation, replacing aerial spraying with manual eradication. In many areas, teams of demobilized paramilitaries have been employed to pull up coca plants by hand. Intense backlash among local populations generated this shift.

Manuel and other residents of Putumayo did not equivocate in their denunciation of fumigation as a regional calamity. Fumigation decimated not only coca and food crops but also pastures, forests, and waterways. Manuel recalled with sorrow the sight of the perpetually green jungle canopy growing withered and brown following fumigation; he mourned the dead birds and monkeys he found. Manuel called fumigation an "organized disaster," because this plague was orchestrated and unleashed according to plan, coordinated by a government that did not see or care about its devastating results.

Fumigation, along with the violence of the drug trade, was one factor pushing Manuel's search for legal alternatives. But fumigation destroyed his legal crops and kept him growing coca. His current coca crop is an insurance policy; he is focused on growing cacao, but he knows that it is not sustainable. The region is too damp, and the harvest is prone to a fungus, rendering it unsellable. "You lose a lot of the harvest, and that is what demotivates people," he told me. He currently has coca bushes scattered among the cacao, which means his crop was likely missed in the estimates of current coca cultivation. Now, instead of making his own coca paste and selling it to a middleman, he dries and sells the coca leaves. This requires less work than tending cacao and produces a harvest every three months, with a guaranteed buyer. "It's not much," he tells me, "but it is the easiest way to work. People have their harvest of 1, 20 or 30 bushels [of coca leaves] and with this they support themselves, they add the money to what they make from cacao, and growing rice, growing corn." After all, as he reminds me with a smile, he has two sons in college now.

Carlos and the Problems of Nation-Building

Although most evaluations agree that Plan Colombia failed to fulfill its counternarcotics goals, they unanimously report success in strengthening the Colombian state. "While trafficking itself remains a problem," Rand Corporation analysts wrote in 2009, "Colombia is no longer in danger of becoming either a 'failed state' or an anemic, low-growth quasi-democracy."[11] According to then-U.S. ambassador to Colombia William Brownfield, "Colombia has been the most successful nation-building exercise by the United States this century."[12] But what kind of nation did the United States help build? The paramilitaries' unprecedented rise coincided with Plan Colombia. Although much of their leadership may have been jailed, extradited, or killed in infighting, the regional power structures linking legal and illegal commerce, official military forces with mercenary assassins, and the rapacious desire to defeat reformists are still intact in many places.

When drug trafficker and paramilitary warlord Salvatore Mancuso boasted in 2005 that he controlled 30 percent of the Colombian Congress, most analysts viewed his claim as wishful thinking.[13] Yet only one year later, Colombian journalist Claudia López's analysis of electoral records revealed "atypical voting patterns" linked to the collusion of paramilitaries and politicians, launching widespread investigations known collectively as the *parapolitica* scandal.[14] By 2011, more than 120 former members of Congress—approximately one third— had come under investigation for paramilitary ties, and more than 40 had been convicted. Approximately one third of Colombia's mayors, governors, and congressmen have been implicated, and investigations remain ongoing as of this writing.[15] Testimony by demobilized paramilitaries has implicated hundreds of members of the armed forces and thousands of private citizens. Paramilitary groups also used bribery and intimidation to influence the judicial system: the so-called corruption by fear, characterized by pervasive threats, intimidation, and physical attacks aimed at the Colombian judiciary.[16] In comparison, during what became known as the 8,000 case (after the case file number) in which President Ernesto Samper was prosecuted for electoral fraud committed during the 1994 presidential campaign—which caused the U.S. State Department to decertify the Colombian government in its annual assessment of counternarcotics cooperation—a total of sixteen politicians were sentenced for illicit enrichment.

Carlos Palacios, former coca farmer, progressive priest, and governor of Putumayo, was one of the many politicians accused of parapolitica. We had first met more than a decade ago at a Washington reception in the home of Colombia Human Rights Committee president Cristina Espinel, where we danced salsa and laughed over empanadas in between advocacy strategy sessions. One of a generation of priests who worked closely with Father Alcides to promote sustainable development in the place of coca, he was charismatic and outspoken in his defense of local farmers. Catholic Relief Services brought him to the United States for a speaking tour, in which he graphically described the impact of fumigation in the region while passionately advocating nonviolent and sustainable alternatives for U.S. policy.

During that trip, Carlos did not reveal that a few months earlier, while in Bogotá completing a degree in political science with a focus on conflict resolution at the country's premier Jesuit University, he had been recruited by a group of local politicians eagerly seeking a candidate for governor. The previous governor had been removed and was serving time for corruption; guerrillas were no longer enforcing an electoral boycott, and these politicians needed a candidate free of the political elite's stigma of corruption and incompetence. A friend and former colleague recalled, "They were adding up the votes in each municipality, how much money each was going to give. I told Carlos, let's go, we should not get involved with this, but he said I am going to stay until the end of the meeting." Father Palacios became the only candidate for the Conservatives and won handily. "Everyone voted for *el padre*," the same friend told me.

Early in his administration, Palacios generated great hopes of a new day in Putumayan politics. As one former colleague recalled, "At the time we thought, with a new bishop, and a new governor, we are going to be able to really improve, *sacar adelante*, this department." Yet his efforts seemed to be quickly derailed. Shortly after resigning the priesthood to run for office, he had married his pregnant girlfriend, and the child was born severely brain damaged. Distraught, he wrote a widely distributed letter attributing this birth defect to the U.S.-sponsored fumigation; it was later revealed that his wife had never been in an area sprayed by the chemicals. He left his wife and took up with a series of younger girlfriends. He took extended trips to Europe, ostensibly to raise funds for local development projects. Palacios was also widely criticized for administrative problems, including hiring family members. In 2006, he was removed from office when the inspector general suspended him for contract irregularities.

However, the most shocking revelation was a statement from paramilitary leader "Ernesto Baez" (Ivan Duque) during a Putumayo demobilization ceremony, held on March 1, 2006, for 504 paramilitaries. According to a *Semana* news article, Baez publicly complained that paramilitaries had financed Palacios's campaign and then been cheated when he failed to meet as requested with paramilitary leaders. The article went on to publish transcripts of recorded conversations, which revealed that Palacios had extorted the owner of the region's lucrative liquor franchise, who also admitted that "30%" of the liquor distribution business went to the paramilitaries. "So I was the one indirectly making those campaign contributions," Baez concluded, referring to the money given Palacios by the paramilitaries.[17] Palacios was brought up on extortion charges in 2009 and sentenced to three years in jail.

In many cases in Colombia, the relationship between paramilitaries and politicians was the inverse of that usually imagined: rather than seeing the paramilitaries as illegal actors buying their way into the political system, politicians saw the growing power of paramilitary forces and approached them about forging an electoral alliance. This was a direct result of the paramilitaries' deep pockets, filled with profits from the drug trade that allowed them to finance political and business projects. At the same time, paramilitary leaders, military officers, and high-ranking politicians held a shared sense of purpose and strategic interests. Like Palacios, politicians saw the opportunity to gain much needed votes and campaign funds in a country with a long history of vote-buying and clientelism.[18] Palacios's defense was that he was simply trapped in a corrupt system. Carlos did not know how to manage the power he had, many of his friends and former colleagues told me. "I had good intentions," he told me over milky coffee and soft bread in his family compound, where he is spending the final months of his sentence under house arrest. "I believed in social and economic development, just like we laid out in the development plan, but that is impossible here. Here political groups are part of very dark forces, and the political groups manage these forces. Anyone elected is a puppet." He made me turn off the tape recorder for the rest of his off-the-record reflections on who was really controlling the political power in Putumayo.

Although Carlos employs a systemic critique to justify his personal malfeasance, many researchers have pointed to the ways in which paramilitaries have capitalized on entrenched structures of clientelism and corruption for personal enrichment and political power.[19] These practices did not disappear with the paramilitary demobilization, but have continued with new, lower profile groups that extort businesses, demand percentages of public contracts, and exercise decision-making power over public administration, in addition to using violence to protect their illegal drug trafficking. Government investigators and others have documented the emergence of reorganized paramilitary forces, which the government calls "emerging criminal bands" (known as Bacrims, a shortening of *bandas criminales*), as evidence of the larger failure of the demobilization process to diminish paramilitary power.[20] As former High Commissioner for Peace Daniel Garcia-Peña wrote in a 2009 editorial,

The truth is that the mass demobilization did not mean the dismantlement of paramilitarism, but instead formed part of its consolidation. Such a large number of armed men was no longer needed. They had already killed the political and social leaders who had to be eliminated, and chopped up and displaced all the *campesinos* who had land that needed to be stolen. Mission accomplished. In addition, to maintain an army of mercenaries, at 500,000 pesos per month (about US$200) times 32,000 heads, requires a respectable amount of money. As a result, the business was an all-around success: the "reinserted" passed into the care of the public treasury and the paramilitary leaders remain with all the treasure they accumulated as a fruit of their terror, keeping only the strictly necessary number of armed men.[21]

According to the former director of the Jesuit think tank, the Center for Grassroots Research and Education,

They have not taken on the same forms of organizing and perpetrating violence, but they are all paramilitaries. Once they take over public posts, thanks to the terror they manage to inspire, the illegal bands re-establish extortion, in the clientelistic manner of traditional politics, but strengthened by the fear that massacres leave floating in the short memory of public opinion. It is a metamorphosis of armed violence into economic and social violence.[22]

In addition to their deep and lasting influence on the Colombian political system, the paramilitaries have transformed Colombian economic life. Paramilitaries appropriated land, repopulating it with people loyal to them while creating sanctuaries for their business interests, including drug trafficking, ranching and mining. Redistribution efforts have been complicated by threats and assassinations against people attempting to reclaim their land. Establishing ownership histories of many properties is very complex, because of their occupation by multiple families through displacement and armed resettlement, as well as the intentional destruction of land titles by burning down land registry offices in several regions.[23] Land tenure, and the return of land stolen by such groups, has become a major priority for the Santos administration (2010–). At the same time, the transformation of the agrarian sector through legislative and financial incentives (including USAID-sponsored programs in some areas) to privilege agribusiness monocrops such as palm oil has contributed to the conservation of paramilitary structures of land ownership and rural economic relationships.[24]

Diana and the Search for Security

The Plan Colombia success story rests on a particular accounting of military forces and combat losses. According to this logic, military expansion translated into guerrilla defeats, and the reduction in accusations of abuses committed directly by the military was attributed to increasing professionalization of the security forces. However, a central factor underlying both accomplishments—the dramatic expansion of paramilitary forces—disappears from these accounts, as do impunity for these crimes and ongoing paramilitary connections to military officers. The security strategies implemented by community residents desperate to survive those bitter years, and their ongoing struggles with multiple forms of abuse and violence, offer a critical take on Plan Colombia's failed security dimensions.

The Colombian military has clearly been transformed in one way: it is now much, much bigger. The expansion of the Colombian security forces made possible by Plan Colombia was begun by Pastrana and continued by his successor, Alvaro Uribe. The number of standing troops increased by 45 percent from 2000 to 2007, from 275,000 to almost 400,000 soldiers; numerous elite special units, including mobile brigades, high mountain battalions, and antiterrorist special forces units, were created during this time period. The military budget grew dramatically, from 3.4 percent of GDP in 2000 to 5.2 percent in 2007, an increase of approximately US$7 billion. During his administration, Uribe increased police coverage to all municipalities and attempted to bring permanent local military outposts into many areas. The use of U.S.-supplied helicopters improved troop mobility, and U.S. intelligence equipment and training increased information-gathering efforts.

U.S. advisors claimed that this military expansion played a pivotal role in counterinsurgency efforts. Beginning in 2004, they helped coordinate a major counterinsurgency campaign called Plan Patriota, targeting guerrilla forces in the south. U.S. officials channeled untold millions through a classified "black budget,"[25] which funded intelligence and weaponry, including laser-guided "smart bombs." The most visible, and devastating, result was a series of military strikes that killed senior FARC leaders (Raul Reyes in 2008, Jorge Briceño in 2010, and Sureshot's successor, Alfonso Cano, in 2011). The group's most senior leader, founder Manuel "Sureshot" Marulanda, had died of natural causes in 2008, the most significant loss in a series of generational shifts—from senior leadership who had risen through the ranks of communist guerrilla fighters to younger commanders focused on criminal enrichment. The number of FARC troops declined from an estimated high of 20,000 in 2002 to 8,000 in 2010.

Diana (not her real name) and other community leaders did not agree with this rosy assessment of improved security. In their recounting, military operations in the region endangered Putumayan women more than they protected them. A coca farm worker turned entrepreneurial housewife, Diana first joined the Women's Alliance of Putumayo on the advice of her friend Ana, the schoolteacher who traveled to Washington in the 2008 delegation analyzed in Chapter 7. They had worked together in a small high school; when Diana started receiving threats from paramilitaries over her cell phone, Ana was the first person she turned to. After leaving her job and then, briefly, the region, Diana returned and discovered through friends that the paramilitaries had decided that the threats were in error and were based on the jealousies of local commanders who were no longer in favor. Ana got Diana a new job in the library of another school and urged her to begin attending meetings of the women's group. While living in a rented room with her son, Diana found her neighbor burying weapons in their shared yard and heard him boast of his previous murders. She received threats and was forced to leave her job.

The women of the Alliance developed an alternative vision of security that focused on strengthening what they called the "social fabric"—women's connections to each other and the wider community. Women sheltered their threatened colleagues, moving them from house to house or farm to farm. They sought international accompaniment, traveling with representatives of international human rights and humanitarian organizations. Women employed complex survival strategies in their daily lives, including lying at roadblocks, staying at home to escape the attention of commanders known to rape residents, avoiding the use of rubber boots and rough appearance associated with rural guerrillas. At times women warned friends and neighbors when their names were mentioned as "on the list," but in other circumstances they abandoned detained friends and neighbors for fear of retaliatory violence. Friends and neighbors were killed, disappeared, and forced to flee the region. Women fled, bargained, and endured.

The full extent of paramilitary crimes will never be known. For the almost 32,000 paramilitaries who passed through the official demobilization process between 2004 and 2007, their crimes fall under the special jurisdiction known as the Justice and Peace law, passed in 2005 and setting out the benefits that accrue for confessing crimes. According to the chief prosecutor of these cases, more than four thousand unmarked graves have yet to be located and exhumed. Government officials estimate that approximately three thousand people from Putumayo alone remain disappeared, their bodies unfound and unidentified. The revelations of the parapolitica scandal offer evidence of paramilitary groups' institutional power, links to politicians, role in electoral politics, and ties to state resources. However, the Justice and Peace process has been pitifully understaffed and underresourced, only able to investigate a tiny fraction of the total crimes.[26] In March 2009, Uribe extradited seventeen of the highest ranking paramilitary commanders to the United States on drug-trafficking charges, in what *Time* magazine reported as "widely interpreted as a move to halt the embarrassing revelations," as their testimony implicated high-ranking politicians and military officers who were also political allies of the president. "The mass extraditions have stymied Colombian prosecutors looking into paramilitary massacres and land grabs and hamstrung their efforts to compensate the victims of these crimes. The extradited might face lengthy prison terms in the United States (some may strike plea deals that result in reduced sentences). But because they only have to answer for their drug crimes, the warlord defendants now have little motive for elaborating on their human rights atrocities back in their homeland."[27] The length of these paramilitary commanders' sentences in the United States has been impossible to track because of the refusal of Department of Justice officials to release any information about possible plea deals.

Plan Colombia supporters point to the lack of current cases of military abuses as proof of military professionalization. However, the decline in reported abuses is more likely the result of shifts in the dynamic of the conflict and the privatization of state violence through the use of paramilitary forces. Numerous studies have pointed to the difficulty of long-term assessment of military reform as a result of U.S. training and funding. The 1995 Rand report, *The Effectiveness of U.S. Training Efforts in Internal Defense and Development: The Cases of El Salvador and Honduras*, noted that many studies have "concluded that US military training and equipment have little or no effect, negative or otherwise, on the institutional behavior of Latin American militaries."[28] The report described the hurdles facing U.S. training efforts:

First, can the United States affect basic attitudinal and behavioral change in the individual soldier who receives the training? Second, assuming the individual soldier internalizes the lessons on "professionalism," can this individual-level metamorphosis be translated into a wide institutional transformation? Third, given the multitude of exogenous factors that affect democratic political development and structurally induced political repression, can the military play an instrumental role in effecting change on a societal level? Strong political, personal, historical, and financial reasons abound for these militaries to remain politically viable and independent. Consequently, it would appear that no amount of U.S. training could persuade them to do otherwise.[29]

What is clear is that, by 2006, there was abundant evidence of ongoing malfeasance by security forces. Under the Uribe government, Colombia's domestic intelligence agency, known as DAS, engaged in widespread illegal surveillance of Supreme Court magistrates, journalists, rights defenders, and government critics. The DAS director from 2002–05 was convicted in 2011 of having put the in-

telligence agency at the service of the AUC. In 2006, journalists and other investigators revealed widespread torture of recruits during training and a massacre
by an army patrol in the pay of drug traffickers of a police anti-narcotics unit;
the first allegations of *falsos positivos* surfaced then. These cases involved young,
poor men disappeared and presented by military units as guerrilla fighters killed
in combat; the name refers to military commanders' relentless demands for "positive" results (i.e., high body counts). The UN High Commissioner for Human
Rights in Colombia estimated that more than three thousand people may have
been victims of extrajudicial executions by state actors and that between 2004
and 2008, the army committed the majority of those executions.

When describing the first Alliance workshops that she participated in, Diana's emphasis was on overcoming a form of lingering trauma that was overlooked by those evaluating security in the region: gendered violence against
women and girls. Anthropologists argue that ethnography can illuminate how
security is conceived of and distributed, how vulnerability is established, and
how protection is appropriated.[30] Security is deeply gendered, and what serves
to advance the security of some, such as demobilization of armed groups, may
reduce the security of others, including the communities and families where such
troops resettle.[31] According to women in the Alliance, domestic violence by intimate partners against women and children is extremely common and remains
significantly underreported in the region. Many of the group's leaders told me
of incidents of domestic violence in their own pasts.

The methodology employed by the Alliance workshops is largely drawn from
feminist psychotherapy models, which emphasize the importance of developing women's self-esteem and supporting their efforts to escape violence in the
home. "In the beginning I was very quiet, I didn't participate much," Diana told
me as we sat together at a small wooden table in her front yard. "That was when
the Alliance was just beginning. [Ana] took me to the meetings, but I didn't participate because I was afraid. I just couldn't—to speak, when anyone could be
listening . . . But little by little I got involved." In describing her ongoing quest for
safety, Diana began with her childhood, which involved extensive physical abuse
and neglect from a young age by her father and mother and sexual abuse by an
uncle. "I didn't tell anyone, [but] when I heard certain songs, I cried. About my
dad, too. I couldn't forgive him; I would go fight with him at the cemetery." She
was only able to speak of it with me because of the work she had done with the
Alliance. "Through the workshops: listening to the women, in the midst of our

tears, the accompaniment, the work with the psychologist . . . Now I am calmer, it is part of my life process." For many women, the paramilitary demobilization has had a negligible impact on the levels of violence in their daily lives; for some, violence has increased as abusive partners, many of them traumatized by their wartime experiences, have returned home.

Diana, like every resident of Putumayo, still must grapple with the ongoing conflict. The guerrillas have not been defeated. As of this writing, FARC and government representatives are holding peace talks in Havana, with many analysts cautiously optimistic that a negotiated settlement is possible. But in many of the most remote regions of Putumayo, the FARC continues to rule daily life, planting landmines along the paths and dictating who can come and go. Landmines have killed farmers and their children; rural communities are periodically forced to abandon their homes because of the fear of such explosions. During fieldwork conversations in August 2010, teachers from rural areas reported that the guerrillas were calling community meetings, at which they threatened forced recruitment and military action.

Demobilized and reconstituted paramilitary groups also continue to target local people. Some of these efforts have the aim of preventing evidence of previous crimes from emerging. Families reported that paramilitaries have dug up the clandestine mass graves identified by the community and scattered or stolen the remains, presumably to prevent revelation of additional crimes that would not be covered by the previous legal agreements. Human rights activists, prosecutors, and investigators continue to receive paramilitary death threats and in some cases have been killed because of their work. During a 2010 research trip to Putumayo, death squads in Puerto Asís released a list of sixty young men designated for "social cleansing," the killing of so-called undesirables such as unemployed youth and small-scale drug vendors. Over the course of the weekend, three young men were shot, two fatally. During a workshop, one woman tearfully recounted how *Los Rastrojos* threatened her husband with death if he refused to serve them as a driver for their drug-trafficking operations. In January 2011, attacks by unknown armed groups against the mayor of Puerto Asís, Putumayo's largest town, resulted in the destruction of his house and the death of his son.

At the same time, the Alliance is taking advantage of the relative calm to focus on playing a more active role in designing local policies, particularly those that affect women. In Alliance workshops, local women learn about rights enshrined in recent legislation and strategize about how to pressure local state officials to comply with their obligations. They also hope to gain material benefits from the state, including a building to serve as their permanent office. For the women of the Alliance, their efforts are now focused less on transnational advocacy and more on local demands for greater accountability, including in municipal policy and budgeting processes. They are working on increasing state funding for women's health, domestic violence programs, and the creation of municipal women's centers, *las casas de la mujer*.

In the last women's meeting I attended, violence was on everyone's mind. The Alliance vice president showed me a photocopied paper, one of many distributed over the weekend. "From today at 6pm," the paper read, "anyone who brings in any unknown person, any informants (*sapos*), and garbage: death." The bottom half of the paper was decorated with images of three skulls surrounded by machine guns. But most of the meeting focused on how to get the mayor to fulfill his promises of support. During his campaign, he had promised municipal funds to help buy a building for the Alliance; now a spirited discussion of possible advocacy strategies focused on what kind of pressure to bring to bear. Following these debates, two community activists described efforts to halt oil exploration on ecologically sensitive lands. They explained their fear of environmental degradation and increased pollution in regional waterways. Working with the local environmental agency, they had secured the commitment of more than twenty hamlets to opposing geological exploration of the area by a Canadian-owned company.

The work of the Women's Alliance illustrates the complex legacy of Plan Colombia's so-called security successes. Many members are consumed with mourning the devastating losses they suffered during the height of the paramilitary and guerrilla violence. As a group, they work to expose and commemorate the multiple forms of violence targeting women in the region. The Alliance has placed permanent memorials in the central plazas of small towns in the region to commemorate assassinated women. The first "wall of truth" includes a mural and 170 bricks, each with the name and date of death of a murdered woman, in one corner of the central park in the state capital; the second was recently completed in Villagarzón. The Alliance, along with other women's groups, have also organized marches and public performances to publicly mourn emblematic

Figure 9   Women of the Alliance in front of the "Wall of Truth" in Mocoa commemorating violence against women in Putumayo.
Photograph by Nancy Sánchez, used by permission.

cases, such as the 2001 disappearance of the four Galarraga sisters by paramilitary forces in La Dorada. At the same time, women must now grapple with new forms of intervention, through massive mining and oil operations that were enabled by Plan Colombia's security "success."

As of this writing in the early days of 2015, the architects of Plan Colombia have largely turned their attention elsewhere. Some are bringing delegations of Colombian National Police to Afghanistan to instruct law enforcement officials on counternarcotics operations. Others are designing military and intelligence assistance for Mexico or managing counterterrorism operations. This history of Plan Colombia allows an understanding not only of their views of Plan Colombia moving forward, but also a model for analysis of these emerging policy endeavors. An ethnographic approach allows an understanding of what policy is, not as a discrete plan for future action but as a set of stories justifying political action in the present by mobilizing imagined pasts and conjuring alternate futures, beginning by categorizing particular kinds of people, products, and practices into problems to be solved by an ever-narrower set of policy prescriptions. An anthropology of policy asks not, did it succeed, but, what work did it do?, excavating the unintended impacts and transformations wrought by such interventions. Such a project interrogates the cultural meanings and assumptions of traditionally defined policymakers, the Department of State representatives officially charged with setting out national foreign policy, but also examines the work of military officers, congressional aides, and the staff of implementing agencies who make policy through the less visible spaces of budget negotiations, official travel, and program management. Casting the net wider still, an anthropology of policy also considers the work of activists and opponents, who attempt to bring alternate visions to bear, in this case most prominently through human rights.

Putumayans' political possibilities continue to be constrained by U.S. militarization, prohibitionist drug policy, and global agricultural markets and trade agreements. In their daily work, the Alliance is now focused on the policy decisions made in the boardrooms of Canadian mining companies as well as the U.S. State Department. Anthropology of policy brings in the targets of foreign policy intervention, the residents of in many cases remote, rural regions that have historically been the primary subjects of anthropological investigation. No longer seen in isolation, the targets of policy are agents of policy transformation, with their own complex political aspirations and agendas. For the women of the Alliance in Putumayo, imaging themselves as policymakers was a transformative project even as they failed to realize their policy objectives. Through multiple fronts, including testimony, advocacy and local organizing, they contest and speak back to policy, offering alternative visions of what the state could be and how governance could be enacted. This ongoing work is also one of the many legacies of Plan Colombia.

Notes

Introduction

1. DeShazo et al. 2007.

2. Stern 2004.

3 Critical works in the anthropology of policy include Shore and Wright 1997; Shore et al. 2011.

4. I conducted more than one hundred oral history interviews with policymakers, analysts, and advocates in the United States. I made more than ten trips to Putumayo to conduct field research since 1999. In Colombia, I conducted more than eighty interviews with local elected officials, including current and former governors and mayors, priests, community leaders, military officials, international aid workers, and coca farmers; I also observed community workshops and public events.

5. Trouillot 2001: 126.

6. Greenhalgh 2008.

7. See Inda 2005; Wedel et al. 2005.

8. Only very rarely does policymaking involve dramatic shifts in state action, and such instances usually involve authoritarian states that can institute such directives. Examples include the Chinese one-child policy explored by Susan Greenhalgh 2008 and the shifts in economic policies during the Southern Cone military dictatorships.

9. Trouillet 2001.

10. Although I did conduct interviews with Colombian foreign policy officials, the bulk of my research focuses on U.S. policymaking and political life in Putumayo. A comprehensive history of the diplomatic role of Colombian senior officials is beyond the scope of this project.

11. Greenhalgh 2008.

12. Crawford 2000, 2002.

13. Rosado 1984: 143.

14. Lutz 1998.

15. Bleiker and Hutchinson 2008.

16. Crawford 2000.

17. Butler 2009.

18. Williams 1977: 132.

19. Butler 1997.

20. Grandin 2007.

21. Lakoff 2007; Masco 2004.

22. Greenhalgh 2008: 13.

23. Gupta 2012; Hertzfeld 1993; Hull 2012.

24. Mitchell 1990: 571; Mitchell 1991.

25. Ballestero 2012; Hetherington 2011; Mathews 2011.

26. Merry 2011; Strathern 2000.

27. Key works in the growing anthropological literature on transparency include Ballestero 2012; Hetherington 2012; and Mathews 2011.

28. Paley 2008.

29. Harvey 2005; Ong 1999 and 2006.

30. For the mechanisms of deniability, see Cohen 2001.

31. This project constitutes a contribution to the growing field of critical security studies, as called for by Daniel Goldstein 2010.

32. Heyman 1999; Tilly 1992.

33. O'Neill and Thomas 2011; Priest 2004; Singer 2007; Simon 2009.

34. Gupta 2014.

35. Key works on expertise include Mitchell 1991; see also Carr 2010.

36. Carr 2010; Mathews 2011; Mosse 2004 and 2007.

37. I left WOLA because I discovered that I was more interested in analyzing political narratives than producing them and in conducting ethnographic research rather than advocating policy changes. I returned to graduate school and then went back to Colombia to complete the fieldwork for my dissertation. Since leaving WOLA, I have worked as a research consultant with a number of organizations, including the Centre for Humanitarian Dialogue, the Latin America Working Group, and Human Rights First, and I continue to serve on the board of directors of the Latin America Working Group.

38. My fieldwork in the region has been circumscribed by security challenges because of the complex and shifting panorama of paramilitary forces, drug-trafficking organizations, and FARC guerrillas. My travel has been restricted to the urban centers, with limited travel into *veredas* (the small hamlets in which the majority of the population live) and has necessarily relied on the assistance of Colombians.

39. For more on the challenges of fieldwork in complex conflicts and transnational bureaucracies, see Greenhouse et al. 2002.

40. Presentation at the Watson Institute for International Studies, Brown University.

41. Ho 2009: ix.

42. For more on activist anthropology, see Checker et al. 2014; Hale 2008; and Sanford and Angel-Ajani 2006.

43. Mosse 2007.

44. Gusterson 1997.

45. This research was carried out before the Wikileaks documents were released, the majority of which dealt with the later period of implementation rather than the initial policy design that was my focus at the time.

46. Chu 2010; Hull 2012; Feldman 2008.

47. Gootenberg 1999 and 2009; Massing 1998; Morone 2004; Reinarman and Levine 1997.

48. The moral weight placed on drug consumption is reflected in the particularly punitive restrictions on drug consumers and sellers who, unlike some more violent felons, are prevented from residing in public housing or receiving student loans. In one minor example, I had to sign a statement that I was drug free to receive funding from the U.S. Institute for Peace, but did not undergo a general criminal background check.

49. Unlike the Incan Empire to the south or the Aztecs and Mayans to the north, Colombia's indigenous population lived in relatively isolated small groups and today only account for approximately 4 percent of the population, one of the smallest percentage of any Latin American country.

50. Courtwright 2002.

51. The Coca-Cola Company reported $1,000,000 in sales by 1903; numerous competitors joined in the coca beverage business, nearly all employing fluid extract of coca, but very little cocaine. Gootenberg 1999.

52. Gootenberg 2009: 207.

53. Gootenberg 2009: 304. Pinochet was himself accused of selling cocaine by the late 1970s. The drug was refined at the Talagante Army chemical plant and used to fund Plan Condor, the overseas anticommunist terror network, and to enlarge his family fortune abroad.

54. Streatfeild 2003: 238.

55. Ramírez 2011.

56. Fumigation is the term widely used in policy discussions of the use of aerially sprayed chemical herbicides as a counternarcotics measure. Defoliation is another appropriate label, but here I use the more commonly used term "fumigation." In Spanish, *fumigación* is used to refer both to the aerial spraying of chemical herbicides and to the use of chemical herbicides to prevent weeds from growing in one's garden or crops.

57. In a few cases, the United States has supported insurgent forces—when U.S. interests have been challenged or in the case of struggles against reformist or communist regimes. Instances include Teddy Roosevelt's support of insurgents in what became Panama after the Colombian congress rejected the U.S. request for canal rights in 1903 and U.S. support for the Contra forces fighting against the Sandinista government and for the Cuban exiles who attempted to ignite an insurrection against Fidel Castro.

58. Anthropologist Lesley Gill (2004) graphically demonstrates the limitations of this training in her ethnographic encounters with U.S. and Latin American officers participating in it. More than 10,000 Colombians have been trained in the past decade by the United States at the Western Hemisphere Institute for Security Cooperation (formerly the School

of the Americas); they make up one of the largest contingent of officers of any country in Latin America.

Chapter 1

1. Full text of the speech is available online from the Dwight D. Eisenhower Presidential library at http://www.eisenhower.archives.gov/research/online_documents/farewell_address/Reading_Copy.pdf. Accessed December 29, 2014.

2. Gusterson 2007.

3. Enloe 2000.

4. Belkin 2012; Lutz 2002; MacLeish 2013.

5. Goldstein 2010.

6. Masco 2006.

7. Gusterson 1998; Lakoff 2007; Masco 2006.

8. Withers et al. 2008.

9. Lutz 2009; Vine 2011.

10. Priest 2004: 97.

11. Priest 2004; Withers et al. 2008.

12. Here I draw on Ana Tsing's analysis of the importance of the "sticky materiality of practical encounters" in her work on the friction in global encounters (2004). See also Peter Andreas and Kelly Greenhill on sticky and magical numbers in "Introduction: the Politics of Numbers," in *Sex, Drugs and Body Counts* (2010).

13. Navaro-Yashin 2006: 282. See also Navaro-Yashin 2012.

14. Massing 1998.

15. Quoted in Morone 2004: 407.

16. Gladwell 1998.

17. Quoted in Massing 1998: 144.

18. Massing 1998: 148.

19. Gladwell 1998.

20. Quoted in Massing 1998: 199.

21. Reinarman and Levine 1997. For more on the impact of drug consumption and counternarcotics policies on poor communities, see Bourgois 2002; Bourgois and Schonberg 2009; Campbell 2009; Garcia 2010; and Hart 2014.

22. FitzGerald 2013; Fleck 2013; Paltrow and Flavin 2013; and Siegel 1997.

23. See Alexander 2012; Beckett and Herbert 2009; Natapoff 2011; Simon 2009; and Wacquant 2009.

24. Crandall 2002: 32.

25. Downie 1998.

26. Cited in Andreas and Nadelmann 2008: 158.

27. Lakoff 2007.

28. Dana Priest quoted chairman of the Joint Chiefs of Staff General Shalikashvili as saying, "Real men don't do MOOTW" (2004: 56).

29. Zirnite 1997: 12.

30. Thomas 1994.

31. Andreas and Price 2001: 40.

32. Crandall 2002: 35.

33. The U.S. Congress requires the State Department to issue a yearly certification of foreign governments, assessing their degree of cooperation with U.S. counternarcotics operations. Failure to be certified results in the suspension of nonmilitary aid, in addition to other sanctions.

34. Crandall 202: 106.

35. The legislation was first passed as an amendment in 1996, and made into permanent law in 2008. For the sake of clarity, the legislation is referred to as the Leahy Law throughout the book.

36. However, even during this period, Colombia did not receive the attention of high-level foreign policy officials; rather, the policy was driven by middle-level officials (Crandall 2002: 4).

37. "International Drug Control Policy: Colombia," Hearing Before the Subcommittee on National Security, International Affairs and Criminal Justice, Committee on Government Reform and Oversight, House of Representatives, 105th Congress. First Session, July 9, 1997. http://www.gpo.gov/fdsys/pkg/CHRG-105hhrg45991/html/CHRG-105hhrg 45991.htm.

38. Directorate of Intelligence, Intelligence Memorandum, Office of Africa and Latin America, "Colombian Counterinsurgency: Steps in the Right Direction," January 26, 1994. Obtained by the National Security Archive, available at http://www2.gwu.edu/~nsarchiv /NSAEBB/NSAEBB266/19940126.pdf.

39. U.S. Embassy Bogotá cable, "Ambassador's January 12 Meeting with New MOD [Minister of Defense] Designate," January 13, 1997, obtained by National Security Archive. http://www.gwu.edu/~nsarchiv/NSAEBB/NSAEBB69/col51.pdf.

40. State Department Embassy cable 1997 0312, "Ambassador's January 12 Meeting with New MOD Designate," January 13, 1997. Secret.

41. Quoted in Youngers 2001: 24.

42. Molano 1989.

43. Dudley 2003; Romero 2005, 2007.

44. Pizarro 2011: 196.

45. Bagley 2001.

46. Chernick 2005.

47. Pax Christi Netherlands 2001.

48. Centro Nacional de Memoria Historica 2013.

49. Pizarro 2011: 232.

50. Lakoff 2007.

51. Caldeira 2001; Comaroff and Comaroff 2006; Goffman 2014; Simon 2009.

52. Feldman 2005.

53. Planned for release in the fall of 2001, the movie was held until late 2002 because of fears that a nation traumatized by the 9/11 attacks would not respond to the theme of domestic terrorism.

Chapter 2

1. Anthropologists have traced the ways in which human rights campaigns have erased cultural difference and local understandings of justice and obligation: Abu-Lughod 2013; Allen 2013; Cowan et al. 2001; Merry 2006; Speed 2007.

2. Talal Asad posited that the critical anthropological question is, what do human rights do? Asad 2000.

3. Davis et al. 2012; Merry 2011; Rosga and Satterthwaite 2009.

4. Congressional approval is required on some foreign policy issues. The Senate must approve the appointments of ambassadors and senior officials, and two-thirds must ratify international treaties. Congressional approval is also required for trade and commercial treaties. Congress can also set statutory guidelines, such as requiring that the State Department submit certification reports confirming that the recipient of the funding has met certain requirements.

5. Singh et al. 2005.

6. Officially known as "Legislative Service Organizations," the caucuses were substantially weakened, and many disbanded, as a result of Speaker of the House (1994–1999) Newt Gingrich's efforts to restructure congressional committee assignments which included precluding member offices from using their budgets to support these groups.

7. Arnson 1993.

8. Drezner 2000; Hartmann 2001.

9. Leogrande 2000.

10. Arnson 1993.

11. Smith 1996: 216.

12. Smith 1996: 227.

13. See Smith 1996.

14. Cunningham 1999.

15. Anthropologists and others exploring the ways in which "credibility" as an epistemological category is culturally produced include Andreas and Greenhill 2010; Comaroff and Comaroff 2006; and Rosa and Satterthwaite 2009.

16. For more on the history of Colombian human rights groups, see Tate 2007.

17. Cohen 1982.

18. According to U.S. embassy cables, the document was prepared in response to a request from the Colombian desk officer in the State Department and was then released to the journalists. 1996 11 21—Bogotá cable, "Amnesty International Statement on U.S. Military Assistance in Colombia" [Sec Asst].

19. Although it did not dispute the information in the list, the embassy claimed that the list "in no way constitutes confirmation on the part of the United States government of

AIUSA's specific allegations of human rights violations by the listed Colombian military units, much less any U.S. equipment my have been involved." 1996 11 27—Bogotá cable, "Correcting the Record Concerning Amnesty International, USA's Press Release that "U.S. Confirms It Armed Colombian Killers." [Sec Asst].

20. Officials note, however, that the embassy cannot prevent training from being provided. Rather, it issues its judgment, and then "the Marines have ten days to tell congress, to go to congress to explain why they went ahead with the training. The burden of proof is on the applicant."

21. Gupta 2012; Goldstein 2012; Herzfeld 1993.

22. Barnett 1997: 562.

23. 1997 04 28—Bogotá cable, "506 and 614: Best and Final Offer to MOD" [Sec Asst].

24. The U.S. Congress requires the State Department to issue a yearly certification of foreign governments, assessing their degree of cooperation with U.S. counternarcotics operations. Failure to be certified results in the suspension of nonmilitary aid, in addition to other sanctions.

25. Avilés 2006.

26. For the history of U.S.-Colombia military relations, see Coleman 2008 and Tate 2007, chapter 8.

27. Isacson 2010; Pardo 1996. The Lleras pact was named for a 1958 speech in which then president Alberto Lleras Camargo urged the military to refrain from political intervention in exchange for institutional autonomy.

28. 1997 04 29—Bogotá Cable, "Ambassador's April 28 Meeting with President Samper" [EUM].

29. 1997 06 16—Cable, "Ambassador's June 13 Conversation with Defmin Echeverri" [Folder: Sec Asst] State Department Embassy Cable 05740, "Ambassador's june 13 conversation with defmin echeverri," June 16, 1997. Confidential.

30. U.S. Embassy Colombia cable, "CODEL [Congressional Delegation] Hastert's May 24–27 Visit to Colombia," May 28, 1997, Secret, 28 pp.

31. 1997 07 08—Bogotá cable, "Bedoya Lawyer Blocks EUM Accord" [EUM] State Department. Embassy Cable 06461, "Bedoya Lawyers blocks EUM accord," July 8, 1997. Confidential.

32. State Department Embassy Cable 006705, "EUM talks with Defmin at Dead End; Recommendation," July 14, 1997. Confidential.

33. Merry 2011; Warren 2012.

34. Ballestero 2012; Hetherington 2011; Li 2007.

35. Human Rights Watch 2002.

36. State Department Embassy Cable 011674, "Ambassador and Minister Lloreda on Leahy Amendment," October 16, 1998. Confidential.

37. U.S. Embassy personnel in-country are unable to conduct independent verification of allegations, because of the lack of personnel, investigative training, and a mandate in foreign countries.

38. Rendón and Lindsay-Poland 2008.

39. For Ambassador meeting with Minister Lloreda, Drafter WSRowland 04/22/99. Confidential.

40. GAO report, p. 55.

41. Haugaard and Nichols 2010.

42. State Department Embassy Cable 002520, "Colombia EUM: Analysis of Specific Human Rights Cases," March 6, 1998. Confidential.

43. The 24th Brigade was listed for conditional aid pending the removal of two individuals and "we leave it to Washington" to determine the aid status of the 3rd, 7th, 12th, and BRIM2State Department Embassy Cable 002520, "Colombia EUM: Analysis of Specific Human Rights Cases," 6 March 1998. Confidential.

44. State Department Embassy Cable 11602, "Colombian Army Counter-Narcotics Battalion Proposed for USG Assistance," October 15, 1998. Confidential.

45. State Department Embassy Cable 011674, "Ambassador and Minister Lloreda on Leahy Amendment," October 16, 1998. Confidential.

46. Schmitt 2013.

Chapter 3

1. Strange 1996.

2. Bornstein 2012; Ferguson 1994; Gupta 2012.

3. Caldeira 2001; Dickins de Girón 2011; Heyman 1999; Singer 2007.

4. Mbembe 2003.

5. O'Neill and Thomas 2011; Poole 2004.

6. Heyman 1999.

7. Deleuze and Guattari 1986.

8. Ballvé 2012; López 2010; Romero 2005, 2007.

9. Rabasa and Chalk 2001.

10. Mathews 2008: 487.

11. Taussig 1999; Green 1999; Feitlowitz 2011.

12. McClintock 1992; Porch 2013.

13. For ethnographic consideration of these issues in other cases, see Starn 1999 on the rondas campesinas (peasant militias) in Peru, and Remijnse 2001 on the civil patrols in Guatemala.

14. Campbell and Brenner 2002; Sluka 1999.

15. Gill 2004.

16. McClintock 1992.

17. LAWG 1997.

18. LAWG 1997.

19. Rempe 2002: 13.

20. Rempe 2002: 17.

21. McClintock 1992.

22. For more on the history of the Colombian military, see Blair Trujillo 1993; Isacson 2010; and Roldán 2002.

23. Richani 2014: 42.

24. Isacson 2010.

25. No charges were ever brought. Jiménez Gómez 1986.

26. Palacios 2006.

27. Dudley 2003; Kirk 2004.

28. Evans 2011.

29. Gill 2004.

30. Human Rights Watch 2001; Ramírez et al. 2012; Taussig 2005.

31. Human Rights Watch 1995, 1998b.

32. Caballero 2000.

33. Garcia-Godos and Lid 2010.

34. Proponents included journalist Robert Kaplan, who originated the most extreme view in his influential 1994 *Atlantic* article, "The Coming Anarchy," which was reportedly faxed to every U.S. embassy and widely circulated within the Clinton administration (Besteman 2005). Beginning in 1994, the CIA funded a research project called "The State Failure Task Force" based at the University of Maryland (Call 2008). By the mid 2000s, World Bank initiatives targeted failed states, and *Foreign Policy* produced a yearly "failed state index."

35. Call 2008.

36. Zackrison and Bailey 1997.

37. Rotberg 2002.

38. DeWinc 1999.

39. Bejarano 2004.

40. Spencer 2001: 2.

41. Spencer 2001: 11.

42. Spencer 2001: 14.

43. For an alternative accounting of the massacre, see "Mapiripán: A Shortcut to Hell," by award-winning Colombian journalist María Cristina Caballero, first published in *Cambio16*, in the July 28 and November 3, 1997, issues and translated and published in the *Colombian Labor Monitor*, August 29, 1999, http://www.hartford-hwp.com/archives/42/074.html.

44. Council on Foreign Relations, "Backgrounder: FARC, ELN, AUC," http://www.cfr.org/publications/colombia. The website was later updated with more extensive background publications on the guerrillas and on the paramilitary demobilization and the *parapolítica* scandal.

45. According to interviews with State Department officials, DRL faced significant pressure to dilute its reporting even further.

46. Taussig 1999.

47. Paragraph 134, "Report of the U.N. High Commissioner for Human Rights on the human rights situation in Colombia," E/CN.4/2001/15, February 8, 2001, http://www.hrw.org /legacy/reports/2001/colombia/2.2.htm - N_77_#N_77_.

48. WOLA sponsored the delegation, which meant covering its costs through special fundraising, organizing the itinerary, and leading the actual trip; as the WOLA Colombia analyst, I organized much of the trip and acted as the group's leader while in Colombia.

49. Oscar Romero was a Salvadoran bishop assassinated by soldiers while saying mass in 1980 after publicly denouncing the military, which was supported by the U.S. government, and demanding they purge its forces of abusive officers.

50. Allen 2013: 131.

Chapter 4

1. It is important to note that there are thirteen officially recognized indigenous groups in the region with distinct forms of indigenous sovereignty exercised within their territories and among community members; these groups are not addressed here.

2. Nordstrom 2004.

3. Centro Nacional de Memoria Historica 2012.

4. Comaroff 1998: 339.

5. Gupta 1995.

6. Reyes Posada 2009.

7. Stanfield 1998; Taussig 1991.

8. Torres Bustamente 2011.

9. For comparative cases see Caldeira 2001 for Brazil, Coutin 2007 for El Salvador, and Goldstein 2012 for Bolivia.

10. Bocarejo 2012; Goldstein 2012; Kernaghan 2009.

11. Ferguson 1994; Gupta 1994 and 2012; Krupa 2010; Nugent 1997; Scott 1999.

12. Reyes Posada 2009; Thomson 2011.

13. Quoted in Thompson 2011.

14. Thomson 2011: 336.

15. Zamosc 2006.

16. Reyes Posada 2009.

17. In 1988, the Gini Coefficient for land in Colombia was .86, with 0.0 being perfect equality and 1.0 representing complete inequality of land distribution. For comparison: Brazil (0.85), Peru (0.91), Korea (0.35), and Taiwan (0.45). See Giugale et al. 2003: 490.

18. In the late 1990s, approximately 75 percent of agricultural land was used for grazing (Deininger 1999).

19. The *Caja Agraria* (established in 1931), a state agency that was the main source of such services, dramatically decreased the amount of credit it provided because of macroeconomic factors including peso devaluation and government restructuring, even as loans available to ranchers through the *Banco Ganadero* increased. The Caja Agraria was liqui-

dated in 1999, replaced by the Banco Agrario, which functions more like a private bank and thereby excluding the majority of small farmers from access to loans because of insufficient collateral (Ardila Galvis 2011).

20. After a final refining process, cocaine is shipped north, where it sells for as much as $2,800 an ounce on the streets.

21. Bowden 2002.

22. Kenney 2008.

23. Transnational Institute 1999.

24. The program was suspended after the 2001 death of a U.S. missionary and her baby in a plane shot down by the Peruvian air force using U.S. intelligence from a CIA contractor.

25. FARC penalties imposed on their own troops were extremely harsh. According to Human Rights Watch, the most serious infractions of the FARC's military code include falling asleep while on guard duty, trying to run away or being absent without leave, surrendering, losing a weapon, being an informer or infiltrator, using a weapon against a fellow FARC combatant, firing guns in populated areas, and committing robbery, extortion, and violence against the civilian population, repeated drug or alcohol abuse, and rape. These "capital offenses" are punishable by execution without regard to the offender's age (Human Rights Watch 1998).

26. Ferro and Uribe Roman 2002: 43.

27. Ferro and Uribe Roman 2002: 43.

28. Within Putumayo, the Catholic Church has played an extremely important role. In a frontier region with minimal state presence, the church was positioned to fully exploit the special powers granted to it by the 1886 Constitution. From 1896 until the early 1970s, the Capuchin Order was authorized to provide education services, build infrastructure, and evangelize and colonize what are now known as Caquetá, Putumayo, and Amazonas. In 1951, the region was upgraded to a new ecclesiastical administrative level, and the three areas were separated, with the Putumayo Apostolic Vicariate operating out of Sibundoy. During this period, the Catholic welfare program Social Action significantly expanded its programs in the region, as it did throughout the country. By the 1970s, the first generation of local boys were educated and consecrated as priests, self-described "native sons" who were then assigned to parishes throughout the region and given significant latitude for local initiatives by then Bishop Arcadio Bernal Supelano. These priests worked to connect Putumayo farmers in remote hamlets to national and transnational networks promoting popular education, sustainable development, and human rights.

29. The FARC's official position is to reject all organized religion; like many guerrilla forces, however, in practice many of the troops retain their religious practices.

30. Bocarejo 2012.

31. Ramírez et al. 2010: 13.

32. Hoyos and Ceballos 2004: 4.

33. Torres Bustamente 2011.

34. Subsequent difficulties in consolidating their political offices included finding people willing to serve as public officials, given the lack of public resources, widespread criminality, and the lucrative alternative of the coca trade. In 1991, a new Constitution allowed the election of governors, as well as enshrining a number of new rights. That year, Putumayo was declared a department, rather than an *intendencia* or nationally administered colony, with the capacity to elect regional assemblies, a governor, and congressional representatives.

35. Gacha opened production operations into Putumayo because of crackdowns on the Medellín Cartel's operations in other regions. A joint DEA-CNP operation in 1984 confiscated 13.8 tons of cocaine from the largest lab, Tranquilandia, located in neighboring Caqueta. Prior to the raid, the site had the capacity to produce 5,000 kilos a week.

36. Ramírez 2011: 45.

37. Ramírez 2011: 49.

38. Ramírez et al. 2010: 15.

39. Comisión Colombiana de Juristas 1993.

40. Tate 2007.

41. The other leader of the committee entered the FARC, and became one of the region's well-known political leaders of the guerrillas.

42. "Ponencia," Movimiento Cívico 1997.

43. Rabasa and Chalk 2001.

44. Alther 2006; Sanford 2003.

45. The FARC was somewhat of an exception; an estimated 40% of its forces are girls and women, although women are not proportionately represented within the command structure.

46. Jansson 2008: 236; see also Ramírez et al. 2012.

47. The Office of the United Nations High Commissioner for Human Rights in Colombia reported repeatedly officially informing the Colombian government of links between paramilitary and military forces in the Putumayo region during this time period, to no effect.

Chapter 5

1. Plan Colombia Fact Sheet, Bureau of Western Hemisphere Affairs, Washington, DC, March 14, 2001.

2. Mosse 2004, 2007.

3. Mosse 2004: 11.

4. For more on frame alignment theory, see David Snow et al. 1986 and Benford and Snow 2000. For an example of a case study of frames used to articulate specific foreign policy alternatives, see Smith, 1996: 231–79. This theory was developed as a bridge between social psychological and resource mobilization views, based on Irving Goffman's "frame," which functions to organize experience and guide action.

5. Felstiner et al. 1980.

6. Mosse 2004.

7. Isikoff and Vistica 2000.

8. Pastrana Arango and Guillén 2014: 51.

9. September 1998, from Embassy bot to Secstate Was DC; Subject: Pastrana mtg w USAID AA/LAC Schneider on Peace, Alternative dev.

10. Godoy 2003: 8.

11. Pastrana's talking points in support to the despeje emphasized that the region, which contained 11 percent of the area known as the Eastern Plains (*Llanos Orientales*), housed only .2 percent of the national population. The largest town, San Vicente del Caguán, had 25,000 inhabitants and only intermittent electricity.

12. Participants Sheridan, Beers, and Bill Brownfield (WHA) were at the assistant secretary level.

13. Fax/Memo May 10, 2000 to OSD/SOLIC, others, from Task Force/Mack; re Colombia trip SVTS May 10, "To discuss Pickering visit to Colombia, WHA Brownfield and Mack chair mtg."

14. Feb 98 from amembassy to sec state wash, Subject: visit by beers.

15. May 1998 from sec state washdc to amembassy bta; Subject: Colombia '98 cn initiative.

16. July 2, 1998 Memo: DOD coordinator for Drug enforcement policy and support; from acting dep asst sec of defense for drug enforcement policy and support; prepared by Salvador Enriquez, DEP&S.

17. July 2, 1998 Memo: DOD coordinator for Drug enforcement policy and support; from acting dep asst sec of defense for drug enforcement policy and support; prepared by Salvador Enriquez, DEP&S.

18. July 2, 1998 DOD Coordinator Drug Enforcement Policy and Support; memo for Sec Defense, deputy sec defense through under secretary of defense for policy; from asst sec of defense fro special op and low intensity conflict; prepared by Salvador Enriquez, DEP&S Subject: read ahead for July 7 1998 principals metc on Panama-Colombia information memo.

19. July 28 1999—Bogotá cable, "A/S Beers Meets with MOD and Armed Forces Chief" [Plan Colombia].

20. General Accounting Office 1999.

21. Douglas Farah, "U.S. Ready To Boost Aid To Troubled Colombia," *Washington Post* (Washington: August 23, 1999): A1. http://www.washingtonpost.com/wp-srv/inatl/daily/aug99/colombia23.htm.

22. Pizarro Leongomez 2011: note 4, p. 273.

23. Tickner 2007.

24. July 17, 2000 to DRL Koh, through DRL Freeman, From DRL Peter Higgins. Subject: mtg with Colombian Ambassador Luis Alberto Moreno, July 18.

25. Davis 2007: A6.

26. Carter campaigned for decriminalization of marijuana for personal use; after being attacked by Republicans, he supported a hard-line drug policy in the second half of his presidency.

27. Shinnick 1999.

28. 11 nov 98 acting A/S Romero's visit to Bogotá, November 8-10 1998. Confidential.

29. Another dispute over the rule of law programs involved their focus. AID and Opdat (Office of Overseas Prosecutorial Development, Assistance and Training of the Department of Justice) wanted to focus on justice reform, strengthening the justice sector in general. INL wanted to use the programs to create prosecutors to investigate drug traffickers and to provide protection for judges in drug-trafficking cases. The debate was over proportion and focus.

30. Cohn 1987.

31. Isikoff and Vistica 2000.

32. Barstow 2008.

33. Wallace-Wells 2007.

Chapter 6

1. Other projects with a similar dynamic include humanitarianism and human rights. Fassin 2011; Ticktin 2011.

2. Stoler 2002, 2010.

3. Bahre 2007; Chomsky and Striffler 2008; Gill 2005 and 2009; Gill and Kasmir 2009.

4. Bob 2012; Rutherford 2009.

5. Masco 2008.

6. Greenhalgh 2008.

7. Babb 2010.

8. Merrill 2009.

9. Pezzullo 2009; Sharpley 2009; Stein 2008.

10. Allen 2009.

11. Perla 2008; Smith 1996.

12. Stern 2006.

13. One of the major legislative strategies pursued by U.S. NGOs was to place conditions in the aid package requiring the State Department to certify Colombian progress on specific human rights measures, as well as mandating periodic meetings with human rights NGOs to discuss these issues. If the conditions were not met, the United States was required to suspend a portion of some aid programs. These conditions were modeled on previous human rights conditions written into aid packages for Serbia and Peru. Human Rights Watch was the primary organization involved in these conditions' creation and monitoring; its strategy focused on building relationships with allied congressional representatives and staff and lacked a significant grassroots component. The first conditions written into the initial Plan Colombia package focused primarily on human rights issues.

The requirements included a presidential decree mandating that military officers accused of human rights abuses be tried in civilian courts; that military officers credibly accused of abuses be suspended from duty; Armed Forces cooperation with investigations of human rights cases; and vigorous prosecution in civilian courts of paramilitary leaders. The final two conditions required the Colombian government to implement a strategy to eliminate poppy and coca production by 2005 and to create and field a Judge Advocate General Corps to investigate military misconduct. Placed in the budget yearly, through the work of Leahy staff, the conditions were adjusted over the coming years to reflect changes in the human rights situation in Colombia.

14. Griffin-Nolan 1991.

15. For an exception, see Chomsky 2008.

16. Cunningham 1995; García 2006; Perla 2008; Perla and Coutin 2010.

17. Even in areas where the United Nation and others anticipated large refugee populations, such as along the border with Ecuador, shelters stood empty for a range of reasons, including the strength of Colombia's economy compared to the neighbors, growing urbanization, and the long history of internal displacement in the face of political violence. (Increasing international awareness of the humanitarian crisis during the 1990s led to an increase in humanitarian assistance provided by international organizations within the country.)

18. This dynamic exists throughout the Americas. In urban Brazil, critics of police brutality have been dismissed by accusations that they care only for the "rights for bandits" and criminals (Caldeira and Holston 2009). In Peru, the human rights community and local communities in conflictive zones engaged in extensive and controversial debates over the importance of innocence in defending victims of abuse (Theidon 2010). After the imposition of sweeping antiterrorist legislation, NGOs adopted a "campaign for the innocents," defending individuals wrongly imprisoned but refusing to take the cases of members of the Shining Path, even if they suffered torture while incarcerated. In the Peruvian case, during the debate over the reach of the truth and reparations committee, legal advisors discussed what is known as the "clean hands doctrine," a legal principle that established eligibility for reparations depending on the degree of criminal involvement. This debate focused on whether to provide reparations to families whose Shining Path relatives had been killed while in government custody (LaPlante 2009). Similarly, there is an extensive literature documenting the importance of the production of specific forms of political identities, including innocence, in political asylum claims (Coutin 2007).

19. Chernick 2005.

20. Perla 2008.

21. Congressional travel is generally ranked in two categories: "windshield tours," luxury junkets in which the local population is observed only from the windshield from the airport to the resort, and trips orchestrated to educate and increase congressional interest and engagement in particular issues.

22. Direct contact with foreign officials allowed members of Congress to express alternative policy priorities and support particular projects that they felt were not sufficiently championed by official State Department policy positions. In some cases, members of Congress went so far as to explicitly oppose official policy or to orchestrate their own policy initiatives, as in the case of Hastert's opposition to the Leahy Law. The most famous example of a member of Congress using travel and his position on Capital Hill to engineer policy was Texas Democrat Charlie Wilson's support for the Mujahedeen in Afghanistan (Crile 2003).

23. Borneman 2011; Kwon 2006, 2008.

24. Davis 2004.

25. Carr 2010: 21.

26. Lutz 2006.

27. Gusterson 1998; Masco 2004, 2006.

28. Masco 2004.

29. Garcia 2010.

30. Bourgois and Shonberg 2009; MacCoun and Reuter 2001.

Chapter 7

1. Ramírez 2010; Jansson 2008.

2. Tsing 1993: 90.

3. Ramírez et al. 2012.

4. Proxy citizenship emerges from the multiple ways in which contemporary citizenship can be disassembled into particular rights and obligations. Histories of citizenship have documented how the rights and obligations conferred by a state to members of the nation have been expanded to new categories of rights-bearing and claiming subjects, producing new forms of citizenship subjectivities. At the same time, ethnographic inquiry illuminates the ways in which citizenship is unevenly accessible to distinct groups, genders, races, and classes within the same nation-state (Fikes 2009), described as disjunctive citizenship in the case of Brazil (Caldeira and Holston 1999; Holston 2008). Migration and flows of labor and capital have created transnational political fields and deterritorialized the lived experiences of citizenship and the legal categories available to migrants (Coutin 2000, 2007), including what Ong (2006) describes as "mutations" disaggregating the component parts of citizenship among mobile populations. Histories of U.S. citizenship struggles reveal how the obligations of citizenship—paying taxes, periodic military service, being subject to restrictive legislation—can be legally and in practice separated from the rights and rewards of citizenship, such as voting, political participation, and entitlement programs (Brodkin 1998).

5. The shift from labor solidarity to labor philanthropy in the case of campaigns to support unionized Colombian Coca-Cola workers (Gill 2009)—what Chomsky and Striffler (2008) call solidarity-charity in the case of coal workers—traces a similar process of political transformation.

6. Strathern 1990.

7. Greenhouse 2002: 196.

8. Cowan 2008: 250.

9. President Alvaro Uribe also refused to address the governors' concerns; Ramírez 2011.

10. Ramírez 2011.

11. Ramírez 2011.

12. Marsh 2004.

13. Gupta 1995: 384.

14. Ferguson 1994.

15. Grisaffi 2010; Ramírez 2011.

16. Checker et al. 2004; Fortun 2001; Nelson 2013.

17. Beverley and Zimmerman 1990; Gugelberger 1996.

18. Keck and Sikkink 1998; Perla 2008.

19. Carr 2010.

20. Andreas and Greenhill 2010; Comaroff and Comaroff 2006; Greenhaghl 2008; Redfield 2006; Rosga and Satterthwaite 2009.

21. Butler 1997.

22. Cowan 2008: 250.

23. Baxstrom et al. 2005.

24. Lorentzen 1991.

25. Perla and Coutin 2010: 12.

26. Arias 2001.

27. Carr 2010: 21.

28. Cockburn 2007.

29. Allen 2009; Fassin 2008.

30. Cattelino 2010; Fortun 2001; Redfield 2012.

31. Feldman 2004; Hinton 2010; Shaw et al. 2010; Theidon 2012; Wilson 2001.

32. Fassin 2008; Redfield 2006; Ticktin 2011; Wilson and Brown 2011.

33. Bishara 2010; Poole 2004.

34. Other work has examined more fully the larger social worlds of these networks, revealing clearly the multiple ways in which such activism is contested and critiqued (Fitz-Henry 2011) as "tourist commissions" or "jet-set campesinos" (Edelman 2005), rather than worthy activist advocacy.

35. Tsing 2004.

Conclusion

1. Coles 2007; Paley 2001, 2008.

2. Guilhot 2005.

3. Kaplan 2008.

4. Boot and Bennet 2009.

5. DeShazo et al. 2007.

6. Bahney and Gereben Schaefer 2009.

7. MacCoun and Reuter 2001.

8. Garcia 2010.

9. Isacson 2006.

10. Ramírez 2011.

11. Bahney and Gereben Schaefer 2009.

12. Boot and Bennet 2009.

13. *Semana* 2006.

14. López 2010: 27.

15. López 2010; Romero, 2007. Colombian investigative journalists with international funding have compiled investigative reporting on the website *Verdad Abierta* (The Open Truth, http://www.verdadabierta.com).

16. López 2010: 461.

17. *Semana* 2006.

18. Evidence that members of Congress tied to paramilitaries followed the executive's lead also raises questions about the role of the Uribe administration in reconfiguring the state. The painstaking analysis in six chapters in *Y refundaron la patria* of legislative action by members of Congress implicated in the scandal leads researchers to conclude that the politicians supported by paramilitaries did not have a collective legislative agenda, but did tend to serve on a specific set of committees, including appropriations, judicial and political reform, and agrarian issues. In this role, they helped consolidate the power of the executive, following Uribe's lead in a series of controversial bills, including the constitutional amendment allowing for his reelection and the so-called Peace and Justice Law, which set the terms for paramilitary demobilization.

19. Romero 2005, 2007, 2011.

20. Human Rights Watch 2005, 2008, 2010; International Crisis Group 2007.

21. García-Peña 2009.

22. Angulo 2009.

23. Reyes Posada 2009.

24. Ardila Galvis 2011; Ballvé 2012.

25. Priest 2013.

26. Human Rights Watch 2005.

27. Otis 2009.

28. Rand Corporation, *The Effectiveness of U.S. Training Efforts in Internal Defense and Development: The Cases of El Salvador and Honduras*, p. 80.

29. Ibid., p. 79.

30. Goldstein 2010.

31. Theidon 2007, 2009.

Bibliography

Abu-Lughod, Lila. 2013. *Do Muslim Women Need Saving?* Cambridge, MA: Harvard University Press.

Alexander, Michelle. 2012. *The New Jim Crow: Mass Incarceration in the Age of Colorblindness.* New York: The New Press.

Allen, Lori. 2009. "Martyr Bodies in the Media: Human Rights, Aesthetics, and the Politics of Immediation in the Palestinian Intifada." *American Ethnologist* 36 (1): 161–80. doi:10.1111/j.1548-1425.2008.01100.x.

———. 2013. *The Rise and Fall of Human Rights: Cynicism and Politics in Occupied Palestine.* Stanford, CA: Stanford University Press.

Alther, Gretchen. 2006. "Colombian Peace Communities: The Role of NGOs in Supporting Resistance to Violence and Oppression." *Development in Practice* 16, no. 03–04: 278–91. doi:10.1080/09614520600694828.

Andreas, Peter, and Kelly M. Greenhill. 2010. *Sex, Drugs, and Body Counts: The Politics of Numbers in Global Crime and Conflict.* Ithaca, NY: Cornell University Press.

Andreas, Peter, and Ethan Nadelmann. 2008. *Policing the Globe: Criminalization and Crime Control in International Relations.* Oxford: Oxford University Press.

Andreas, Peter, and Richard Price. 2001. "From War Fighting to Crime Fighting: Transforming the American National Security State." *International Studies Review* 3 (3): 31–52. doi:10.1111/1521-9488.00243.

Angulo, Alejandro. 2009. *The Rearrangement.* Bogotá: Centro de Investigación y Educación Popular.

Ardila Galvis, Camilo Andrés. 2011. *Agrarian Change and Rural Poverty in Colombia.* The Hague: Erasmus Unviersitieit Rotterdam Graduate School of Development Studies. oaithesis.eur.nl.

Arias, Arturo, ed. 2001. *The Rigoberta Menchú Controversy.* Minneapolis: University of Minnesota Press.

Arnson, Cynthia. 1993. *Crossroads: Congress, the President, and Central America, 1976–1993.* University Park: Penn State University Press.

Asad, Talal. 2000. "What Do Human Rights Do? An Anthropological Enquiry." *Theory & Event* 4 (4).

Avilés, William. 2006. *Global Capitalism, Democracy, and Civil-Military Relations in Colombia*. Albany: State University of New York Press.

Babb, Florence. 2010. *The Tourism Encounter: Fashioning Latin American Nations and Histories*. Stanford, CA: Stanford University Press.

Bagley, Bruce. 2001. "Drug Trafficking, Political Violence and U.S. Policy in Colombia in the 1990s." University of California at Berkeley. http://clasarchive.berkeley.edu/Events /conferences/Colombia/workingpapers.html.

Bahney, Benjamin, and Agnes Gereben Schaefer. 2009. "Assessing Mexico's Narco-Violence | RAND Blog." The *San Diego Union-Tribune*. May 19. Accessed September 16, 2014. http:// www.rand.org/blog/2009/05/assessing-mexicos-narco-violence.html.

Bähre, Erik. 2007. "Reluctant Solidarity." *Ethnography* 8 (1): 33–59. doi:10.1177/1466138107076136.

Ballestero S., Andrea. 2012. "Transparency Short-Circuited: Laughter and Numbers in Costa Rican Water Politics." *PoLAR: Political and Legal Anthropology Review* 35 (2): 223–41.

Ballvé, Teo. 2012. "Everyday State Formation: Territory, Decentralization, and the Narco Land-grab in Colombia." *Environment and Planning D: Society and Space* 30 (4): 603–22.

Barnett, Michael N. 1997. "The UN Security Council, Indifference, and Genocide in Rwanda." *Cultural Anthropology* 12 (4): 551–78.

Barstow, David. 2008. "One Man's Military-Industrial-Media Complex." *New York Times*, November 29.

Baxstrom, Richard, Naveeda Khan, Deborah Poole, and Bhrigupati Singh. 2005. "Networks Actual and Potential: Think Tanks, War Games and the Creation of Contemporary American Politics." *Theory & Event* 8, no. 4. http://muse.jhu.edu/journals/theory_and _event/v008/8.4singh.html.

Beckett, Katherine, and Steve Herbert. 2009. *Banished: The New Social Control in Urban America*. New York: Oxford University Press.

Bejarano, Ana Maria. 2004. "Colombia: The Partial Collapse of the State and the Emergence of Aspiring State-Makers." In *States Within States: Incipient Political Entities in the Post-Cold War Era*, edited by Paul Kingston and Ian Spears. 99–118. New York: Palgrave Macmillan.

Belkin, Aaron. 2012. *Bring Me Men: Military Masculinity and the Benign Facade of American Empire, 1898–2001*. New York: Oxford University Press.

Benford, Robert D., and David A. Snow. 2000. "Framing Processes and Social Movements: An Overview and Assessment." *Annual Review of Sociology* 26, no. 1: 611–39. doi:10.1146/ annurev.soc.26.1.611.

Besteman, Catherine. 2005. "Why I Disagree with Robert Kaplan." In *Why America's Top Pundits Are Wrong: Anthropologists Talk Back*, edited by Catherine Besteman and Hugh Gusterson. Berkeley: University of California Press.

Beverley, John, and Marc Zimmerman. 1990. *Literature and Politics in the Central American Revolutions*. Austin: University of Texas Press.

Bishara, Amahl. 2010. "Weapons, Passports, and News: Palestinian Perceptions of U.S. Power as a Mediator of War." In *Anthropology and Global Counterinsurgency*, edited by John

Kelly, Sean Mitchell, Beatrice Jauregui, and Jeremy Walton. 125–36. Chicago: University of Chicago Press.

Blair Trujillo, Elsa. 1993. *Las fuerzas armadas: Una mirada civil.* Bogotá: Cinep.

Bleiker, Roland, and Emma Hutchison. 2008. "Fear No More: Emotions and World Politics." *Review of International Studies* 34 (Supplement S1): 115–35.

Bob, Clifford. 2012. *The Global Right Wing and the Clash of World Politics.* 1st ed. Cambridge: Cambridge University Press.

Bocarejo, Diana. 2012. "Longing for the State." Unpublished manuscript.

Boot, Max, and Richard Bennet. 2009. "The Colombian Miracle." *The Weekly Standard*, December 14. http://www.weeklystandard.com/Content/Public/Articles/000/000/017/301nyrut.asp.

Borneman, John. 2011. *Political Crime and the Memory of Loss.* Bloomington: Indiana University Press.

Bornstein, Erica. 2012. *Disquieting Gifts: Humanitarianism in New Delhi.* Stanford, CA: Stanford University Press.

Bourgois, Philippe, and Jeffrey Schonberg. 2009. *Righteous Dopefiend.* Berkeley: University of California Press.

Bowden, Mark. 2002. *Killing Pablo: The Hunt for the World's Greatest Outlaw.* New York: Penguin Books.

Brodkin, Karen. 1998. *How Jews Became White Folks and What That Says About Race in America.* New Brunswick, NJ: Rutgers University Press.

Butler, Judith. 1997. *Excitable Speech: A Politics of the Performative.* New York: Psychology Press.

———. 2009. *Frames of War: When Is Life Grievable?* New York: Verso.

Caballero, Maria Cristina. 2000. "A Journalist's Mission in Colombia: Reporting Atrocities Is Not Enough." *Columbia Journalism Review*, Vol. 39, Issue 1, page 66.

Caldeira, Teresa P. R. 2001. *City of Walls: Crime, Segregation, and Citizenship in São Paulo.* Berkeley: University of California Press.

Caldeira, Teresa P. R., and James Holston. 1999. "Democracy and Violence in Brazil." *Comparative Studies in Society and History* 41 (4): 691–729.

Call, Charles T. 2008. "The Fallacy of the 'Failed State.'" *Third World Quarterly* 29 (8): 1491–1507.

Campbell, Bruce B., and Arthur D. Brenner. 2002. *Death Squads in Global Perspective: Murder with Deniability.* New York: Palgrave Macmillan.

Campbell, Howard. 2009. *Drug War Zone: Frontline Dispatches from the Streets of El Paso and Juárez.* Austin: University of Texas Press.

Carr, E. Summerson. 2010. "Enactments of Expertise." *Annual Review of Anthropology* 39 (1): 17–32.

Cattelino, Jessica R. 2010. "The Double Bind of American Indian Need-Based Sovereignty." *Cultural Anthropology* 25 (2): 235–62.

Centro Nacional de Memoria Historica. 2012. *Basta Ya!.* Bogotá: Imprenta Nacional.

————. 2013. *Una Sociedad Secuestrada*. Centro Nacional de Memoria Historica. Bogotá: Imprenta Nacional.

Checker, Melissa, Dana-Ain Davis, and Mark Schuller. 2014. "Anthropological Superheroes and the Consequences of Activist Ethnography." *American Anthropologist* 116 (2): 416–20.

Chernick, Marc. 2005. "Economic Resources and Internal Armed Conflicts: Lessons from the Colombian Case." In *Rethinking the Economics of War: The Intersection of Need, Creed, and Greed*, edited by Cynthia Arnson and I. William Zartman, 178–205. Washington, DC: Woodrow Wilson Center Press.

Chomsky, Aviva. 2007. *Linked Labor Histories: New England, Colombia, and the Making of a Global Working Class*. Durham, NC: Duke University Press.

Chomsky, Aviva, and Steve Striffler. 2008. "Solidarity and Divisions: Challenges to Solidarity in the Global Coal Industry." Paper presented at the Empire and Solidarity in the Americas conference, University of New Orleans.

Cockburn, Cynthia. 2007. *From Where We Stand: War, Women's Activism and Feminist Analysis*. London: Zed Books.

Cohen, Stanley. 2001. *States of Denial: Knowing about Atrocities and Suffering*. Hoboken, NJ: Wiley.

Cohen, Stephen B. 1982. "Conditioning U.S. Security Assistance on Human Rights Practices." *The American Journal of International Law* 76, no. 2 (April): 246. doi:10.2307/2201453.

Cohn, Carol. 1987. "Sex and Death in the Rational World of Defense Intellectuals." *Signs* 12, no. 4 (July 1): 687–718.

Coleman, Bradley Lynn. 2008. *Colombia and the United States: The Making of an Inter-American Alliance, 1939–1960*. Kent, OH: Kent State University Press.

Coles, Kimberley. 2007. *Democratic Designs: International Intervention and Electoral Practices in Postwar Bosnia-Herzegovina*. Ann Arbor: University of Michigan Press.

Comaroff, Jean, and John L. Comaroff. 2006. "Figuring Crime: Quantifacts and the Production of the Un/Real." *Public Culture* 18 (1): 209–46.

Comaroff, John L. 1998. "Reflections on the Colonial State, in South Africa and Elsewhere: Factions, Fragments, Facts and Fictions." *Social Identities* 4, no. 3 (October 1): 321–61. doi:10.1080/13504639851663.

Comisión Colombiana de Juristas. 1993. *Putumayo*. Informes Regionales de Derechos Humanos. Bogotá: Comisión Colombiana de Juristas.

Courtwright, David T. 2002. *Forces of Habit: Drugs and the Making of the Modern World*. Cambridge, MA: Harvard University Press.

Coutin, Susan Bibler. 2000. *Legalizing Moves: Salvadoran Immigrants' Struggle for U.S. Residency*. Ann Arbor: University of Michigan Press.

————. 2007. *Nations of Emigrants: Shifting Boundaries of Citizenship in El Salvador and the United States*. Ithaca, NY: Cornell University Press.

Cowan, Jane K. 2008. "Fixing National Subjects in the 1920s Southern Balkans: Also an International Practice." *American Ethnologist* 35 (2): 338–56.

Cowan, Jane K., Marie-Bénédicte Dembour, and Richard A. Wilson. 2001. *Culture and Rights: Anthropological Perspectives*. Cambridge: Cambridge University Press.

Crandall, Russell. 2002. *Driven by Drugs: US Policy Toward Colombia*. Boulder, CO: Lynne Rienner.

Crawford, Neta. 2000. "The Passion of World Politics: Propositions on Emotion and Emotional Relationships." *International Security* 24 (4): 116–56.

———. 2002. *Argument and Change in World Politics: Ethics, Decolonization, and Humanitarian Intervention*. Cambridge: Cambridge University Press.

Crile, George. 2003. *Charlie Wilson's War*. Washington, DC: Atlantic Monthly Press.

Cunningham, Hilary. 1995. *God and Caesar at the Rio Grande: Sanctuary and the Politics of Religion*. Minneapolis: University of Minnesota Press.

———. 1999. "The Ethnography of Transnational Social Activism: Understanding the Global as Local Practice." *American Ethnologist* 26 (3): 583–604.

Davis, Bob. 2007. "Colombia Goes Full Tilt to Return to Grace." *Wall Street Journal*.

Davis, Kevin E., Benedict Kingsbury, and Sally Engle Merry. 2012. "Indicators as a Technology of Global Governance." *Law & Society Review* 46 (1): 71–104.

Davis, Tom. 2004. *The War Against Drugs and Thugs: A Status Report on Plan Colombia Successes and Remaining Challenges*. Washington, DC: U.S. Government Printing Office.

Deininger, Klaus. 1999. "Making Negotiated Land Reform Work: Initial Experience from Colombia, Brazil and South Africa." *World Development* 27 (4): 651–72.

Deleuze, Gilles, and Félix Guattari. 1986. *Nomadology: The War Machine*. New York: Columbia University Press.

DeShazo, Peter, Tanya Primiani, and Phillip McLean. 2007. *Back from the Brink: Assessing Progress in Plan Colombia*. Washington, DC: Center for Strategic and International Studies.

DeWine, Michael. 1999. "Future Challenges to Secure Democracy in Latin America." Presented at the Heritage Foundation, Washington, DC.

Dickins de Girón, Avery. 2011. "The Security Guard Industry in Guatemala." In *Securing the City: Neoliberalism, Space, and Insecurity in Postwar Guatemala*, edited by Kevin Lewis O'Neill and Kedron Thomas. 103–26. Durham NC: Duke University Press.

Downie, Richard Duncan. 1998. *Learning from Conflict: The U.S. Military in Vietnam, El Salvador, and the Drug War*. Westport, CT: Praeger Publishers.

Drezner, Daniel W. 2000. "Ideas, Bureaucratic Politics, and the Crafting of Foreign Policy." *American Journal of Political Science* 44 (4): 733.

Dudley, Steven. 2003. *Walking Ghosts: Murder and Guerrilla Politics in Colombia*. London: Routledge.

Edelman, Marc. 2005. "When Networks Don't Work: The Rise and Fall and Rise of Civil Society Initiatives in Central America." In *Social Movements: An Anthropological Reader*, edited by June Nash, 29–45. Malden, MA: Blackwell.

Enloe, Cynthia. 2000. *Maneuvers: The International Politics of Militarizing Women's Lives*. Berkeley: University of California Press.

Evans, Michael. 2011. *The Chiquita Papers*. National Security Archive Electronic Briefing Book No 340. Washington, DC: National Security Archive.

Fassin, Didier. 2008. "The Humanitarian Politics of Testimony: Subjectification Through Trauma in the Israeli–Palestinian Conflict." *Cultural Anthropology* 23 (3): 531–58.

———. 2011. *Humanitarian Reason: A Moral History of the Present*. Berkeley: University of California Press.

Feitlowitz, Marguerite. 2011. *A Lexicon of Terror: Argentina and the Legacies of Torture, Revised and Updated with a New Epilogue*. Oxford: Oxford University Press.

Feldman, Allen. 2004. "Memory Theatres, Virtual Witnessing, and the Trauma-Aesthetic." *Biography* 27 (1): 163–202.

———. 2005. "The Actuarial Gaze: From 9/11 to Abu Ghraib." *Cultural Studies* 19 (2).

Felstiner, William L. F., Richard L. Abel, and Austin Sarat. 1980. "The Emergence and Transformation of Disputes: Naming, Blaming, Claiming . . ." *Law & Society Review* 15 (3/4): 631.

Ferguson, James. 1994. *The Anti-Politics Machine: Development, Depoliticization, and Bureaucratic Power in Lesotho*. Minneapolis: University of Minnesota Press.

Ferro Medina, Juan, and Graciela Uribe Ramon. 2002. *El Orden de La Guerra, Las FARC-EP: Entre La Organizacion Y La Politica*. Bogota: Centro Editorial Javeriano.

Fikes, Kesha. 2009. *Managing African Portugal: The Citizen-Migrant Distinction*. Durham, NC: Duke University Press.

Fitz-Henry, Erin E. 2011. "Distant Allies, Proximate Enemies: Rethinking the Scales of the Antibase Movement in Ecuador." *American Ethnologist* 38 (2): 323–37.

FitzGerald, Susan. 2013. " 'Crack Baby' Study Ends with Unexpected but Clear Result." *The Inquirer*, July 22.

Fleck, Alexine. 2013. "The Return of the Crack Baby. Again. | Points: The Blog of the Alcohol and Drugs History Society." *Points: The Blog of the Alcohol and Drugs History Society*. http://pointsadhsblog.wordpress.com/2013/06/07/the-return-of-the-crack-baby-again/.

Fortun, Kim. 2001. *Advocacy After Bhopal: Environmentalism, Disaster, New Global Orders*. Chicago: University of Chicago Press.

Garcia, Angela. 2010. *The Pastoral Clinic: Addiction and Dispossession Along the Rio Grande*. Berkeley: University of California Press.

García, Maria Cristina. 2006. *Seeking Refuge*. Berkeley: University of California Press.

García-Godos, Jemima, and Knut Andreas O. Lid. 2010. "Transitional Justice and Victims' Rights Before the End of a Conflict: The Unusual Case of Colombia." *Journal of Latin American Studies* 42 (3): 487–516.

García-Peña, Daniel. 2009. "Los Mal Llamado 'Grupos Emergentes.'" *El Espectador*, March 10.

General Accounting Office. 1999. *Military Training: Management and Oversight of Joint Combined Exchange Training*. Washington, DC: General Accounting Office.

Gill, Lesley. 2004. *The School of the Americas: Military Training and Political Violence in the Americas*. Durham, NC: Duke University Press.

———. 2005. "Labor and Human Rights: The 'Real Thing' in Colombia." *Transforming Anthropology* 13 (2): 110–15.

———. 2009. "The Limits of Solidarity: Labor and Transnational Organizing Against Coca-Cola." *American Ethnologist* 36 (4): 667–80.

Gill, Lesley, and Sharryn Kasmir. 2009. "Forum: Solidarity." *Dialectical Anthropology* 32 (3): 175.

Giugale, Marcelo M., Olivier Lafourcade, and Connie Luff, eds. 2003. *Colombia: The Economic Foundation of Peace*. Washington, DC: World Bank Publications.

Gladwell, Malcolm. 1998. "Just Say 'Wait a Minute.'" *New York Review of Books*, December 17.

Godoy, Horacio. 2003. "Plan Colombia's Strategic Weakness." Paper presented at the Latin American Studies Association meeting, Dallas.

Goffman, Alice. 2014. *On the Run: Fugitive Life in an American City*. Chicago: University of Chicago Press.

Goldstein, Daniel M. 2010. "Toward a Critical Anthropology of Security." *Current Anthropology* 51 (4): 487–517.

———. 2012. *Outlawed: Between Security and Rights in a Bolivian City*. Durham, NC: Duke University Press.

Gootenberg, Paul, ed. 1999. *Cocaine: Global Histories*. London: Routledge.

———. 2009. *Andean Cocaine: The Making of a Global Drug*. Chapel Hill: University of North Carolina Press.

Grandin, Greg. 2007. *Empire's Workshop: Latin America, the United States, and the Rise of the New Imperialism*. New York: Holt Paperbacks.

Green, Linda. 1999. *Fear as a Way of Life*. New York: Columbia University Press.

Greenhalgh, Susan. 2008. *Just One Child*. Berkeley: University of California Press.

Greenhouse, Carol J. 2002. "Citizenship, Agency and the Dream of Time." In *Looking Back at Law's Century*, edited by Austin Sarat, Bryant G. Garth, and Robert A. Kagan, 184–209. Ithaca, NY: Cornell University Press.

Greenhouse, Carol J., Elizabeth Mertz, and Kay B. B. Warren, eds. 2002. *Ethnography in Unstable Places: Everyday Lives in Contexts of Dramatic Political Change*. Durham, NC: Duke University Press.

———. 2011. *The Paradox of Relevance: Ethnography and Citizenship in the United States*. Philadelphia: University of Pennsylvania Press.

Griffin-Nolan, Ed. 1991. *Witness for Peace: A Story of Resistance*. Louisville, KY: Westminster John Knox Press.

Grisaffi, Thomas. 2010. "We Are Originarios . . . 'We Just Aren't from Here': Coca Leaf and Identity Politics in the Chapare, Bolivia." *Bulletin of Latin American Research* 29 (4): 425–39.

Gugelberger, Georg M., ed. 1996. *The Real Thing: Testimonial Discourse and Latin America*. Durham, NC: Duke University Press.

Guilhot, Nicolas. 2005. *The Democracy Makers: Human Rights and the Politics of Global Order*. New York: Columbia University Press.

Gupta, Akhil. 1995. "Blurred Boundaries: The Discourse of Corruption, the Culture of Politics, and the Imagined State." *American Ethnologist* 22 (2): 375–402.

———. 2012. *Red Tape: Bureaucracy, Structural Violence, and Poverty in India.* Durham, NC: Duke University Press.

———. 2014. "Gupta, Akhil 2012 Red Tape: Bureaucracy, Structural Violence, and Poverty in India, Response by Akhil Gupta: Arbitrariness, Structural Violence, and State Theory." *Society and Space.* http://societyandspace.com/reviews/reviews-archive/gupta -akhil-2012-red-tape-bureaucracy-structural-violence-and-poverty-in-india-response -by-akhil-gupta/. Last accessed December 29, 2014.

Gusterson, Hugh. 1997. "Studying Up Revisited." *PoLAR: Political and Legal Anthropology Review* 20 (1): 114–19.

———. 1998. *Nuclear Rites: A Weapons Laboratory at the End of the Cold War.* Berkeley: University of California Press.

———. 2007. "Anthropology and Militarism." *Annual Review of Anthropology* 36 (September): 155–75.

Hale, Charles R. 2008. *Engaging Contradictions: Theory, Politics, and Methods of Activist Scholarship.* Berkeley: University of California Press.

Hart, Carl. 2014. *High Price: A Neuroscientist's Journey of Self-Discovery That Challenges Everything You Know About Drugs and Society.* New York: Harper Perennial.

Hartmann, Hauke. 2001. "US Human Rights Policy under Carter and Reagan, 1977–1981." *Human Rights Quarterly* 23 (2): 402–30.

Harvey, David. 2005. *The New Imperialism.* Oxford: Oxford University Press.

Haugaard, Lisa, and Kelly Nichols. 2010. *Breaking the Silence: In Search of Colombia's Disappeared.* Washington, DC: Latin America Working Group Education Fund.

Herzfeld, Michael. 1993. *The Social Production of Indifference.* Chicago: University of Chicago Press.

Hetherington, Kregg. 2011. *Guerrilla Auditors: The Politics of Transparency in Neoliberal Paraguay.* Durham, NC: Duke University Press.

Heyman, Josiah, ed. 1999. *States and Illegal Practices.* New York: Berg Publishers.

Hinton, Alexander Laban, ed. 2010. *Transitional Justice: Global Mechanisms and Local Realities After Genocide and Mass Violence.* New Brunswick, NJ: Rutgers University Press.

Ho, Karen. 2009. *Liquidated: An Ethnography of Wall Street.* Durham, NC: Duke University Press.

Holston, James. 2008. *Insurgent Citizenship: Disjunctions of Democracy and Modernity in Brazil.* Princeton, NJ: Princeton University Press.

Hoyos, Diana, and Marcela Ceballos. 2004. "Working Paper 57: Electoral Behaviour Trends and Decentralization in Colombia's Municipalities, 1988–2000." Translated by Judy Butler. Crisis States Program, London School of Economics, December.

Hull, Matthew S. 2012. *Government of Paper: The Materiality of Bureaucracy in Urban Pakistan.* Berkeley: University of California Press.

Human Rights Watch. 1995. *Colombia's Killer Networks.* New York: Human Rights Watch.

———. 1998a. *War Without Quarter: Colombia and International Humanitarian Law*. New York: Human Rights Watch.

———. 1998b. *Ties That Bind: Colombia and Military-Paramilitary Links*. New York: Human Rights Watch.

———. 2001. *The Sixth Division: Military-Paramilitary Ties and US Policy in Colombia*. New York: Human Rights Watch.

———. 2002. *A Wrong Turn: The Record of the Colombian Attorney General's Office*. New York: Human Rights Watch.

———. 2005. *Letting Paramilitaries Off the Hook*. New York: Human Rights Watch.

———. 2008. *Breaking the Grip: Obstacles for Justice for Paramilitary Mafias in Colombia*. New York: Human Rights Watch.

———. 2010. *The Paramilitaries' Heirs*. New York: Human Rights Watch.

Inda, Jonathan Xavier, ed. 2005. *Anthropologies of Modernity: Foucault, Governmentality, and Life Politics*. Malden, MA: Wiley-Blackwell.

International Crisis Group. 2007. *Colombia's New Armed Groups*. Washington, DC: International Crisis Group.

Isacson, Adam. 2006. "Plan Colombia Six Years Later." Washington, DC: Center for International Policy, November. http://www.ciponline.org/images/uploads/publications /0611ipr.pdf. Last accessed December 29, 2104.

———. 2010. "Enmendando El 'Pacto': El Cambio En El Equilibrio Civil-Militar En La Colombia de Álvaro Uribe." In *Influencias Y Resistencias. Militares Y Poder En América Latina*. Quito: FLACSO.

Isikoff, Michael, and Gregory Vistica. 2000. " 'The Other Drug War: Is a $1.3 Billion Colombia Aid Package Smart Policy, Dirty Politics, Good Business or a Costly Mistake?' " *Newsweek*, April 3.

Jansson, Oscar. 2008. *The Cursed Leaf: An Anthropology of the Political Economy of Cocaine Production in Southern Colombia*. Uppsala: Uppsala Universitet.

Jiménez Gómez, Carlos. 1986. *Una Procuraduria de Opinion Informe Al Congreso Y El Pais*. Bogotá: Editorial Printer Colombiana Ltda.

Kaplan, Robert. 2008. "A Colombian Vision for Iraq." *The Current, The Atlantic*, April 30. http://thecurrent.theatlantic.com/archives/2008/04/alvaro-uribe.php. Accessed February 20, 2013.

Keck, Margaret E., and Kathryn Sikkink. 1998. *Activists Beyond Borders: Advocacy Networks in International Politics*. Ithaca, NY: Cornell University Press.

Kenney, Michael. 2008. *From Pablo to Osama: Trafficking and Terrorist Networks, Government Bureaucracies, and Competitive Adaptation*. State College: Penn State University Press.

Kernaghan, Richard. 2009. *Coca's Gone: Of Might and Right in the Huallaga Post-Boom*. Stanford, CA: Stanford University Press.

Kirk, Robin. 2004. *More Terrible than Death: Drugs, Violence, and America's War in Colombia*. New York: Public Affairs.

Krupa, Christopher. 2010. "State by Proxy: Privatized Government in the Andes." *Comparative Studies in Society and History* 52, no. 02: 319–50. doi:10.1017/S001041751000006X.

Kwon, Heonik. 2006. *After the Massacre: Commemoration and Consolation in Ha My and My Lai*. Berkeley: University of California Press.

———. 2008. *Ghosts of War in Vietnam*. New York: Cambridge University Press.

Lakoff, Andrew. 2007. "Preparing for the Next Emergency." *Public Culture* 19 (2): 247–71.

LaPlante, Lisa. 2009. "The Law of Remedies and the Clean Hands Doctrine: Exclusionary Reparation Policies in Peru's Political Transition." *American University International Law Review* 23 (1): 51–90.

LAWG. 1997. *Declassified Army and CIA Manuals Used in Latin America: An Analysis of Their Content*. Washington, DC: Latin America Working Group. http://www.lawg.org/our -publications/72-general/319-declassified-army-and-cia-manuals.

LeoGrande, William M. 2000. *Our Own Backyard: The United States in Central America, 1977–1992*. Chapel Hill: University of North Carolina Press.

Li, Tania Murray. 2007. *The Will to Improve: Governmentality, Development, and the Practice of Politics*. Durham, NC: Duke University Press.

López, Claudia, ed. 2010. *Y Refundaron La Patria? De Como Mafiosos Y Politicos Reconfiguraron El Estado Colombiano*. Random House Mondadori S. A. Barcelona, Espana, Debate.

Lorentzen, Robin. 1991. *Women in the Sanctuary Movement*. Philadelphia: Temple University Press.

Lutz, Catherine. 1988. *Unnatural Emotions: Everyday Sentiments on a Micronesian Atoll and Their Challenge to Western Theory*. Chicago: University of Chicago Press.

———. 2002. *Homefront: A Military City and the American Twentieth Century*. Boston: Beacon Press.

———. 2006. "Empire Is in the Details." *American Ethnologist* 33, no. 4 (November 1): 593–611. doi:10.1525/ae.2006.33.4.593.

———, ed. 2009. *The Bases of Empire: The Global Struggle Against U.S. Military Posts*. New York: New York University Press.

MacCoun, Robert J., and Peter Reuter. 2001. *Drug War Heresies: Learning from Other Vices, Times, and Places*. Cambridge: Cambridge University Press.

MacLeish, Kenneth T. 2013. *Making War at Fort Hood: Life and Uncertainty in a Military Community*. Princeton, NJ: Princeton University Press.

Marsh, Betsy. 2004. *Going to Extremes: The Aerial Spraying Program in Colombia*. Washington, DC: Latin America Working Group.

Masco, Joseph. 2004. "Nuclear Technoaesthetics: Sensory Politics from Trinity to the Virtual Bomb in Los Alamos." *American Ethnologist* 31 (3): 349–73.

———. 2006. *The Nuclear Borderlands: The Manhattan Project in Post-Cold War New Mexico*. Princeton, NJ: Princeton University Press.

———. 2008. " 'Survival Is Your Business': Engineering Ruins and Affect in Nuclear America." *Cultural Anthropology* 23 (2): 361–98.

Massing, Michael. 1998. *The Fix*. Berkeley: University of California Press.

Mathews, Andrew S. 2008. "State Making, Knowledge, and Ignorance: Translation and Concealment in Mexican Forestry Institutions." *American Anthropologist* 110 (4): 484–94.

———. 2011. *Instituting Nature: Authority, Expertise, and Power in Mexican Forests*. Cambridge, MA: MIT Press.

Mbembe, Achille. 2003. "Necropolitics." *Public Culture* 15 (1): 11–40.

McClintock, Michael. 1992. *Instruments of Statecraft: U.S. Guerilla Warfare, Counter-Insurgency, Counter-Terrorism, 1940-1990*. New York: Pantheon Books.

Merrill, Dennis. 2009. *Negotiating Paradise: U.S. Tourism and Empire in Twentieth-Century Latin America*. Chapel Hill: University of North Carolina Press.

Merry, Sally Engle. 2006. *Human Rights and Gender Violence: Translating International Law into Local Justice*. Chicago: University of Chicago Press.

———. 2011. "Measuring the World: Indicators, Human Rights, and Global Governance: With CA Comment by John M. Conley." *Current Anthropology* 52 (S3): S83–S95.

Mitchell, Timothy. 1990. "Everyday Metaphors of Power." *Theory and Society* 19 (5): 545–77.

———. 1991. *Colonizing Egypt*. Berkeley: University of California Press.

Molano, Alfredo. 1989. *Siguiendo El Corte: Relatos de Guerras Y de Tierras*. Bogotá: El Ancora Editores.

Morone, James A. 2004. *Hellfire Nation: The Politics of Sin in American History*. New Haven, CT: Yale University Press.

Mosse, David. 2004. *Cultivating Development: An Ethnography of Aid Policy and Practice*. New York: Pluto Press.

———. 2007. "Notes on the Ethnography of Expertise and Professionals in International Development." Paper presented at the Ethnografeast, Lisbon.

———. 2011. "Politics and Ethics: Ethnographies of Expert Knowledge and Professional Identities." In *Policy Worlds: Anthropology and Analysis of Contemporary Power*, edited by Cris Shore, Susan Wright, and Davide Però. New York: Berghahn Books.

Natapoff, Alexandra. 2011. *Snitching: Criminal Informants and the Erosion of American Justice*. New York: New York University Press.

Navaro-Yashin, Yael. 2006. "Affect in the Civil Service: A Study of a Modern State-System." *Postcolonial Studies* 9, no. 3: 281–94. doi:10.1080/13688790600824997.

———. 2012. *The Make-Believe Space: Affective Geography in a Postwar Polity*. Durham, NC: Duke University Press.

Nelson, Diane. 2013. " 'Yes to Life = No to Mining:' Counting as Biotechnology in Life (Ltd) Guatemala." *S&F Online* 11, no. 3. http://sfonline.barnard.edu/life-un-ltd-feminism-bioscience-race/yes-to-life-no-to-mining-counting-as-biotechnology-in-life-ltd-guatemala/. Accessed December 29, 2014.

Nordstrom, Carolyn. 2004. *Shadows of War: Violence, Power, and International Profiteering in the Twenty-First Century*. Berkeley: University of California Press.

Nugent, David. 1997. *Modernity at the Edge of Empire: State, Individual, and Nation in the Northern Peruvian Andes, 1885–1935*. Palo Alto, CA: Stanford University Press.

O'Neill, Kevin Lewis, and Kedron Thomas. 2011. *Securing the City: Neoliberalism, Space, and Insecurity in Postwar Guatemala*. Durham, NC: Duke University Press.

Ong, Aihwa. 1999. *Flexible Citizenship: The Cultural Logics of Transnationality*. Durham, NC: Duke University Press.

———. 2006. *Neoliberalism as Exception: Mutations in Citizenship and Sovereignty*. Durham, NC: Duke University Press.

Otis, John. 2009. "Colombia's Drug Extraditions: Are They Worth It?" *Time*, February 25.

Palacios, Marco. 2006. *Between Legitimacy and Violence: A History of Colombia, 1875–2002*. Durham, NC: Duke University Press.

Paley, Julia. 2001. *Marketing Democracy: Power and Social Movements in Post-Dictatorship Chile*. Berkeley: University of California Press.

———. 2008. *Democracy: Anthropological Approaches*. Santa Fe: School for Advanced Research Press.

Paltrow, Lynn M., and Jeanne Flavin. 2013. "Arrests of and Forced Interventions on Pregnant Women in the United States, 1973–2005: Implications for Women's Legal Status and Public Health." *Journal of Health Politics, Policy and Law* 38 (2): 299–343.

Pardo, Rafael. 1996. *De primera mano. Colombia 1986–1994: Entre conflictos y esperanzas*. Bogotá: Grupo Editorial Norma.

Pastrana Arango, Andrés, and Gonzalo Guillén. 2014. *Memorias olvidadas: Episodios personales de la historia de colombia, relatados a Gonzalo Guillén*. Bogotá, Colombia: Debate.

Pax Christi Netherlands. 2001. *The Kidnap Industry in Colombia*. Utrecht: Pax Christi Netherlands. http://www.paxforpeace.nl/media/files/the-kidnap-industry-in-colombia-our -business-112001_0.pdf.

Perla, Hector, Jr. 2008. "Si Nicaragua Venció, El Salvador Vencerá: Central American Agency in the Creation of the U.S.–Central American Peace and Solidarity Movement." *Latin American Research Review* 43 (2): 136–58.

Perla, Hector, Jr., and Susan Bibler Coutin. 2010. "Legacies and Origins of the 1980s US-Central American Sanctuary Movement." *Refuge: Canada's Journal on Refugees* 26 (1).

Pezzullo, Phaedra Carmen. 2009. *Toxic Tourism: Rhetorics of Pollution, Travel, and Environmental Justice*. Tuscaloosa: University of Alabama Press.

Pizarro Leongomez, Eduardo. 2011. *Las FARC, 1949–2011: De Guerrilla Campesina a Maquina de Guerra*. Bogotá: Grupo Editorial Norma.

Poole, Deborah. 2004. "Between Threat and Guarantee: Justice and Community on the Margins of the Peruvian State." In *Anthropology in the Margins of the State*, edited by Deborah Poole and Veena Das, 35–66. Santa Fe: SAR Press.

Porch, Douglas. 2013. *Counterinsurgency: Exposing the Myths of the New Way of War*. New York: Cambridge University Press.

Priest, Dana. 2004. *The Mission: Waging War and Keeping Peace with America's Military*. Reprint edition. New York: W. W. Norton.

———. 2013. "Covert Action in Colombia: US Intelligence, GPS Bomb Kits Help Latin American Nation Cripple Rebel Forces." *Washington Post*, December 21. http://www.washingtonpost.com/sf/investigative/2013/12/21/covert-action-in-colombia/.

Rabasa, Angel, and Peter Chalk. 2001. *Colombian Labyrinth: The Synergy of Drugs and Insurgency and Its Implications for Regional Stability*. Santa Monica, CA: Rand Corporation.

Ramírez, Maria Clemencia. 2010. "Maintaining Democracy in Colombia Through Political Exclusion, States of Exception, Counterinsurgency, and Dirty War." In *Violent Democracies in Latin America*, edited by Enrique Desmond Arias and Daniel M. Goldstein, 84–107. Durham, NC: Duke University Press.

———. 2011. *Between the Guerrillas and the State: The Cocalero Movement, Citizenship, and Identity in the Colombian Amazon*. Durham, NC: Duke University Press.

Ramírez, Maria Clemencia, Ingrid Bolivar, Juliana Iglesias, Maria Clara Torres, and Teofilo Vasquez. 2010. *Elecciones, Coca, Conflicto Y Partidos Políticos En Putumayo, 1980–2007*. Bogota: CINEP/PPP, ICANH, Colciencias.

Ramírez, Maria Clemencia, María Luisa Moreno, and Camila Medina. 2012. *El Placer: Mujuers, Coca Y Guerra En El Bajo Putumayo*. Bogotá: Centro de Memoria Historica. http://www.centrodememoriahistorica.gov.co/.

Redfield, Peter. 2006. "A Less Modest Witness." *American Ethnologist* 33 (1): 3–26.

———. 2012. "The Unbearable Lightness of Ex-Pats: Double Binds of Humanitarian Mobility." *Cultural Anthropology* 27 (2): 358–82.

Reinarman, Craig, and Harry G. Levine, eds. 1997. *Crack in America: Demon Drugs and Social Justice*. Berkeley: University of California Press.

Remijnse, Simone. 2001. "Remembering Civil Patrols in Joyabaj, Guatemala." *Bulletin of Latin American Research* 20, no. 4: 454–69. doi:10.1111/1470-9856.00025.

Rempe, Dennis. 2002. *The Past as Prologue? A History of U.S. Counterinsurgency Policy in Colombia, 1958–66*. Carlisle, PA: Strategic Studies Institute, U.S. Army War College. http://www.strategicstudiesinstitute.army.mil/pdffiles/pub17.pdf.

Rendón, Renata, and John Lindsay-Poland. 2008. *Assisting Units That Commit Extrajudicial Killings: A Call to Investigate US Military Policy Towards Colombia*. Washington, DC: Fellowship of Reconciliation and Amnesty International.

Reyes Posada, Alejandro. 2009. *Guerreros Y Campesinos: El Despojo de La Tierra En Colombia*. Buenos Aires: Grupo Editorial Norma.

Richani, Nazih. 2014. *Systems of Violence: The Political Economy of War and Peace in Colombia*, 2nd edition. Albany: State University of New York Press.

Roldán, Mary. 2002. *Blood and Fire: La Violencia in Antioquia, Colombia, 1946–1953*. Durham, NC: Duke University Press.

Romero, Mauricio. 2005. *Paramilitares Y Autodefensas, 1982–2003*. 2nd ed. Bogota: Editorial Planeta-IEPRI.

————. 2007. *Parapolitica: La Ruta de La Expansion Paramilitar Y Los Acuerdos Politicos*. Bogota: Corporacion Nuevo Arco Iris and Intermedio.

————, ed. 2011. *La Economia De Los Paramilitares*. Bogotá: Debate.

Rosado, Michelle. 1984. "Toward An Anthropology of Self and Feeling." In *Culture Theory: Essays on Mind, Self, and Emotion*, edited by Richard A. Shweder and Robert Alan LeVine, 137–57. New York: Cambridge University Press.

Rosga, AnnJanette, and Margaret Satterthwaite. 2009. "The Trust in Indicators: Measuring Human Rights." *Berkeley Journal of International Law* 27 (2): 253.

Rotberg, Robert I. 2002. "The New Nature of Nation-State Failure." *Washington Quarterly* 25 (3): 83–96.

Rutherford, Danilyn. 2009 "Sympathy, State Building, and the Experience of Empire." *Cultural Anthropology* 24, no. 1: 1–32. doi:10.1111/j.1548-1360.2009.00025.x.

Sanford, Victoria. 2003. "Eyewitness: Peacebuilding in a War Zone: The Case of Colombian Peace Communities." *International Peacekeeping* 10, no. 2: 107–18. doi:10.1080/714002455.

Sanford, Victoria, and Asale Angel-Ajani. 2006. *Engaged Observer: Anthropology, Advocacy, and Activism*. New Brunswick, NJ: Rutgers University Press.

Schmitt, Eric. 2013. "Military Says Law Barring U.S. Aid to Rights Violators Hurts Training Mission." *New York Times*, June 20.

Scott, James C. 1999. *Seeing Like a State: How Certain Schemes to Improve the Human Condition Have Failed*. New Haven, CT: Yale University Press.

Semana. 2006. "¿Quién Manda Aquí?" *Semana.com*, August 19, 2006. http://www.semana.com//nacion/articulo/quien-manda-aqui/80533-3. Accessed December 29, 2014.

Sharpley, Richard. 2009. *The Darker Side of Travel: The Theory and Practice of Dark Tourism*. Bristol: Channel View Publications.

Shaw, Rosalind, Lars Waldorf, and Pierre Hazan. 2010. *Localizing Transitional Justice: Interventions and Priorities After Mass Violence*. Stanford, CA: Stanford University Press.

Shinnick, Julie. 1999. "Bureau of the Month: Bureau for International Narcotics and Law Enforcement Affairs: More Than Narcotics." *State Magazine*, December. http://www.state.gov/www/publications/statemag/statemag_dec99/bom.html. Accessed April 8, 2008.

Shore, Cris, and Susan Wright. 1997. *Anthropology of Policy: Perspectives on Governance and Power*. London: Routledge.

Shore, Cris, Susan Wright, and Davide Pero. 2011. *Policy Worlds: Anthropology and the Analysis of Contemporary Power*. New York: Berghahn Books.

Siegel, Loren. 1997. "The Pregnancy Police Fight the War on Drugs." In *Crack In America: Demon Drugs and Social Justice*, edited by Craig Reinarman and Harry G. Levine, 249–59. Berkeley: University of California Press.

Simon, Jonathan. 2009. *Governing Through Crime: How the War on Crime Transformed American Democracy and Created a Culture of Fear*. New York: Oxford University Press.

Singer, P. W. 2007. *Corporate Warriors: The Rise of the Privatized Military Industry, Updated Edition*. Ithaca, NY: Cornell University Press.

Singh, Bhrigupati, Deborah Poole, Richard Baxstrom, and Naveeda Khan. 2005. "Networks Actual and Potential: Think Tanks, War Games and the Creation of Contemporary American Politics." *Theory & Event* 8 (4).

Sluka, Jeffrey A. 1999. *Death Squad: The Anthropology of State Terror*. Philadelphia: University of Pennsylvania Press.

Smith, Christian. 1996. *Resisting Reagan: The U.S. Central America Peace Movement*. Chicago: University of Chicago Press.

Snow, David A., E. Burke Rochford, Steven K. Worden, and Robert D. Benford. 1986. "Frame Alignment Processes, Micromobilization, and Movement Participation." *American Sociological Review* 51, no. 4: 464. doi:10.2307/2095581.

Speed, Shannon. 2007. *Rights in Rebellion: Indigenous Struggle and Human Rights in Chiapas*. Stanford, CA: Stanford University Press.

Spencer, David. 2001. *Colombian Paramilitaries: Criminals or Political Force?* Carlisle, PA: Center for Strategic Studies of the U.S. Army War College.

Stanfield, Michael Edward. 1998. *Red Rubber, Bleeding Trees: Violence, Slavery, and Empire in Northwest Amazonia, 1850–1933*. Albuquerque: University of New Mexico Press.

Starn, Orin. 1999. *Nightwatch: The Politics of Protest in the Andes*. Durham, NC: Duke University Press.

Stein, Rebecca L. 2008. *Itineraries in Conflict: Israelis, Palestinians, and the Political Lives of Tourism*. Durham, NC: Duke University Press.

Stern, Steve J. 2004. *Remembering Pinochet's Chile: On the Eve of London, 1998*. Durham, NC: Duke University Press.

———. 2006. *Remembering Pinochet's Chile: On the Eve of London 1998*. New edition edition. Durham: Duke University Press.

Stoler, Ann Laura. 2002. *Carnal Knowledge and Imperial Power: Race and the Intimate in Colonial Rule*. Berkeley: University of California Press.

———. 2010. *Along the Archival Grain: Epistemic Anxieties and Colonial Common Sense*. Princeton, NJ: Princeton University Press.

Strange, Susan. 1996. *The Retreat of the State: The Diffusion of Power in the World Economy*. New York: Cambridge University Press.

Strathern, Marilyn. 1990. *The Gender of the Gift: Problems with Women and Problems with Society in Melanesia*. Berkeley: University of California Press.

———, ed. 2000. *Audit Cultures: Anthropological Studies in Accountability, Ethics and the Academy*. London: Routledge.

Streatfeild, Dominic. 2003. *Cocaine: An Unauthorized Biography*. Reprint. New York: Picador.

Tate, Winifred. 2007. *Counting the Dead: The Culture and Politics of Human Rights Activism in Colombia*. Berkeley: University of California Press.

———. 2009a. "U.S. Human Rights Activism and Plan Colombia." *Revista Colombia Internacional-Revista* 69 (Enero-Junio): 50–69.

———. 2009b. "From Greed to Grievance: The Shifting Political Profile of Colombian Paramilitaries." In *Colombia: Building Peace in a Time of War*, edited by Virginia M. Bouvier, 111–32. Washington, DC: United States Institute of Peace.

———. 2010. "Accounting for Absence: The Colombian Paramilitaries in U.S. Policy Debates." In *Sex, Drugs, and Body Counts: The Politics of Numbers in Global Crime and Conflict*, edited by Peter Andreas and Kelly M. Greenhill, 215–46. Ithaca, NY: Cornell University Press.

———. 2011. "Human Rights Law and Military Aid Delivery: A Case Study of the Leahy Law." *Political and Legal Anthropology Review* 34 (2): 337–54.

———. 2013a. "Proxy Citizenship and Transnational Advocacy: Colombian Activists from Putumayo to Washington, DC." *American Ethnologist* 40 (1): 55–70.

———. 2013b. "Congressional 'Drug Warriors' and U.S. Policy Towards Colombia." *Critique of Anthropology* 33 (2): 214–33.

Taussig, Michael. 1991. *Shamanism, Colonialism, and the Wild Man: A Study in Terror and Healing*. Chicago: University of Chicago Press.

———. 1999. *Defacement: Public Secrecy and the Labor of the Negative*. Stanford, CA: Stanford University Press.

———. 2005. *Law in a Lawless Land: Diary of a Limpieza in Colombia*. Chicago: University of Chicago Press.

Theidon, Kimberly. 2007. "Transitional Subjects: The Disarmament, Demobilization and Reintegration of Former Combatants in Colombia." *International Journal of Transitional Justice* 1, no. 1: 66–90. doi:10.1093/ijtj/ijm011.

———. 2009. "Reconstructing Masculinities: The Disarmament, Demobilization, and Reintegration of Former Combatants in Colombia." *Human Rights Quarterly* 31, no. 1: 1–34. doi:10.1353/hrq.0.0053.

———. 2010. "Histories of Innocence: Post-War Stories in Peru." In *Localizing Transitional Justice: Interventions and Priorities after Mass Violence*, edited by Rosalind Shaw, Lars Waldorf, and Pierre Hazan. Stanford, CA: Stanford University Press.

Thomas, Paulette. 1994. "Making Crime Pay: Triangle of Interests Creates Infrastructure to Fight Lawlessness—Cities See Jobs; Politicians Sense a Popular Issue—And Businesses Cash In—The Cold War of the '90s." *Wall Street Journal*, May 12.

Thomson, Frances. 2011. "The Agrarian Question and Violence in Colombia: Conflict and Development." *Journal of Agrarian Change* 11 (3): 321–56.

Tickner, Arlene B. 2007. "Intervention by Invitation: Keys to Colombian Foreign Policy and Its Main Shortcomings." *Colombia Internacional*, no. 65 (June): 90–111.

Ticktin, Miriam I. 2011. *Casualties of Care: Immigration and the Politics of Humanitarianism in France*. Berkeley: University of California Press.

Tilly, Charles. 1992. *Coercion, Capital and European States: AD 990–1992*. Revised edition. Cambridge, MA: Wiley-Blackwell.

Torres Bustamente, Maria Clara. 2011. *Estado Y Coca En La Frontera Colombiana*. Bogotá: Odecofi-CINEP.

Transnational Institute. 1999. *The US "Air Bridge Denial" Strategy: The Success of a Failure.* Amsterdam: Transnational Institute. http://www.tni.org/article/drug-war-skies.

Trouillot, Michel Rolph. 2001. "The Anthropology of the State in the Age of Globalization: Close Encounters of the Deceptive Kind." *Current Anthropology* 42 (1): 125–38.

Tsing, Anna Lowenhaupt. 1993. *In the Realm of the Diamond Queen: Marginality in an Out-of-the-Way Place.* Princeton, N.J: Princeton University Press.

———. 2004. *Friction: An Ethnography of Global Connection.* Princeton, NJ: Princeton University Press.

Vine, David. 2011. *Island of Shame: The Secret History of the U.S. Military Base on Diego Garcia.* Princeton, NJ: Princeton University Press.

Wacquant, Loïc. 2009. *Punishing the Poor: The Neoliberal Government of Social Insecurity.* Durham, NC: Duke University Press.

Wallace-Wells, Ben. 2007. "How America Lost the War on Drugs." *Rolling Stone*, December 13. http://www.rollingstone.com/politics/news/how-america-lost-the-war-on-drugs-20110324. Accessed July 21, 2013.

Warren, Kay B. 2012. "Troubling the Victim/Trafficker Dichotomy in Efforts to Combat Human Trafficking: The Unintended Consequences of Moralizing Labor Migration." *Indiana Journal of Global Legal Studies* 19 (1): 105–20.

Wedel, Janine R., Cris Shore, Gregory Feldman, and Stacy Lathrop. 2005. "Toward an Anthropology of Public Policy." *Annals of the American Academy of Political and Social Science* 600 (1): 30–51.

Weldes, Jutta, ed. 1999. *Cultures of Insecurity: States, Communities, and the Production of Danger.* Minneapolis: University of Minnesota Press.

Williams, Raymond. 1977. *Literature and Marxism.* Oxford: Oxford University Press.

Wilson, Richard A. 2001. *The Politics of Truth and Reconciliation in South Africa: Legitimizing the Post-Apartheid State.* Cambridge: Cambridge University Press.

Wilson, Richard Ashby, and Richard D. Brown. 2011. *Humanitarianism and Suffering: The Mobilization of Empathy.* Cambridge: Cambridge University Press.

Wilson, Scott. 2001. "Chronicle of a Massacre Foretold." *Washington Post*, January 28.

Withers, George, Adam Isacson, Lisa Haugaard, Joy Olson, and Joel Fyke. 2008. *Ready, Aim, Foreign Policy: How the Pentagon Takes over More and More Areas of Foreign Policy.* Washington, DC: Center for International Policy, the Latin America Working Group Education Fund, and the Washington Office on Latin America. http://www.wola.org/sites/default/files/downloadable/Regional%20Security/past/LAWG-Combo-ForeignPolicy-6.pdf.

Youngers, Coletta. 2001. "Collateral Damage: US Drug Control Efforts in the Andes." Presented at the 2001 Latin American Studies Association meeting, Washington, DC. http://lasa.international.pitt.edu/Lasa2001/YoungersColetta.pdf.

Zackrison, James, and Eileen Bradley. 1997. *Colombian Sovereignty Under Siege.* Washington, DC: National Defense University Institute for National Strategic Studies.

Zamosc, Leon. 2006. *The Agrarian Question and the Peasant Movement in Colombia: Struggles of the National Peasant Association, 1967–1981*. Cambridge: Cambridge University Press.

Zirnite, Peter. 1997. *Reluctant Recruits: The US Military and the War on Drugs*. Washington, DC: Washington Office on Latin America. http://www.tni.org/report/reluctant-recruits-us-military-and-war-drugs. Accessed September 28, 2011.

Index

Page numbers in italic indicate photographs.

Anthropology of Policy